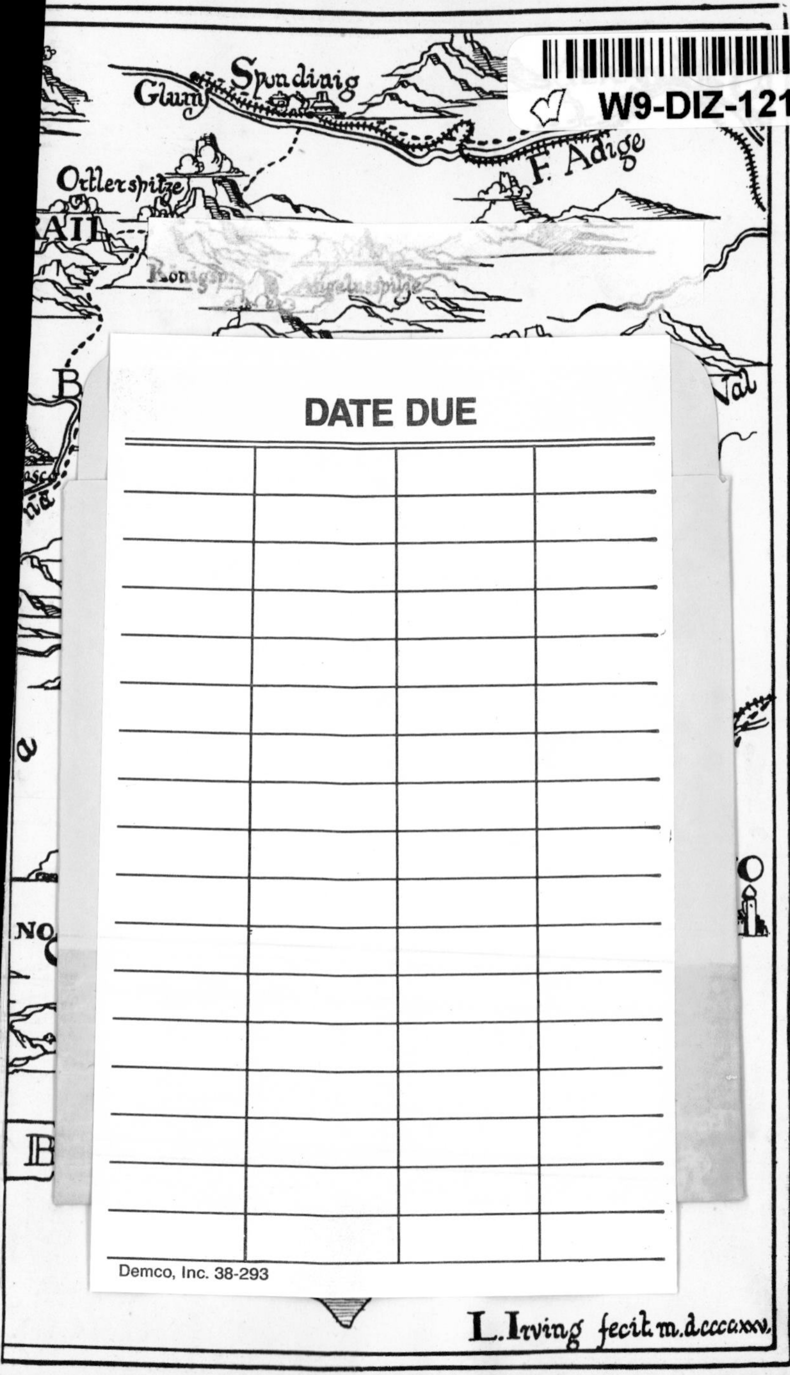
Glurn
Spondinig
Ortlerspitze
F. Adige
Val
L. Irving fecit m.dcccaxxv.

LOMBARDY, TYROL AND THE
TRENTINO

THE HEART OF CADORE

MONTE CIVETTA FROM PIEVE DI LIVINALLONGO

LOMBARDY TYROL
AND THE TRENTINO

BY

HUGH QUIGLEY

WITH TWELVE ILLUSTRATIONS AND TWO MAPS

METHUEN & CO. LTD
36 ESSEX STREET W.C.
LONDON

First Published in 1925

PRINTED IN GREAT BRITAIN

PREFACE

THE travel sketches given in this volume were undertaken in a moment of enthusiasm, when sufficient leisure intervened from more arduous and less attractive duties, and they represent the fruit of years of communion with the beauty and culture of the Italian mountain land. There may be slight faults of perspective, slight moments of overpraise, but the substance of the book is born of sincere conviction. I have had no desire to embellish for the sake of embellishment, and even in the more enthusiastic passages description lags painfully behind reality. The fashion has been to wander south to Florence, Rome and Naples, or east to Venice, and become lyrical on their beauties, when a wonderland of a more lasting attraction lies unexplored to the north among the valleys and peaks of the Italian Tyrol. Perhaps some of the freshness and vivacity of this region would disappear if it became the centre of a pilgrimage, but even æsthetics must give way sometimes to less selfish motive, and this book is the result. An inadequate but a sincere tribute to a rich experience !

I have retained, in spite of the fulminations of
Mussolini and the more extravagant fascisti, the
name " Tyrol," since it means something a title
sanctified and confirmed by history, while " Upper
Adige " means exactly nothing. The love and
affection of Tyrol will never be gained through
imposition of irritating minor legislation ; it can
only come through persuasion and through force
of conviction. It is impossible to tear up every
element in the history of Tyrol and rechristen it
with an Italian name ; such a course leads to
confusion and distrust. I have retained, therefore,
the old German names wherever the Italian version
is obscure or misleading. *Klausen* as *Chiusa*,
for example, loses its individuality entirely and
Waidbrück as *Ponte all'Isarco* is actually misleading.

LONDON, S.W. 15.

CONTENTS

                                                                    PAGE
FOREWORD V

CHAPTER

I. NORTHERN ITALIAN CITIES AND TYROL . . 1

II. BERGAMO AND THE BERGAMASCANS . . . 19

III. A SOLDIER OF THE RENAISSANCE : BARTOLOMEO
COLLEONI 34

IV. CHURCHES, PALACES AND FOUNTAINS OF
BERGAMO 52

V. BERGAMO AND BRESCIA IN LITERATURE AND ART 68

VI. BRESCIA 95

VII. THE VAL CAMONICA IN HISTORY AND ART . 115

VIII. THE ROUTE OF THE ALPS—EDOLO AND TIRANO 129

IX. THE ROUTE OF THE ALPS—BORMIO, TRAFOI AND
THE ORTLER 145

X. THE CASTLES OF SOUTHERN TYROL . . . 160

XI. THE HEART OF TYROL : MERANO AND BOLZANO 179

XII. THE DOLOMITES 192

XIII. CADORE—THE LAND OF TITIAN . . . 220

XIV. A MOUNTAIN PARADISE—SAN MARTINO DI
CASTROZZA 239

XV. TRENTO 254

INDEX 270

LIST OF ILLUSTRATIONS

*THE HEART OF CADORE.   MONTE CIVETTA FROM PIEVE
  DI LIVINALLONGO .   .   .   .   *Frontispiece*

                                        FACING PAGE
*THE ROSENGARTEN WITH THE VAJOLET TOWERS .   14

THE TOMB OF BARTOLOMEO COLLEONI   .   .   .   40

THE PORTAL OF S. MARIA MAGGIORE, BERGAMO .   56

IN A VILLAGE OF THE VAL CAMONICA   .   .   .   116

*COMING DOWN FROM THE STELVIO.   THE ORTLER IN
  FULL VIEW.   156

*CASTLE TYROL   174

*MERANO   186

*TOFANA AND THE AMPEZZO ALPS FROM THE PORDOI
  PASS   202

*CRODA DA LAGO FROM THE CORTINA ROAD   .   .   216

PIEVE DI CADORE.   THE BIRTHPLACE OF TITIAN   .   226

THE CATHEDRAL OF TRENTO   254

MAP OF NORTHERN LOMBARDY, ADAMELLO AND
  ORTLER MOUNTAINS (DRAWN BY L. IRVING)
                                    Front end-paper

MAP OF DOLOMITES AND CADORE (DRAWN BY L.
  IRVING) .   .   .   .   *Back end-paper*

* Reproduced from photographs by Leo Baehrendt, Merano.

PLACE NAMES IN ITALIAN TYROL AND TRENTINO [1]

Italian Version.	*German Version.*
Bolzano	Bozen
Branzollo	Branzoll
Brennero	Brenner
Bressanone	Brixen
Brunico	Bruneck
Caldaro	Kaltern
Caminato	Kematen
Cardano	Kardaun
Castello Firmano	Sigmundskron
Castelrotto	Kastelruth
Catinaccio	Rosengarten
Chiusa	Klausen
Ciaro	Tschars
Cima Undici	Elfer Kofel
Colalbo	Klobenstein
Cornedo	Karneid
Curaces	Gratsch
Dobbiaco	Toblach
Egna	Neumarkt
Giogo dello Stelvio	Stilfserjoch
Giogo di San Vigilio	Vigiljoch
Glorenza	Glurns
Gudon	Gufidaun
Lago di Braies	Pragser Wildsee

[1] This list is not complete but it gives a clue to some of the more important changes caused by substitution of Italian names in place of the original German.

xi

Italian Version.	*German Version.*
Lago di Carezza	Karersee
Laives	Leifers
Lazze	Latsch
Maia	Mais
Malesio	Mals
Merano	Meran
Monte Donna	Ciampedie Hütte
Monte Pez	Schlern
Novacella	Neustift
Nuova Levante	Welschnöfen
Ora	Auer
Ortelio	Ortler
Pieve di Tures	Taufers
Ponte all' Isarco	Waidbrück
Roda di Vael	Rotewand Spitze
Sasso Lungo	Langkofel
Sass Platt	Plattkofel
Le Scale	Hohe Gaisl
Scena	Schönna
Slandro	Schlanders
Sluderno	Schluderns
Soprabolzano	Oberbozen
Spondigna	Spondinig
Tires	Tiers
Torri di Vajolet	Vajolettürme
Tre Cime di Lavaredo	Drei Zinnen
Val d'Ega	Eggenthal
Vipiteno	Sterzing

LOMBARDY, TYROL AND THE TRENTINO

CHAPTER I

NORTHERN ITALIAN CITIES AND TYROL

THERE is a peculiar fascination in the towns of Northern Lombardy which impresses them more deeply on the memory than even the richer towns of Central and Southern Italy, and the traveller passing through Brescia, Verona and Vicenza on his way to Venice is apt to allocate only a few hours to each of those towns, confident that in doing so he has savoured all their beauty and breathed in the full warmth of intimacy all the pleasure that they can give him.   Such a belief only indicates that impressions have been fleeting and sympathy superficial, that the real vibrant spirit of those towns has escaped him ; the deeper and more lasting appreciation is still to be felt—that appreciation which once experienced acts as an irresistible magnet in all subsequent travel.   Venice may be more strikingly beautiful, more richly endowed with the glamour of the past, but there are elements in the Italian genius which found expression in those towns ranged along the foot of the Alps quite foreign to either Venice or Milan.

The mountains have contributed their share to the

more peaceful instincts inspired by the green plains of Lombardy, and some of the fierce independence which characterized the Northern Italian States, not only during the Middle Ages but also during the more recent struggle for national assertion, can be traced to the sterner influence of the Alps and the high hills dipping into the plain.   Each town along the meeting line of the Alps— Como, Lecco, Bergamo, Brescia, Verona and Vicenza, with Rovereto, Trento and Bassano—has its own contribution to make to the history of Italian art and Italian civilization ; each contribution is unique and entirely individual, so that, in the final evaluation of those fundamental elements which, taken together, form the strength of Italy in the eternal things of history, the share of Northern Lombardy is very great indeed.

It is not the intention of the writer to explore the history of those towns in close detail, but to show the district bounded by Bergamo, Brescia and Verona on the south, Rovereto, Trento, Feltre, Belluno, Pieve di Cadore and Bolzano on the east, Merano, Spondinig and Schluderns on the north, and the Stelvio Pass, Bormio, Tirano, Sondrio and Edolo on the west, in such a light that something like affection may be inspired for its history and a desire engendered to appreciate, in full intimacy, the rare wealth of beauty it offers to the traveller.

There are certainly few places in Europe with a richer and more varied wealth of natural beauty than the block of mountain land contained in this area ; on the south, the cities of Lombardy with the full traditions of Italian culture and history behind them ; on the east, the Trentino with its echoes of the struggle between Emperor and Pope and, more recently, between Austria and Italy ; on the north, the Southern Tyrol with its historical background as ancient as that of Lombardy but totally different, expressed in a different art and a different literature ; and in the east, the most impressive mass of the whole Italian Alps coming over the Dolomites, the Brescian Alps, to end in the jewel lake of Iseo and the vine-clad hills of Bergamo.

The interest of such a region is something more than purely scenic ; the transformation of so many different civilizations, so many traditions derived from the long evolution of centuries and the interchange of conflict, into a single Italianized civilization constitutes a problem of intense attraction. The Upper Trentino, as the new Italian province is now termed beyond Trento, has a deeper fascination through this effort towards conversion of a whole people than the wonderful alternation of mountain and valley could give.

History moves from the past into a different present, and the change causes peculiar modifications of existing institutions, abolishing some and glorifying others. The movement also from a purely agricultural state to an industrial can be seen more clearly perhaps in some of the towns of Northern Lombardy than in any other region of Italy, in Bergamo, Brescia and the Valley of the Oglio as far as Edolo, and this movement is in itself of importance even to the traveller. Some elements in the life of those towns and districts can only be fully appreciated in reference to this. A new civilization, a new tradition, is emerging, a new attitude to art and life.

The difference between the northern towns and the towns in the centre and south of Italy, not only from the purely historical or artistic standpoint but also from the psychological, is very real. The peculiar sensation felt on entering the old Romanesque churches of Verona,

San Zeno especially, is entirely different from the impression made by churches of equal antiquity farther south, and it is only when we come again to the churches of the Rhineland, even as far north as Cologne, that the feeling is reproduced.

The atmosphere remains more Gothic and romantic than purely Italian ; the sense of continuity disappears even when we pass from Brescia or Verona to Venice. In the one case, the northern civilization has been predominant in shaping the artistic genius of the people, in the other case, the eastern and south-eastern.

The great communes of Central Italy, Florence and Pisa especially, constituted in themselves a single, self-governing, self-sufficing state ; the mediæval conception of the town entered more fully into their administration than into the administration of any other town or state, even after the mediæval civilization had passed away. The result of this was the creation of a definite municipal ideal which was strong enough to preserve the southern towns and the southern civilization from disaster ; our conception of a modern state found something like direct realization in Florence, Pisa and even Naples.

We may trace to this the strong artistic and architectural renaissance which raised the central and southern towns of Italy into the forefront of the development of their time ; the intense municipal ideal, associated with guilds and guild administration, which continued uninterrupted through the period between the 13th and 17th centuries, led to advocacy and immediate support of the arts. The building of a magnificent church or palace meant something more than satisfaction of an individual desire for salvation or luxury ; it was a true addition to the assets of the town.

It is necessary to dwell on this point, as some part of the contrast between the northern towns of Lombardy and even the southern towns of the same province is due to the conditions caused by the penetration of the municipal ideal. We find in Florence and in Siena a strong interest in art fomented actively by official public support, while in Brescia and Verona this support was either refused or came sporadically. The conception of the town as self-sufficient and a source of ideal came only later in the north, in the 16th and 17th centuries, when the great municipalities of the south had already lost their strength.

Certain elements caused this difference in the attitude to the commune. The position of the towns of Northern Lombardy and the Trentino laid them open immediately to invasion from beyond the Alps ; the wars of the Investitures, the struggle between pope and emperor, were fought not at Rome nor Florence, nor even Bologna, but in the neighbourhood of Brescia, Mantua and Verona, and even as far north as Trento.

Lombardy lay eternally in fear of an armed invasion, against which the resistance of one town would mean only a few days' delay consummated in a general massacre. The strength of Lombardy itself was never sufficiently mobilized under one ruler to make this subjection less complete. Under such a regime, the opportunity and leisure for cultivation of the arts and the creation of an immense monument to the splendid ambitions of a commune were entirely lacking. The palace as apart from the church was only built in Lombardy in a magnificence of style similar to that of Venice, Bologna or Florence, during the late Renaissance period and the 17th century. The one great exception to this is Bergamo, where the position of the city, built on the last spurs of the Alps and surrounded by immensely strong walls, made it almost impregnable. In Bergamo, the flourishing of art and architecture on a scale similar to that of Florence gave rise to a very definite municipal ideal at a time when Lombardy itself was torn through the war of factions, both religious and political.

If, however, the corporate ideal never quite flourished in Northern Lombardy, the natural advantages enjoyed by the province combined to give to its development a unique direction. The interchange of trade, carried out under conditions much less exacting than those obtaining in the southern towns, like Bologna or Florence where the guilds maintained a very close system of supervision, led very soon to enrichment of the Lombardy towns ; the town became more and more valuable as a market, and the market-place itself assumed a new importance.

It is only in Verona, Brescia, Padua and Vicenza that we find now the mediæval market as the centre of the town. This activity of trade caused a special type of architecture, the trade hall or exchange such as we find it in the Sale della Ragione in Verona and Padua.

The liberal habit of mind came as an inevitable consequence. Even in the early centuries of the Renaissance, when Dante came as an exile to Verona, the north of Italy was known as distinctly less autocratic than the south. The revolt of a Rienzi or a Masaniello would have been impossible in Verona or Brescia, simply because conditions never reached an extreme stage where revolution would have been necessary.

*   *   *   *   *

The idea of the state had little support in Lombardy, and had consequently little real influence on the

development of art and literature until the 17th century;
but the intensity of religious conviction which inspired
the early inhabitants of the province gave to it its
peculiar strength and, from the modern point of view,
its peculiar value.

The old churches of Verona, Brescia and Bergamo
are among the most precious possessions of Italy;
the Romanesque architecture reached, in San Zeno,
San Fermo and the cathedral of Verona, a height which
was seldom reached before or after in Europe; even in
Milan where the architectural revival, which swept over
the main cultural states, France, Germany, and Italy,
found expression in churches like St. Ambrose or in
churches like St. Ursula, in Cologne, the enthusiasm
seems to be less impassioned and the noble simplicity
of feeling less inspired by overwhelming conviction.

To the social reformers of Naples, Rome and Florence
bent on establishing the first version of a modern
democratic state, Brescia could only present Arnaldo,
a religious fanatic preaching a revival of faith. This
religious strength may be due to the position of Lombardy, even as its prosperity in trade was due. The
incessant struggles for domination between the condottieri rulers of the early centuries of the Renaissance,
the Scaligers of Verona followed later by the Visconti
of Milan, the Esti of Ferrara and Bartolomeo Colleoni
of Bergamo, although they bore directly on the government of the north of Italy, were never solely aimed
against the temples of the Catholic faith. Pillage
and destruction spared them as much as conditions
would permit of a policy of mercy.

The sanctity of the architectural memorials of the
Church remained practically untouched, the tombs of
the past were honoured with due reverence and the

condottieri themselves occasionally assisted the Church
directly. The sense of reward and of expiation consequent on material gifts was always present in the most
bloodthirsty leaders ; the building of the church of
San Francesco at Rimini by Sigismond Malatesta was
paralleled by the Colleoni Chapel in Bergamo and the
Scaliger Church at Verona. It may have appeared
impossible to reconcile the cold-blooded brutality of the
actions performed by the condottieri themselves with
the whole tenets of the Church, but the Church itself
was not guiltless of similar actions as contemporary
accounts of massacres, like that which took place at
Lodi, prove.

The inspiring motive in church architecture came from
the north rather than from the south. In the creation
of a definite tradition, the builders of Verona in the
10th, 11th and 12th centuries were inspired by the
Gothic spirit almost entirely—not the crudely realistic
force visible beyond the Alps, but a more refined, a more
delicate perception of values. The beauty of the tombs
of the Scaligers at Verona lies, not so much in rich
arabesque of detail or in symmetry of form, as in the
immediate force of detail ; everything conforms to the
feeling of life now brought to repose. It is realism
softened into a delicate harmony, an ennobled version
of actual life to conform to the higher conception inspired
by faith.

This feeling of a softened and harmonious realism
gives a rare splendour to the older Romanesque churches,
not in Verona alone, but also in Bergamo, Trento and
Como ; the tradition is not yet formulated, the living
force of conviction has been dominant in art, and there
is no sense of contrast or distortion. The curious
sculptures on the doors of San Zeno are raised above

crudity and even comedy by the strong feeling of life in those little figures hammered out in bronze ; the frescoes on the walls never jar with the simple memorial beneath. The lions at the portals have the entire freshness of original inspiration, they have ceased to be a convention as at Parma. The northern spirit, the spirit of the mountains, breathes in those memorials. The same may be said of the fine details shown in some of the churches of Brescia, in the windows of the Broletto and in the older palaces of Bergamo. The Gothic spirit has fused into the more classical spirit of the south and produced something quite unique in the history of art.

The distinction made by Heinrich Wölfflin between the art of the North and of Italy loses its force when the art of the 12th, 13th and 14th centuries, as it came to expression in Northern Lombardy, is studied. "The essentials of art " are not here so much the " enjoyment of perfect form and the satisfaction given by pure proportions " as the immediate conversion into a plastic form of a strong emotion felt as the dominating purpose of life. The harmony achieved by classical art through the simplicity and direct value of form and line is reached here by the simplicity of emotion finding utterance in art. The naïve, in this latter case, has a finer beauty than the studied excellence of the former. The lions in the portals of the cathedrals of Verona or of Trento have more abiding beauty than the lions under the pulpit in the Baptistry of Siena sculptured there in the highest period of the Renaissance.

In addition to the great contribution to early architecture, each town had fame through the work of local artists all contributing to that immense revival of Italian painting which lasted more than two centuries, from the end of the 14th to the beginning of the 17th

—Brescia through Moretto and Romanino, Verona through Liberale and Girolamo dei Libri, Bergamo through Previtali, Moroni and even Lorenzo Lotto. The support given by the cities of Northern Lombardy to the development of art can be seen directly in the splendour of the frescoes painted by Tiepolo in the Colleoni Chapel at Bergamo, in the works of Luini scattered over a number of churches in the smaller hill towns even as far north as Como and Lugano, in the rare frescoes visible in the Sala della Ragione and the Romanesque churches of Verona. The full wealth of this movement in the north of Italy can never wholly be assessed, however, by the traveller, since the finer works of many of the Italian masters are still enshrined in the palaces where they were originally painted, and those palaces lie in quiet side streets, in silent corners where only the birds make sound and time itself has dropped to sleep.

The feeling of essential fitness, the work of art held and ennobled in its true setting, lends to the cities of the Lombardy hills a significance deeper and richer than that of the more ostentatious cities farther south ; the memorials are rarer, the frescoes less numerous, the paintings less thickly crowded together, but the impression made by them is all the more memorable.

I can never forget the pleasure given me by a simple small marble god, worn, but still living in its just sweep of line and perfect massing of shadow, seen in a court-yard of old Bergamo against a background of immense blue plain beneath. Everything came to expression in that single figure ; the courtyard with its pillars on three sides hiding spaces of sun-filled shadow had a more peaceful beauty ; the vines seemed to cling from the walls of the palace on each side across the open space in a grace that was almost symbolical, while the plain below, drenched in sun from a cloudless sky, had a sparkle of colour intensified and deepened through the shadow of that figure designing a simple gesture with an upraised arm.

The church, as San Giorgio in Verona with its superb Veronese, may have only one picture to show, but this picture is a culmination, a single final expression to the message contained in every pillar and every stone ; it sets the seal on the beauty lying round it.

*　　　*　　　*　　　*　　　*

A characteristic shared by the main towns of Northern Lombardy and Venetia lies in the creation in the very centre of the town of an asylum of quiet beauty where the wealth of the past can be appreciated with a full sympathy of understanding. While modern industry has extended the boundaries of the city, brought into being miles of streets bordered by lofty buildings and made the whole atmosphere vibrate with the sound of activity and hurried movement, the centre remains untouched in its suggestion of the peace of centuries.

In the Broletto of Brescia, the palaces of the Scaligers at Verona, the Piazza del Duomo at Bergamo and, above all, in the square at Feltre above the old town, the fine flavour of the Renaissance can be appreciated without a check ; the present yields to the past immediately without any feeling of transition, and the past itself dwells in a glory of remembrance.

An afternoon spent in the courtyard of the Scaliger palaces in Verona beneath the statue of Dante, or at Feltre beside the image of Vittorino, brings understanding of the past more vividly into the memory than prolonged study of ancient documents or even frescoes ; the atmosphere conveys the message directly to the emotions and every detail gains a new significance from this.

The 17th and 18th centuries contributed more than even the 19th century to the present position of Bergamo, Brescia and Verona ; the importance assumed by the north in the expansion of religion and literature over the south can be seen in the work of the Venetian press, in the historical and archæological school grouped in Verona round Scipione Maffei, in the movement of the great Roman prelates northwards, the Pallavicini among others, in the creation of drama and dramatic criticism. The balance of culture seemed to have moved from Rome to Bologna, to Venice, Verona, and even to Brescia.

With this, and perhaps the main cause of this, came the movement towards internationalism in thought and in trade. The trade of Brescia, Bergamo, Verona and the towns along the Brenner Pass began to revive with the interlinking of communications with the north ; the recovery of Germany after the Thirty Years War only began to have full effect a century later, and something like a powerful movement towards the south took place. Switzerland formed closer connections with Lombardy through Bergamo and Austria through Verona.

With this revival in trade and international communication, the character of the towns changed, and the first traces of industrialism appear. At the same time, the power of the great families, the Tiraboschi, the Locatelli, the Calepii in Bergamo especially, who took the place of the single dominating chiefs of the Middle Ages and Renaissance like the Scaligers and the Colleoni, began seriously to decline.

The end of the 18th century showed the rise of the

municipality to something like full domination in the
cities, and with it a change in the art and architecture
of the towns themselves ; education became an object
of public attention and the library or museum came
definitely into being as an important feature of the life
of the city. Archæological research in the 18th century
preserved for us an immense number of *lapide*, statues,
ruins of antiquity which were in danger of total
extinction.

The Church itself began to establish local printing
presses of wonderful excellence, although few of the
presses established in Northern Lombardy could rival
the work of the Seminarium of Padua. The 18th century, although less spectacular than previous centuries,
was of more importance owing to the preparation it
made for the industrial activities of a later century.

The Napoleonic epoch and the long period of revo-
lutions against the tyranny of Austria, beginning from
the end of the Napoleonic wars and ending only in 1860,
when the campaign of Victor Emmanuel in the north
came to an end, gave a new importance to Northern
Lombardy. The arena on which the whole question of
Italian Independence was fought to a triumphant conclusion was situated in the range of country between
Verona and Brescia. In this region the battles of Cus-
tozza, Solferino and Magenta were fought, and the
betrayal of Italy by France at Villafranca signed ; it is
the sacred ground of Italian Independence, the centre
of the pilgrimages of the Italians desirous of living again
in the past. At Bergamo, Brescia and the hill towns,
Garibaldi recruited a considerable part of The Thousand
which set out to conquer Sicily.

In more recent years the utilization of the immense
power contained in the water falling from the Alps

has developed to such an extent that since 1910, to confine attention to the present, the population of Bergamo and Brescia has more than doubled and the outcrop of engineering, textile and chemical factories has been formidable. With this rapid growth of industrialism, all the usual phenomena have taken place, the loss of the old simplicity and the introduction of a more artificial and more hectic life.

The memorials of the centuries stand in constant danger of uprootal, but it is still possible to renew communion with the achievements of the past in old Bergamo and live again some part of that simpler existence. The beauty of the limitless plain, lying like a blue sea beneath the ramparts of old Bergamo or the vine-clad hills with their sudden movements of storm at evening beyond the Adige at Verona, can still be enjoyed in delight unmixed with dismay at intrusion of discordant things.

*   *   *   *   *

The welding of the new Italian provinces into a unity, if not of race at least of administration, can never be achieved in the space of a few years; the racial differences between the inhabitants of the Southern Tyrol and the natives of Trento are fundamental. The whole strength of Austrian history and civilization, of Austrian art and literature, is thrown into the balance against the policy of unification. As far north as San Michele the population has been Italian in history and in sympathy; Trento is closer to Milan or Venice from every point of view but that of mere distance than Bolzano, and Bolzano, on the other hand, has a closer affinity to Innsbruck or even Munich than Trento.

The landscape changes with the change of race; the Brenta Alps differ in structure and in colour from

THE ROSENGARTEN WITH THE VAJOLETT TOWERS

the Dolomites ; the somewhat arid vine-clad slopes of Rovereto and Trento yield to the luscious vineyards and rich orchards of the Southern Tyrol.

The memorials left by the centuries have little in common ; the painted palaces of Venice, although the moist air from the lagoons has washed away their frescoes, come irresistibly to memory when the palaces of Trento are seen, with their frescoes still visible in a flaky beauty, but Merano or Bolzano has no echo of Italian culture or art beyond a colonnaded street and an occasional arcade.

The north, with its high-peaked gables and its Gothic decoration in church and palace, has stamped its design on those towns so completely that the Italian architecture of Trento would appear wholly at variance in every detail. The native of the Trento, seeing the statue of Dante silhouetted against the hills, hails him with reverence as a national symbol, but the Bozener knows nothing of Dante and places his faith in Walther von der Vogelweide ; for him, Dante is representative of an entirely foreign culture.

This antagonism of the centuries may never wholly be eliminated but, for the traveller, the great interest of the whole province lies exactly in this division ; he moves at once from the classical serenity of the sun-filled arcades of Trento to the more imaginative and more tormented world of Tyrol, from the deliberate simplicity of the Italian palace and church to the grotesque fantasy of the Tyrol memorials. The feeling of change quickens imagination and strengthens vision even for the slightest details, the inscription on a tombstone, the fount in a church, the picture behind an altar, the statue on a fountain.

Tyrol is steeped in legend bequeathed from the past

and cherished by the present with an enthusiasm unknown to the southern provinces ; each mountain always wears the aspect of familiar friend with no dangerous moments. The Rosengarten, with its serrated peaks where colour appears to be held in a radiance of tone incredible to anyone who has not seen it in morning or the full noonday sun, lives and palpitates through the legendary armies of fairies living within it ; the mountaineer, looking up from the mirror of the Karersee towards the high wall of the hills before him rich with the majesty of sheer precipice and sharp uplift of rock against the sky, feels in his heart a sudden intimacy of communion, and gives to that vision the significance of an eternal religion.

Only in the valley north of the Val di Non does the true spirit of the mountain country become apparent ; at Trento the plain of Lombardy still seems to cast a suave listlessness over the hills, thinning the blue of the peaks beyond the valleys and softening the tones of the rocks, but beyond it the sudden uplift and glow of passion becomes intensely real. The castle overlooking from its heights the quiet little town of Klausen or the strangely impressive crosses on the Kalvarienberg at Bolzano, have a definite message for the Tyrolese ; they remind him of a history passing from the long centuries behind him towards the future beyond him, a history of struggle and passionate assertion of faith either for a feudal lord or a sorely stressed church, and of a religion with an appeal never silent and never wholly extinguished in his heart.

Such an attitude may appear unreal now, but the main characteristic of the Tyrolese is exactly intense conservatism, a reliance on tradition and precept rather than on individual action.

The historical sense exerts a powerful influence even when the material conditions of life have changed ; it acted in the affirmation of liberty in the Revolution of 1809 when Andreas Hofer resisted the French domination ; it acted during the whole of the earlier centuries of Tyrolese history when Bavaria strove to annex Tyrol and Austria schemed for expansion to the west. The Counts of Tyrol were something more than local dignitaries ; they affirmed and held their position of equality with the reigning princes of Europe ; they formed a tradition of chivalry which the years have not entirely swept away.

The knightly figure on the wall of the church at Bolzano, the innumerable tombs in the churches scattered through Tyrol at Brixen, Klausen, St. Leonard, the strangely realistic frescoes painted in the Neustift at Brixen, or on the church walls at Stegen, came together in the vision of Castle Tyrol perched above the vineyards of Merano, and gave to Tyrol its strength to inspire affection and its power to cause unquestioning loyalty in the emotions of its inhabitants.

Tyrol is quite dead to the traveller without some perception of those influences. Beside the glory of mountain and still lake, there is the glory of the achievement of the past, the flavour of a unique art visible not only in altars, altar screens and frescoes, but also in cloisters and in castles, in the simple decoration of a room or the wooden balcony of a cottage, and the flavour of a history, part true and part legend, enshrined in the landscape itself.

The Romanesque sculpture of Castle Tyrol or the pillar of St. Leonard is no longer the sculpture of a period which found expression in the churches of Verona or laid a decoration on the windows of the Duomo at Trento ;

c

the spirit has changed, the figures are cruder but the passion shown in them is more intense.

The gracious beauty of the portal of the Duomo of Trento or the chaste simplicity of the fountain close to it, where a single figure of a child is kneeling on a pillar of exquisitely chased marble, find no counterpart in the stronger and cruder art of the Southern Tyrol, but in their place there is always a sense of effort, of yearning, of everlasting endeavour. The crudeness we see is a crudeness of desire, of vision beyond the range of achievement, and this is, in many things, a finer excellence than the perfect accuracy of shadow and line admired farther south.

Tyrol has inexhaustible treasures beyond the glowing landscape and the wonders of the sky in the morning and evening hours; it speaks always of a past glory that is a present glory, of a past beauty which has become a nobler present beauty. The change in government does not touch those eternal issues; Italian or Austrian, the appeal of Tyrol remains unchanged, unbroken.

CHAPTER II

BERGAMO AND THE BERGAMASCANS

THE Alps disappear from view as the traveller leaves Turin on the way to Milan, and only reappear when Milan is left behind and Treviglio is reached. There is a feeling of renewing old associations when the faint blue of the hills rises on the faint purple of the horizon, and provides a delicate contrast to the immense sea of green or yellowish brown, as the seasons may come ; the immensity becomes bounded, and a sense of familiarity takes the place of inadequacy and even monotony.

There is no longer any need to reconstruct a vision of beauty from small details, a vine-festooned villa with shadowy clusters of grapes, a farm-house decorated with scarlet pepper pods laid out to dry in the sun, a clump of canes bending gracefully over a dark pool or a quiet river moving through willows. The plain of Lombardy has its own power of attraction, if only through its evenly spaced mulberry-trees or through isolated rows of poplars ranged beside the grey-green waters of the Po or glittering fields of rice, where the sun strikes down to the water and throws a reflected gleam into the grasses above, but it is less impressive through this wealth of detail than the plains of the Romagna or the marshy levels round Ferrara.

In the Romagna the sky comes down directly to the

fields, and everything becomes suggestive through the complete harmony of immense stretches of warm brown colour fading into the purple above, and then cooling off to the rich blue overhead. In this landscape, everything moving becomes almost symbolical ; the oxen driver with his white oxen taking pine trunks from the Pineta, the herdsman driving small groups of swine over the green margins by the roadside ; the churches seem to be balanced between earth and sky when the twilight comes, and only the red roofs take the gleam.

This aspect of the Romagna moved Carducci most of all even as it moved Dante. The picture of the peasant girl standing in the cornfield in " Idillio Maremmano," with the immense summer flaming round her, is unforgettable :

> Com'il ciano seren tra'l bondeggiante
> Or de le spicche, tra la chioma flava
> Fioria quell' occhio azzurro ; e a te d'avante
> La grande estate, e intorno, fiammeggiava.[1]

This impression can only be recaptured with difficulty on the plain farther north under special conditions of light and colour, and the feeling is rather of movement in a rich historical place beside broad rivers and before the distant shadow of the hills.

The hill towns have a greater significance than the towns of the plain, for they represent the older traditions when the wars of the Middle Ages made the plain dwellers defenceless against barbarism and the more lasting elements in progress could only exist in the security afforded by the mountains. The plain loses its power to inspire confidence through its accessibility

[1] As the tranquil cornflower among the billowing gold of the corn, so that blue eye flowered among the yellow hair ; and around thee and before thee the immense summer flamed.

to the invaders from the north and the condottieri from the south, and, of the civilization of the past, only a few traces remain. The towns existing at present are comparatively modern successors of towns destroyed in previous centuries.

In the hill towns, however, the past has still many of its most cherished memorials complete, and it is possible to reconstruct with some measure of truth the life of the earlier centuries when war and pestilence ravaged the plain beneath. Of those hill towns, Como, Bergamo, Brescia, and Verona are, perhaps, the most significant, although of the four, the first two are alone hill towns proper, the other two being ranged at the foot of the Alps within easy distance of the last spurs of the mountains as they grade down into the plain.

*　　　*　　　*　　　*　　　*

Before passing through directly to Bergamo from Milan, the traveller should spend a few hours examining the altar of the church of San Martino and the frescoes in the organ chapel in the cathedral at Treviglio.

Although Treviglio has not the same romantic past as Monza with the famous " iron crown " of Lombardy preserved in its cathedral, it contains in the church of San Martino and the cathedral some of the most important work of the two Lombardian artists of the 15th century, Butinone and Zenale, who, with Foppa and Giovanni della Chiesa, were the only artists of distinction Lombardy could show as its contribution to the Renaissance of Italian art during the Quattrocento.

Both Zenale and Butinone were pupils of Foppa, as observation of the paintings in Treviglio can show at the first glance, but it is unjust to term them mere imitators. The altar in San Martino bears comparison with the magnificent altar of Mantegna in San Zeno, and has undoubtedly been modelled on it in many essentials. The convention of angels singing and playing musical instruments on each side of the Madonna has been adopted without, however, the exquisitely natural gestures and poses of the Mantegna angels. The influence of Foppa has been sufficient to coarsen the treatment and weaken the delicacy of suggestion which gives to Mantegna's choir the interest and even humour of an interlude.

The altar in San Martino is built in two stages of equal value divided into two main pictures, the Madonna enthroned with angels above, by Butinone, and St. Martin tearing his cloak, by Zenale below; on the right side of the Madonna is a panel showing St. John the Baptist, St. John the Evangelist and St. Stephen; on the left, Saints Lucca, Catherine and Magdalene; on the right side of St. Martin, Saints Gustavus and Peter, and on the left, Saints Paul, Antony of Padua and Sebastian.

The whole altar is conceived in almost exactly the same architectural design as Mantegna's altar at San Zeno, the panels are separated by gilded wooden pillars of an intricate design with rich arabesque of gold, and the whole is surmounted by a richly decorated " gable " in accordance with convention. The simplicity of Mantegna has given way here, however, to decoration, excessive in the case of the St. Martin picture, and the figures themselves contrast too suddenly with the golden background.

The characteristics of Foppa, crude contrast of light and shade with a strong feeling for anatomy, a strained composition based on unnatural posing of the principal figures within an architectural scheme, have been retained, but there is a surer feeling for the purely decorative, the careful placing of figures within a beautiful frame against minute architectural detail, and the lowering of colour tones towards a greater unity and harmony of effect show individuality on the part of both painters.

The intensity of living force, the direct, if harsh, expression of emotion which gave to Foppa his unique position in the history of Northern Italian art has been weakened down to symbolism and even convention. The figure of St. Martin on his horse is stiff and unnatural, while the horse itself has been crushed into the space left within the archway ; there is no room for gesture or movement.

In the Cappella del Organo in the cathedral, there are shadowy frescoes visible in the vaulted roof, relics of what was once a series of frescoes covering the walls of the whole chapel. The feeling for architectural detail is visible here again in the painting of the ribs of the ceiling, meeting in a centre-piece showing God. The figures of angels flying from billowy draperies towards the centre from the open sides of the ribs have a delicate grace more poetical than that shown in the altar of San Martino. The tendency, however, to sacrifice anatomy and natural gesture to decoration can be seen in the deliberate swelling-out of the angels' robes and in the naked cherubs at each corner.

There are traces still on the walls of the early frescoes which were swept away through neglect or through the efforts of decorators intent on applying a more garish splendour to the simplicity and beauty of the older paintings. In the church of the Madonna delle Lagrime there is also a " predella " by a Lombardian artist of the 16th century worthy of examination, if only through the picture it gives of contemporary life.

Treviglio, beyond those paintings of the Quattrocento

and Cinquecento, has little further to offer, and the traveller can pass on to Bergamo, now visible in the distance against the blue and shadowy purple of the hills. The plain becomes dotted with more and more villages, each with their church and bell tower, brown tiled, and always echoing to the sound of bells.

*   *   *   *   *

Like Orvieto and Perugia, Old Bergamo is still a walled town, and like them enjoys a position of unique advantage for the appreciation of beautiful panorama. The city itself is split up into the old town proper, built on a hill with its *ceinture* of walls making it self-contained, and Bergamo Piana built on the plain beneath.

While the old town has remained unchanged during the centuries with the atmosphere of the Middle Ages and Renaissance clinging round it and giving it a rare attraction, the lower town throbs with a busy commercial life, and is in fact one of the most flourishing financial and business centres of Lombardy. Bergamo Piana pushes out each year farther and farther into the plain, factories crop up in unsuspected corners and power stations supplied from the Alps ; the feverish, and somewhat artificial, activity of modern industrial life robs it more and more of that leisurely enjoyment of existence which can only be relished in some districts of Italy.

While Old Bergamo dreams of the Sforza, the Visconti and Colleoni, and treasures its manuscripts in the Civic Library once the Palace of the Commune, New Bergamo honours Donizetti in the Teatro Donizetti or erects new schools of technology and agriculture in the ambition to be the most progressive town in Italy. It is a piquant contrast of civilizations and cultures, a Manchester asserting itself against Oxford, and it is doubtful whether, in moving forward towards intenser industrialism, something of great value has not been sacrificed.

The traveller may find in the new city some clue to the modern Italian spirit, perhaps more clearly shown here than in any other town in Italy, and, with the knowledge of this spirit, climb up the steep hillside, over flights of cobbled steps, to Old Bergamo, and compare the present with the past. To the modern Italian, as we find him in Bergamo, the memory of Francesco Nullo and the contribution of Bergamo to the Risorgimento, especially to the expedition of The Thousand under Garibaldi is only second in importance to the memory of the achievement of Donizetti.

A successful reproduction in the Opera House of " Lucia di Lammermoor " is of greater significance to him than the beauty of the Cappella Colleoni, and the scientific exploitation of agriculture in the surrounding country with its greater influx of wealth into the provincial capital means more than the pious conservation of a few historical relics.

The difference in outlook is sufficiently clear ; a band of scholars, artists, historians, teachers, mostly descendants of the great families, the Pesenti, the Locatelli, the Tiraboschi, the Caversassi, still treasure every single relic of the past, keep the memorials of Old Bergamo in perfect conservation, seek out and comment on every single picture, or carving, or document reminiscent of the past and so, from year to year, reconstruct the life of Bergamo as it was in the earlier centuries. On the other hand, the new generation willingly forgets all those things, goes periodically to Milan for inspiration, shares with enthusiasm in every political, every literary and every artistic movement of the time.

The rôle played by Bergamo in common with Brescia

and Verona in the development of Fascism was only exceeded in importance by the rôle played by the Socialists when the factories of Bergamo were occupied by the workmen in 1921. The Circolo Artistico has its band of artistic enthusiasts, extravagant with gesture, but somewhat sparing in actual achievement, while the new Technical College built beside the chestnut-lined Viale Roma points to a powerful municipal interest in industrial and scientific matters.

In Old Bergamo, on the other hand, it is still possible to avoid those confusing issues and regain that simplicity of outlook, which seems to have disappeared from modern life, to look down in full tranquillity on the new city spread out into the green plain, and wonder, with a placid curiosity, what new spirit will emerge from this confusion of ideas and ideals.

The fascination of Bergamo lies as much in this contrast as in the beauty of landscape or the rich memorials of a past history. " The old gods, shorn of their mystery and reduced to impersonal forces, rise from their graves, strive for control over our life and begin anew their eternal struggle." The struggle can be seen almost clearly before the eyes, and the sense of change becomes acute, an old civilization, an old tradition yielding reluctantly to the new.

* * * * *

The designers of the walls of Old Bergamo had evidently in mind the infinite possibilities for beauty afforded by the contrast between plain and mountain, for the outer walls open out at intervals into bays commanding a view on three sides at once—in front, the infinite sea of plain broken in its exquisite harmony of blue and pale purple by an occasional campanile or spire, and only interrupted in its even gradation into the sky by the roofs and towers of Milan, and, on both sides, vine-covered hillsides with white villas encircled by poplars rising to the foot of the walls.

Beyond them, to the north, lie the Alps in masses of subdued colour warming to purple above the lower slopes where vines are grown, and rising, beyond valleys, to snow-crested peaks.

The contrast between the warm red of the roofs, the delicate green of the verdure in the near distance and the purple of the mountains is singularly beautiful, especially in the morning, when a cooling breeze comes from the Alps, and the sparkle of the sun lies on every leaf and every tile.

Century-old chestnuts are ranged in symmetry along the path inside the outer wall, so that an asylum of shade can always be found in the warm summer days when the sun lies in a white glare on the roads and the heat rises in waves from the pavement ; the entire length of the wall is shaded by those trees, and it is possible to sit on the broad coping and dream in the silence beside the radiant beauty of hill and plain.

There are few places in Italy so rich in the suggestion of peace, in the recollection of historical actions brought to tranquillity as the ramparts of Old Bergamo ; beside the gateway, that gives on the Colle Aperto, where only a few nuns with heavy black dresses pass, or an occasional priest, and the fruit-seller by the entrance seems to be stationed merely as a part of the general decoration, one can remain in the cool shadow of the foliage and enjoy the shimmer of colour in the valley beneath.

Beyond this valley the hills rise immediately, and in the early autumn mornings the white mist rising over the fields seems to be a mighty river opening out to the plain. The situation of Bergamo is almost perfect in this respect; the last spurs of the Alps come into the plain behind the town, but Bergamo itself is perched on an island of rock which forms broad valleys with those mountains. The pedestrian can leave the town by the Porta San Alessandro, climb up the hillside over the Colle Aperto and walk in a continual glory of panorama for hours, the mountains with their changing forms and colours on the one side and river-streaked plain on the other.

At the farther end of the island he can gaze into an immense sea of plain with a continual series of hills on the right, moving down into this sea. The Valle Brembana opens up before him, and beyond it the valley leading to Lecco and Lake Como. Beside the Bremba river lie clumps of poplars and alders, and beyond them the quaint buildings of Brembate, so that the eye can rest on them before gazing into the radiance beyond.

The island is criss-crossed with mule tracks and roads, through wild spaces of bush and flower or beside cool villas festooned with vines, where a fountain or a small garden statue, or even a door knocker, testifies to the loving art of past centuries.

The variety of picture obtained at every turn of the road is bewildering, and the background of plain acts as a setting of rare splendour. There are stairs from the higher roads to the lower with broad walls where the lizards bask in the sun; it is a joy to sit even on those cobbled levels, and follow the movements of a labourer pruning the vines or digging up the ground beneath.

The similarity between Amalfi and Bergamo is striking in this respect, only with the difference that the deep turquoise Bay of Salerno is replaced here by the paler tinted plain of Lombardy. In wealth of picturesque detail, in the suggestion of peace, both landscapes are the same. The old town harmonizes with the landscape ; the squares keep their fountains unchanged and the streets are darkened by the palaces that darkened them in the 15th and 16th centuries.

The contrast between the modern spirit and the spirit dwelling in the memorials of the past can be seen in one very small detail in Bergamo. On the open space in front of the church of San Agostino, with its simple romanesque façade, the Bergamascans have placed the ground for a peculiarly Bergamascan game, a long-distance tennis with no courts where the four players stand from one hundred to one hundred and fifty yards apart, and strike the ball with a small drum attached to the hand and wrist. The main principle is to keep the ball in the air as long as possible, and strike it as high as the strength of the wrist will permit. The dexterity shown is often remarkable, and the combination of flitting figures and sharp booming of the drums have a strange fascination, especially towards sunset, when the quaint buildings of the old town to the right are outlined against gold and the valley to the left below the walls fills with rich purple colour.

A further game is played with large stone balls, similar to bowling without a green, where the policy of striking away the opponent's ball is adopted. The green in front of San Agostino acts as an excuse for both games, and the peacefulness suggested by the church contrasts with the active spirit seeking expression before it. On feast days, the Bergamascans put on their rucksacks and go off towards the Alps, towards San Pellegrino, and thence trace out a day's ramble among the mountains, returning in a joyous crowd to the cafés at night. The Bergamascan character resembles more

closely the Tyrolese or the Swiss in this love of the Alps
than the typical Italian; the whole province becomes
mapped out for him in a series of mountain rambles,
and every beautiful haunt where the glory of the
panorama comes close to vision appears almost as
familiar to him as the Piazza Garibaldi or the Sentirone.

*　　　*　　　*　　　*　　　*

The history of Bergamo is largely a history of
conflicting forces, using the hill town as a basis for
operations, southward into Italy or for defence against
the hostile armies coming from beyond the Alps; the
Romans placed in it one of their main outposts in
Cisalpine Gaul, and relics of the Roman occupation can
be seen in the lower sections of the outer wall near the
Porta San Giacomo, where ten arches of the ancient
town wall can still be seen. The entrance to the Civic
Library in the Piazza Garibaldi has many stones on its
walls indicating the importance of Bergamo under the
Roman regime.

Bergamo, in common with Aquileia, Verona and Milan
was governed by a quadrumvir, or main provincial
governor, and it acted also as a religious centre. The
vision of Bergamo from the plain must have been
superb in Roman times—an immense structure of
strongly fortified walls topped by palaces of the
provincial Roman dignitaries, by temples to Venus,
Neptune, Jupiter and the immortal gods, by the Capitol, the Forum and the numerous trading institutions
where the whole of the northern part of Cisalpine Gaul
was represented. There are still traces of those temples
in the column visible at San Alessandro, of those palaces
in the ruins in Via Bartolomeo Colleoni, while the
Rocca, now the headquarters of the military division,
was once the site of the Capitol. The fall of the Roman

Empire led almost at once to abandonment of the provincial administration, but the Bergamascans, in virtue of their position, were able to protect the town from destruction.

This element contributed greatly to the value of Bergamo in the eyes of the early Lombard princes as a centre for dominating surrounding territory. The Vandals, the Goths, the Longobards and the Franks contributed in turn to the moulding of the town ; it has been suggested that even Charlemagne visited Bergamo on his way south to Rome. The destruction of the town, after the defeat of Gottfried and Ambrogio in 894, by Arnolfo would have meant total extinction of Bergamo, and its disappearance from history, if the Bishop Adalbert had not begun again the rebuilding of the walls and attracted new forces from the provinces. The Middle Ages were peculiarly rich in stories of revolting massacre, when the policy of extermination formed an essential part of the theory of military domination, but Bergamo, with Lodi, was specially unfortunate even in this age.

The wars of the Investitures coming after the struggle for the possession of Lombardy, and the rise of the Communes in Northern Italy quenched in blood by Frederick Barbarossa, brought new fame to the town. The Diet of Roncaglia, formed after the destruction of the Communes, simply forced the cities of Bergamo, Cremona, Brescia, Mantua and Milan to sign an agreement of mutual protection in 1167. The result of the struggle between Barbarossa and the Lombard League, supported by the Pope, can be seen in the pavement in front of St. Mark's, Venice, where the defeat of Barbarossa led to a humiliation unequalled in history.

The struggle between the Guelfs and Ghibellines under

Frederick II and his successors, interspersed by the domination of Northern Italy through John of Bohemia, Azzo and Barnabo Visconti, brought a succession of disasters to the provincial capital. The reign of Gian Galeazzo, described by Marjorie Bowen in the *Viper of Milan*, followed by that of Martino Visconti, Pandolfo Malatesta, Facino Cane, Sigismund Malatesta and Filippo Mario Visconti, simply meant a continual oppression of every element tending towards freedom and culture— a long progression of shadows veiled in blood.

Finally, as a measure of protection against this continual invasion and destruction, Bergamo decided, in 1428, to dedicate itself spontaneously to the Venetian Republic. In return for this voluntary dedication to Venice, the city of Bergamo was allowed to retain all its ancient prerogatives, and the cathedral of Santa Maria Maggiore received each year seventy-three golden florins, the Ospedale Maggiore, thirteen ducats and the churches of the Santi Protettori forty-six imperial lire. The period then ensuing was notable in Bergamascan annals for the rise to power of Bartolomeo Colleoni, whose influence is sufficiently important in the history of Venetia to merit a more detailed study.

After Colleoni, Lodovico il Moro, the successor of the Sforza of Milan, invaded Bergamo, and his French allies sacked it after him in turn. The French were twice in occupation between 1509 and 1529, and Maximilian seven times. In the period 1561–88 the city became fortified and took on the appearance we now see, with a double ring of walls opening out into powerful bastions and accessible through four gates, the Porta San Alessandro, San Giacomo, San Agostino and San Lorenzo, each designed in Renaissance style by different architects. This series of fortications has since undergone no change, and can be appreciated almost as vividly as it was appreciated in the 16th century.

The vicissitudes of Bergamo during the 17th and 18th centuries were less noteworthy than in the previous centuries, and the town enjoyed a period of comparative tranquillity. The fall of the Venetian Republic in 1797 initiated that period of French and Austrian domination, which culminated in 1870 in the formation of the new Italian State under Victor Emmanuel. In the struggle for independence, Bergamo played an important part, and in the person of Francesco Nullo contributed to the Garibaldian epic one of its noblest characters.

D

CHAPTER III

A SOLDIER OF THE RENAISSANCE :
BARTOLOMEO COLLEONI

ALTHOUGH the greatest figures of the Italian Renaissance were to be found farther south than Bergamo at Milan, Venice, Ferrara and Bologna, one hero stands out in Bergamascan history, unique almost in that early Renaissance period, Bartolomeo Colleoni. Colleoni has been ennobled for ever in the wonderful equestrian statue by Verrocchio in Venice where, in the imagination of the sculptor, the Roman tradition had been transmuted intact in this general of the Venetian Republic, and in the architectural gem built beside Santa Maria Maggiore in Old Bergamo, the Capella Colleoni, where a northern counterpart of the Capella Medici in Florence perpetuates the memory of the founder.

The life of Colleoni possesses even now for us an absorbing interest if only through the light it casts on that period when the condottieri came to full splendour and horror of achievement ; he has been described as the last of the classical condottieri in Italy, although this assertion may be doubted when we consider the struggles which continued all through the 15th and 16th centuries farther south, in Florence, Naples and Sicily.

The Papacy could never quite dispense with a hired

general, which was the true designation of a condottiere, and kept the tribe alive long after it had been extinguished alsewhere. It was certainly responsible, as Burckhardt has pointed out, for the introduction of the condottieri on a large scale into Italy. Gregory XI granted the overlordship of the two towns, Bagnacavello and Cotignola, to the first of the condottieri, John Hawkwood, and this example was decisive for other rulers in Italy.

The period between Hawkwood and Colleoni, almost the entire 15th century, constitutes one of most fascinating and most bloody chapters in Italian history, as well as its richest time of blossom in literature, art and sculpture. The age itself was responsible for the peculiar mentality it produced in its warriors and rulers; the duplicity and political rapacity of the various princes of Italy which made Machiavelli advocate the establishment of a central despotic government as the only hope for Italy, acted also in the case of the condottieri, and produced in them what we may now consider as the most truly representative product of the 15th century.

It is difficult to see how the condottieri could preserve any real nobility of character and service ; the fate of Carmagnola shows how a leader of fairly high standard of honour fared with the unscrupulous seigneurs of the Quattrocento. The peculiar conditions under which Italy lay as a prey for the two contending forces, the Empire and the Papacy, produced a peculiar mentality in the rulers who lived under this perpetual menace of destruction from one side or the other. It was absolutely vital for those seigneurs to be efficient to the last degree in the practical art of statesmanship or, if incapable of becoming efficient to this extent, to employ someone to make good their deficiencies.

The deficiencies of the Papacy from the temporal as apart from the spiritual point of view were met as we have seen by employing mercenaries under a hired general; the time when the power of the Church was sufficient to summon nations and national armies in its defence had disappeared entirely; a repetition of Canossa was impossible in the logical Italy of the 15th century, and the Pope was forced to rely on condottieri. In this sense, the Papacy set the fashion, and the practice of hiring condottieri to protect their towns spread to almost every overlord.

The conflict between the various overlords was only rivalled by the conflict between the overlord himself and his defender; if successful, the condottiere became too powerful, and it was necessary to get rid of him, usually by poison or a judicious dagger-thrust; if unsuccessful, the sins of the overlord were passed on to the condottiere and he was sacrificed, as a rule, to appease the discontent of the subjects nominally protected by him.

The change from autonomous and republican government in the Communes to an overlordship as practised in Milan, Cremona, Brescia, Verona, Perugia, Siena, Genoa and many other towns was caused largely through the necessity for some unity of command against the invasion from the north or from neighbouring towns. The existence of the overlord depended, therefore, on his capacity to carry out this function, and the condottiere gave him a convenient foil to ward off criticism.

The condottiere himself, faced with the prospect of disaster, no matter how events developed, temporized with opposing condottieri, and we have the extraordinary spectacle in the 15th century of two enemy armies fraternizing with each other and arranging together the plan of campaign. Pius II describes one piquant episode. When it was a question of routing Giacomo Piccinino out of Siena, the troops sent against him decided it would be better for both sides to keep him in Siena. " If he were to be defeated, we would have to return to the plough." During the siege of Orbetello, where Piccinino took refuge after Siena, the besieging army kept the garrison supplied with food, and they had no difficulty in arranging matters to the satisfaction of everyone.

The loss of his army meant disaster and death for the condottiere, and it was therefore a matter of immediate concern to obtain victory with a minimum of casualties, however much the civilian population should suffer. The history of the 15th century was a history of massacre, but not of great casualties in battle, of intrigue against the condottieri by their employers, but seldom of the condottieri against each other. Treachery was recognized as good policy where events made treachery profitable, while the amassing of wealth was held to justify any foul action. The history of the Venetian Republic in this last respect is not edifying.

The campaign of murder and treachery culminated at last in elimination of the smaller overlords themselves and, with them, of the less important condottieri, so that, at the end of the 15th century something like a balance of power existed in Italy between the four great States—Milan, Venice, Naples and the Papacy.

The position of the condottieri in the development of Italian history can never be exactly defined owing to the fact that, for the majority of the successful condottieri, this period of activity signified merely a transitional period towards something more stable and more permanent. The Sforza, for example, were condottieri only until they became rulers in Milan. From that moment onwards, the duty of the Sforza lay in suppressing entirely the condottiere movement since the main strength of their rivals depended on a constant and abundant provision of armed mercenaries. The first principle of the condottiere was to ensure some such definite position, and expand from that centre outwards. The Sforza occupied Milan, and from it spread their net over Lombardy as far north as Bergamo and the Valley of the Adda ; Piccinino found headquarters in Bologna, and from that stronghold waged incessant war on the inhabitants of the Marches, strugling over possession of the Romagna with Sigismund Malatesta of Rimini.

Before the end of the 15th century, the transformation of the condottieri into regional potentates was virtually complete, and the *raison d'être* of the condottiere disappeared. In place of the former princes who had employed these mercenaries, Italy was supplied with a new set of rulers, worse even than the rulers displaced ; the history of the Baglioni of Perugia, of Ferrante of Aragon at Naples, of the Malatesta at Rimini is a history inscribed in blood. Ferrante of Aragon must surely belong to the chosen band of murderers of all time.

The transition was therefore unfortunate for Italy as a whole, and the rise to power of the condottiere seldom contributed in any one district to the maintenance of that glory in literature and art which had already given to Italy a position unique in modern history. There are few cases on record of condottieri encouraging art and literature to the same degree as the Medici of Florence, the Esti of Ferrara, the Gonzagas of Mantua, or the first Aragon at Naples. They were exceptional in this. Mention may be made here of the *Tempio*

Malatestiano at Rimini erected by Sigismund Malatesta, where the simple beauty of the interior is marred by a continual series of inscriptions to the effect that Sigismund Malatesta caused the church to be erected, and the Cappella Colleoni in Bergamo, where a genuine love of art has brought into existence one of the architectural jewels of the Renaissance.

It is important to dwell on the distinction between the memorial erected by Malatesta and the memorial erected by Bartolomeo Colleoni, since it provides a clue to the character of both men. The *Templo Malatestiano* would appear now, if bereft of the ennobling and softening influence of time, as merely a vulgar exhibition of the fame of Malatesta without taste and without the simplicity of a true conviction ; the long inscriptions on the arches before each altar and over the portals are so many claims to the attention of God. Malatesta did not raise this church to satisfy an inner desire for salvation ; it was rather a crude statement of his claim to charitable judgment on the part of posterity, and at the same time a triumphant affirmation of his own position on earth.

The Temple set a seal on a career of triumphant rascality, without refinement and without soul. The atmosphere speaks of this more than words, even the beautiful fresco of Pier della Francesca, where Sigismund Malatesta, a pious figure in a simple cloak, kneels before Saint Sigismund, suffers in its appeal through the association of the saint and sinner. The pose is too artificial. The conflict between the paganism shown in the sculpture of the altars, in the groups of *putti* (cherubs) carved in the marble of the pillars, and on the altar rails weakens the unity of effect and the sensation of truth disappears— truth as conviction, as a surrender to an eternal faith.

On the other hand, the keynote of the Cappella

Colleoni is unity of impression, of inspiration, of trust ; there is immensely more detail in it than in the *Tempio Malatestiano*, but it is a complexity united in vision. The sensation on entering the Chapel is, on a smaller scale, the sensation felt on entering the Medici Chapel in Florence ; everything grades into the single effect of beauty, a cultivated, smoothly shining beauty where everything is in perfectly good taste. There is no attempt to claim the undivided attention of God ; the Chapel was conceived as a memorial to Colleoni and a memorial it remains, nothing more, nothing less.

Malatesta would appear to be therefore of a totally different type from Colleoni, more primitive, more passionate, more brutal, but also more naïve ; there is a certain pathos in those inscriptions in the church of Rimini, the feeling that Malatesta himself had little faith in his power, through erection of this memorial to himself and to God, to turn away the wrath that would befall him. Through this alone, the church has more force of appeal to the emotions than the Colleoni Chapel.

Colleoni was evidently satisfied with his part of life, reposefully confident of an adequate return for services performed on earth. The feeling of rest after a life-time of arduous struggle, the suggestion of a powerful mentality, come here to tranquillity, give a certain finite beauty to the chapel not without appeal, but without that appeal that arises from a tragic renunciation, a bitter expression of ultimate defeat.

Examination of the statue made by Verrocchio for the Republic of Venice to commemorate the services of Colleoni for the *Serenissima* confirms this reflection. The sculptor had evidently modelled from the life, since it would be difficult to imagine so clearly and so vividly the lineaments of this warrior mounted on a charger ;

THE TOMB OF BARTOLOMEO COLLEONI

the expression of relentless bravery coupled with a certain cruelty in the mouth is tempered, however, by the justice seen in the eyes. The feeling of one who, even in the midst of treachery, would uphold whatever policy convention decided, with rugged honesty in the performance of his duty gives to the statue a living force which we miss in the memorials to the courtlier princes farther south.

The simplicity we admire and even reverence at times in the mounted figures of the Scaligers at Verona is repeated here with modifications ; Colleoni comes closer than the Scaligers to the Roman ideal, not only in the shrewd handling of business affairs and in the direct knowledge of military tactics, but also in the sensuous love of women, represented in the statue by the lips themselves and the folds of the chin and throat. Verrocchio ennobles him as a perfect leader, of a commanding presence, a powerful fighting machine, strong in physique, but, with those attributes, some of those weaknesses which darkened the character of other condottieri for us.

Even in Colleoni, the soldier of fortune was not a noble type, and, although Spino states him to be of a masculine dignity accompanied by kindness and prudence, it is scarcely credible that such an age, with its daily narration of massacre and desecration, of pillage and murder, could allow any decent feeling to survive. The fact that one writer of authority can speak thus of Colleoni shows that the iron had not wholly entered into the soul of Colleoni, and made him as consummate a villain as Sigismund Malatesta.

Unlike his peers, Colleoni preserved some of the vivacity and energy of the mountains, and Gian Galeazzo Maria Visconti, according to one legend, expressed surprise at the Bergamascan leading his army into action on foot. This habit of abandoning the position which riding into battle would have given him, points rather more to the caution of Colleoni than to his physical vigour. It is refreshing to find among warriors who believed in the motto—" Tout s'arrange "—one for whom the shining sword meant a real weapon and not a pretty symbol.

Colleoni, unlike his fellow condottieri, preferred a fair, clean fight to assassination or poisoning, and this hatred of subterfuge may well have explained his lack of success in gaining an independent State where he would be his own ruler, as Piccinino at Bologna or Sforza at Milan. His one opportunity for seizing Milan came when the last of the Visconti was overthrown, but he had decided by this time that the fate that befell Carmagnola at Venice might well be his at Milan and wisely refrained.

The Colleoni family was Ghibelline, a dangerous fault in a town so close to Milan, which from time immemorial had been Guelf, and resented any movement towards association with the Empire or its representatives. The Soardi family, an ardent group of Guelfs, expelled the Colleoni from Bergamo, and forced them to take refuge at Rocca di Trezzo on the banks of the Adda ; at Rocca di Trezzo, a general massacre left only Bartolomeo and his mother as survivors, and they fell in turn into the hands of the tyrant of Cremona who, by some fortunate chance, let them go after a time. From Cremona, Colleoni went to Piacenza and enlisted in the army of Braccio di Montone. Profiting by the example of Montone, he became a captain himself, and soon gathered together sufficient men to make it a matter of sound policy to hire him or at least to keep him neutral.

In his varying capacity as associate or as enemy, according to the seigneur employing him, he came into intimate relations with Carmagnola, Francesco Gonzaga and Gattamelata, the last named of whom has been ennobled for ever in the statue by Donatello at the Santo of Padua. From Braccio di Montone he gained his first insight into the value of the modern policy of strong mobile reserves supporting a comparatively weak front line. The tactics generally adopted at that time consisted merely in one overwhelming assault with every available soldier ; Colleoni, however, avoided the initial assault, and launched his reserves at the moment when the enemy had spent his force in attack.

With Braccio, Colleoni took place in the wars of Queen Joanna, in the battles at Riccardina against Gian Galeazzo Visconti and at Caravaggio, in the assault on Cremona and later, in the service of the Venetian Republic, acted under Sforza on the attack on Milan defended by Piccinino and Gonzaga. In common with other condottieri, he had no difficulty in changing banners, from Venice to Milan, from Milan to Venice with Sforza and again to Venice, but it is permissible to see in this a fairly steady attachment to the *Serenissima*. In 1451, for example, the sentence of death passed on him by the Council of Ten made desertion of Venice a vital necessity, while, on another occasion, the lack of activity of Venice threw him into unemployment from which the only escape lay in joining Filippo Maria Visconti. It is certainly true that his greatest successes were achieved under Sforza rather than under the Venetian generals and, in the war of 1452–53, against Venice.

The fame of Colleoni as a politician in the service of Venice was only rivalled by his reputation as a military tactician ; he acted as an intermediary between the Republic and the Fieschi of Genoa, the Overlord of Mantua, the Princes of Ferrara and Modena, treated with the emissaries of the Angevins against Naples, with the exiles from Florence against the Medici, and formed cordial relations with the Dukes of Burgundy and Savoy. The balance of power, always a difficult matter in the greater States of Europe, demanded genius of the first order in intrigue, and Colleoni had in this more success than his more polished brethren, largely through the impression he disseminated of the will being preliminary to the deed.

As a Bergamascan, he remained true to tradition by demanding and obtaining fabulous sums for his intervention, military or political ; the Governor of Verona complained to Venice of the exactions of Colleoni, the most rapacious condottiere who had ever despoiled the population of the lands of the Adige. Princes, like the Duke of Modena, borrowed freely from him at profitable terms, for Colleoni, and we know that even the Popes were among his debtors. According to Burckhardt, the fortune left by him at his death amounted to 216,000 ducats, or almost £300,000 in our money, an enormous sum in the 15th century, and quite notable even now. Part of this wealth went to the building of the Colleoni Chapel.

Like the Sforza, Colleoni, though comparatively uneducated himself and capable only of using the Bergamascan idiom, liked association with men of letters and artists, and, with the extraordinary facility of the Renaissance, could speak intelligently with some of the leading philosophers of his time.

The faculty of caution and objective criticism let him see when the whole tendency of his period was changing

and the internecine policy, which had made the condottiere system possible, was yielding to comparative
tranquillity consequent on the establishment of a balance
of power among the more powerful princes of Italy, and
we see him retiring in full middle age to the hill-town
of Bergamo to enjoy the leisure rendered possible by his
military career.

Some writers have looked on this as a disastrous
culmination, a swift sunset to a career full of splendour,
but we may regard it as a recognition of a greater
conjunction of forces than any Colleoni had to face and
defeat before ; the fate of Carmagnola was still too fresh
in his memory to make him trust his whole existence
to the Venetian Republic.

The retreat to Bergamo was undoubtedly an act of
profound wisdom, and allowed him to end his life in
a peace enjoyed by none of his contemporaries. At
Bergamo, now almost thirty years under Venice, he
lived in retirement for eighteen years, surrounded by
his veterans, discussing philosophy with the *litterati* of
Venetia, and planning new methods of communication
by water between Bergamo, Milan and Venice. In the
last years of his life, he arranged the details of the
Cappella Colleoni, his tomb and his memorial to posterity, and on his death, in 1475, bequeathed to the
Signoria of Venice a sufficient sum to raise in Venice
an equestrian statue. This statue, by Verrocchio, as
we now see it before the School of St. Mark's, forms
with Donatello's Gattamelata one of the finest achievements in bronze of the Italian Renaissance.

*   *   *   *   *

The first view of the chapel through the pillars
supporting the Civic Library across the Piazza Garibaldi,
is very striking through the contrast between the dark

shadow of the frame and the vivid colours of the marble forming the façade.

The attempt to combine the Gothic arabesque of detail, re-forming the rose-window in its exquisite tracery of marble, and the successive biforia in a row beneath the cornice especially, with the more obvious decoration of the classical Renaissance has given to the façade an originality of conception almost unique in the 15th century. The struggle between the horizontal and the vertical line is more acute here than even in the façade of the cathedral of Orvieto, and the unity of artistic effect suffers accordingly.

The feeling that the process of distillation in the mind of the architect has never been completed, and that the perception of beauty has been obscured in the too close observance of detail—a feeling that disappears entirely when we are confronted by the radiant splendour of the façade of the Certosa di Pavia, a façade conceived by the same architect, Amadeo, in a similar style of architecture on an immensely larger scale—intensifies the sensation of an architectural jewel with every detail a brilliant facet.

The groundwork of diamond-shaped tiles of red, dusky green and white marble is almost Oriental in suggestion, and throws into relief the white medallions on the side pillars and the white marble of the doorway and windows.

The suave use of colour has undoubtedly brought everything into a finer proportion ; without the alternation between the white of the roses and the green of the plaques in the outer section of the rose-window, the whole window would appear impossibly heavy, while the exquisitely beautiful colonnades stretching beneath the cornice to form a loggeta would be too massive in effect without the alternation of red and white. In a single tone of white, the architectural defects would stand out at once, and the whole chapel become top-heavy.

To heighten the sensation of exquisitely just balance in decoration, the architect, instead of bringing the façade without interruption to the cornice beneath the dome, has stepped back the upper section above the loggeta, forming an intermediate stage. The façade, then, presents one single exquisitely designed lower section completely finished with a heavy cornice supporting small bell turrets, the façade proper, while the upper sections are graded back to throw it into relief. It is necessary to stress this point since the architect has solved here an almost insuperable problem, and redeemed the whole chapel from failure architecturally.

The mixture of the Gothic and Renaissance in architecture is paralleled by the mixture of the pagan and Christian elements in the decoration ; the busts of the Cesars on each side of the rose window and on the front face of the dome-support, and the stories of Hercules (Hercules and the hydra, Hercules and the Cretan bull, Hercules and Anteaus, Hercules and the lion) on the square marble plaques at the base of the façade contrast with the biblical stories represented in single scenes above the Herculean legends beneath the windows. Those scenes from the Old Testament, the creation of Adam, of Eve, the Original Sin, the Expulsion from the Garden, Adam and Eve, the Death of Abel, the Slaughter of the Innocents, the Presentation of Gifts to God and the Sacrifice of Isaac, testify to a skill and beauty of sculpture rare even at that period (1475), when the Renaissance in art as in architecture was only beginning to move northwards from Florence, Siena, Pisa and Rome.

The beauty of decoration on the pilasters and rose-window, with its single little figure breaking the sharp line of contact between the window and the surface of the façade, is remarkable, and surpasses in sheer delicacy of line the decoration on the Protiro of the Chiesa dei Miracoli at Brescia ; it is only necessary to think of the *putti* in the Tempio Malatestiano at Rimini to appreciate the grace and *gagliardezza* of the cherubs seated on the cornices of the windows.

The two groups of cherubs at the sides of the door on the bases of the statues show a mastery of art almost on a level with that of Donatello and Agostino di Duccio ; the wealth of detail on the pilasters, foliage, fruit, small lions, cherubs, medallions of Colleoni's exploits, dolphins in all their delicious agility, makes of the façade a pure joy. Amadeo evidently had a finer inspiration here, in these details, than even at Pavia, and the mixture of pagan and classical, demanded by Colleoni, who, in his humanistic enthusiasm, had given to his children the classical names of Medea and Cassandra, evidently suited his genius. When Colleoni died in 1475, the chapel and the tomb were practically complete, so that it is permissible to see in the work of Amadeo some part of the inspiration of Colleoni himself.

The interior of the chapel is notable above all for the tomb of Medea Colleoni, a lovely vision drawn in stone by Amadeo in 1470 at the very height of his artistic career when he had abandoned the school of Mantegazza, and studied the works of Donatello and Bellano. The tomb was originally in the church of Santa Maria della Basella and was transported to the chapel in 1842, where it now forms a noble contrast to the more ornate tomb of Colleoni himself. It is impossible to pass this figure lying on a bier, carved to a perfection of loveliness scarcely conceivable, without experiencing the reverence expressed by Ruskin before the tomb of Ilaria del Carretto in the cathedral of Lucca. There are no flaws in that perfection, no marring touches.

Even the bier appeals to the spirit, for its border of marble filigree has lines in it fine as hair and simplicity of design so harmonious that, not by one single detail, is one allowed to forget that the mission of this tomb was not the expression of art, but a confession of trust— a last, grave, serene resignation at the consummation of the haunting mystery of life now closed for ever on earth, and the fervent hope of that new radiance of life to come, repose and a chaste dream of glory. Even in death, there is an eagerness in that taut figure, in the straight folds of the dress rising over the feet, in the crossed hands as if, at a sign, it would spring up naturally to clutch that beautiful illusion of eternity within a gleam.

Gabrielle d'Annunzio commemorates the tombs of Medea and Bartolomeo in a sonnet of the " Città del Silenzio " :

> Destarsi la dormente, qual la pose
> su l'origlier di marmo l'Amadeo ;
> gli occhi aprirsi, le labbra *Laus Deo*
> clamare, le due mani sparger rosi ;
> quest'opre vid'io meravigliose
> del lene April, ma in vetta al mausoleo,
> tutt'oro l'arme, il gran Bartolomeo
> pronto imperar tra le virtu sue spose.[1]

---

[1] The sleeping lady may awaken from the marble pillow where Amadeo placed her, open her eyes and, singing *Laus Deo*, scatter roses with both hands.

I saw those wonder works of the soft April but, on the peak of the mausoleum, all golden in armour, the great Bartolomeo preparing to reign among his peers.

E

The simplicity of the tomb of Medea is lost in the more ornate memorial to Colleoni himself, where the mingling of the sacred and the profane forms with the gilt of the equestrian statue itself a strange mixture. The soldiers guarding the sepulchre are Roman soldiers, while in the bas-reliefs there is a series of pictures from the Passion—the Annunciation, the Adoration of the Child, Advent of the Wise Men, the Way of the Cross, the Crucifixion and the Deposition. The art of these bas-reliefs is conceived in a spirit of exquisite repose, of resignation mellowed to a serene beauty, with the crowning glory in the figure of the Madonna seated on a throne in the first relief, adoring the Child in an attitude of simple grace in the second relief, and receiving the homage of the kings in the third.

This series contrasts in its serenity and quiet simplicity with the movement and anguish of the three bas-reliefs below where the tragedy of Christ is enacted ; the rhythm of line and shadow is quickened here, and the sense of movement yields to them a greater force than the simpler pictures above. The architectural setting for those bas-reliefs is purely classical in its perfection of line and decoration, and the classical spirit has entered into the sculpture sufficiently to bring everything into harmony ; with it, however, the gracious impression of religious faith is preserved.

The four symbolical figures between the scenes in the lower series, Justice, Charity, Temperance and Faith, in their appropriate architectural frame serve as a commentary to the scenes of passion beside them, and ennoble the decorative setting of the sarcophagus. The bottom frieze with its cherubs is delicate almost as a flower of poetry, music and dancing represented in those joyous figures ; Donatello or Lucca della Robbia have little to show more exquisitely beautiful.

The frescoes on the walls weaken to some extent the whole effect of the interior through the flamboyant 18th-century art they represent, but the ceiling is a glory of vivid colouring wrought by Tiepolo at his most genial moment ; the feeling of life is quickened on gazing at the pictures drawn there in a splendid vivacity of light and shadow. The fresco showing the preaching of St. John the Baptist, a solemn figure designing a passionate gesture against a radiant sky witnessed by an interested crowd of Jews almost grotesque in their freshness and vivacity of attitude, is specially noteworthy—not so much as a realization in paint of the New Testament scene as an illustration of the somewhat satirical, almost frivolous life of Venice.

Some breath of this gay spirit lives in the symbolical figures at the corners, Justice and Prudence especially, and the chapel seems to move with them into a space of more dazzling splendour, into a brighter sea of light and colour. The classical ideal honoured at a distance by Bartolomeo, and expressed in the chapel beside the ancient cathedral where the Romanesque simplicity still ennobles the lions of the portals, comes in Tiepolo into contact with some of the ideals which enter into modern art and life. The sunlight of the past has mellowed to the warmer glory of the present.

CHAPTER IV

CHURCHES, PALACES AND FOUNTAINS OF BERGAMO

THE beauty of the Cappella Colleoni may obscure the more modest splendour of the church or basilica of Santa Maria Maggiore beside it, but the significance of this church for the history of architecture in Northern Italy is only paralleled by the Duomo of Verona. The Colleoni Chapel represents the Bergamascan spirit in a moment of victory when the enthusiasm of a sudden accession to tranquillity and wealth spilled over in a luxury of decoration, but Santa Maria Maggiore breathes of that time of struggle and danger when the spirit of the Bergamascans seemed to be overwhelmed in despair.

Even now, the Bergamascan looks on the Colleoni Chapel with detachment as on a memorial far removed from him in time and inspiration, while Santa Maria Maggiore summons up immediately in him a feeling of reverence and trust. The origin of the Basilica is romantic enough ; a horrible period of drought in 1133 caused such misery and desolation that the people of Bergamo, in the midst of starvation and pestilence, decided in 1135 to raise a votive temple to the Virgin. The temple, consecrated by the tears of a whole city, began to take shape in 1137 under the plans of Maestro Fredi, and, although we may doubt the reality of such an origin and rather look on the structure as a monument to civic pride similar to the cathedral of Parma or of Verona, the thought of desolation blossoming into stone still ennobles the vision and glorifies the architectural detail.

It is impossible now to reconstruct entirely the form of the original church owing to the continued incrustation of the interior with new styles, new fashions in decoration as the centuries advanced from 1400 to 1700 ; the most important additions were made, in all probability, between 1550 and 1620. The exterior was never entirely finished and the peculiar grouping of the buildings round the basilica, the Capella Colleoni closing in on one side, the cathedral on the other side of the square shutting out the perspective from the Piazza Garibaldi and houses built up closely all round, forces the attention away from the general shape of the church to the octagonal dome, rising in tiers of graceful arcades to a finely pointed spire, one of the few successful spires in Italy.

This dome and the abside where the stone has been rounded off into delicate arches under the roof with a cornice fine as lace and the pillars forming the loggetta beneath, are of an exquisite symmetry, symptomatic of Romanesque architecture at its best period.

The crowning glory of all lies in the two side portals executed, towards the middle of the 14th century, by Giovanni Campilione and his son of the same name. The northern portal beside the Colleoni Chapel, by the father, is reminiscent, in the use of white marble and the red Veronese marble of Santa Anastasia at Verona but shows, however, a richer beauty of decoration, the corded pillars inside the *protiro* being conceived in a wonderful variety of form and design. The dominating colour, red, gives warmth to the lace-like arch of the portal and life to the statues above, the equestrian figure of San Alessandro, flanked by Saint Barnabas and another protective saint.

On the second stage, above those statues, is a statue of the Virgin and Child in the midst of Saints Esther and Grace. These form, with the remarkable cross inside Santa Maria Maggiore, the main artistic achievement of Andreolo de Blanchis, a Lombardian sculptor of a slightly later date than the Campilioni. The portal to the south is less ornamental but more truly artistic in its beautiful frieze of saints above the arch ; the design is simpler but nobler. On the wall above is a *guglia*, a Gothic spire of as pure a style as the spire in the church of St. Lorenz in Nuremberg, carried out by Antonio of Germany (d'Alemagne) towards the end of the century ; it enshrines the effigy of the Holy Father seated on a throne, with the Virgin and the angel Gabriel on either side.

From the purely romantic point of view, the lions supporting the main columns of the portals are remarkable ; they show, in the groups of smaller lions and clinging figures, a power of imaginative design encountered in few other churches of the Romanesque period. The convention has ceased to be a convention and forms, in itself, a definite artistic achievement ; the suggestion of life is delicious, especially in those mighty guardians which stare defiantly into the square beside the suave loveliness of the Colleoni Chapel.

A third portal, towards Via Arena, ignored hitherto, but interesting through its refined elegance of detail, has since been found to be the work of Pietro Cleri, who executed it in 1521, or almost two hundred years after the completion of the other portals. It illustrates in its simplicity of decoration something of the pure Renaissance spirit shown in a state of transition in the Cappella Colleoni, and the fresco of the Nativity over the doorway belongs to the school of Previtali, if not by Previtali himself. Other work by Cleri, although the architect Pietro Isabello has hitherto been credited with them, may undoubtedly be seen in the side chapels of Santo Spirito, where the same love of elegant line and quiet massing of decoration on a larger scale glorifies the main pillars, and, in the cortile of the Palazzo Grataroli in Via Pignolo, where it gives a tranquil loveliness to the supporting pillars with their single decorative motif.

The art of Cleri, although restricted in range and only visible in a few memorials, belongs to the most exquisite achievement of the Bergamascan architects of the Renaissance ; the pediments of the columns in Palazzo Grataroli are delightful through the sheer simplicity and change of motif.

There are traces still of 14th-century frescoes on the outer walls of Santa Maria Maggiore, shadowy heads in a flaky glory, and inside the church, over the doorway to the right of the main altar, an almost perfectly preserved fresco, the Tree of Saint Bonaventura, carried out in 1347 to the orders of Walther de Soardi, a knight shown kneeling in front of the Virgin. The influence of Giotto can scarcely be denied in the force and stern vivacity of expression of the faces of the saints turned towards the Virgin, in the stiffness of attitude and, above all, in the sober harmony of colour, and we may attribute it rather to a southern artist than to a Bergamascan.

Apart from this fresco, the magnificent work of Luca Giordano behind the main altar, where the splendid warmth of colour and gesture lightens up the whole altar, Moses describing one noble gesture in his effort to lead the children of Israel through the Red Sea, is undoubtedly one of the great pictorial visions of the 17th century and Giordano's most impressive work; more impressive in the modelling of flesh and in rhythm of gesture than the more famous efforts of the Caracci. Other pictures, covering the organ, represent the Birth of Christ, a fresh work by Cavagna, with some of the *brio* of Veronese, and the Adoration of the Magi, a somewhat sugary creation of Talpino.

Apart from the frescoes, Santa Maria Maggiore is notable for the singularly beautiful *arazzi* covering its walls, and for the exquisite intarsia and wood carving of the choir stalls carried out by Capodiferro according to the designs of Lorenzo Lotto. It is only necessary to compare the work of a German artist of the same period in the cathedral of Ulm, or even the choir stalls of San Domenico in Bologna, with the masterpiece of Capodiferro, to appreciate the beauty of every single detail—the arms of the stalls, the richly decorated arches above and the scenes from the Old and New Testament depicted in a series of intarsia panels of a great splendour of execution. The decorative spirit of the Renaissance has found here a worthy embodiment, and something of the fire and profound conviction of a true religious ideal lives again in those single moments of vision enshrined in wood, almost palpitating with the suggestion of air and colour.

The arras tapestries take the place of the ancient frescoes that once entirely covered the walls as in Duomo of Verona, and it can scarcely now be said that the church has lost by the substitution. The tapestries were the product of the Florentine school

THE PORTAL OF S. MARIA MAGGIORE, BERGAMO

working on the Flemish model from cartoons designed by Bronzino, Bachiacca, Salviati and, above all, by Alessandro Allori, who flourished after 1576. The first series of arazzi, the Nativity, the Adoration of the Magi and the Flight into Egypt, were carried out in the studio of Allori; then the five tapestries, the Annunciation, the Marriage of the Virgin, the Visitation, the Circumcision and the Assumption, a trifle later; and the nineth tapestry, the Presentation of the Virgin in the Temple, after a longer period. The friezes, bordering the actual scenes, were executed according to cartoons by Allori to be seen still in the Uffizi at Florence and constitute in themselves notable achievements in decoration. The impression felt on seeing those arazzi in the half-light of the interior can never wholly be forgotten—a riot of suavely radiant blues and purples and browns with an infinite variety of background, trees on hillsides and cherub-starred skies with huge clouds, plains and temples embroidered with loving skill, window by window, stone by stone, miracles of patient craftsmanship. In one, a futurist landscape in glory like a Gaugain can be seen.

As a last memory of all, the monument to Cardinal Longhi, who died at Avignon in 1319, the Chancellor of Charles II of Naples and nominated cardinal by Celestine V, may be revered as an austerely beautiful example of 14th-century sepulchral art, a simple statue beneath a Gothic arch, with the solemn figures of two angels consecrating the dead.

Santa Maria Maggiore and the Cappella Colleoni are the outstanding architectural achievements of Bergamo, but several other churches merit examination. The façade of the Chiesa San Agostino silhouetted against the blue of the distant hills always evokes a feeling

of admiration and reverence through the beautiful
windows with their two tiers of arches exquisitely
balanced, where the Gothic spirit has been sweetened
by the new spirit of the Renaissance, and through the
suggestion it still gives, in its cornice and in the statues
over the small rose-window, of a chaste art once expressed in a quiet splendour in every detail of the
church. The door and windows of the refectory preserve some beautiful details of this transitional architecture. The history of the church is the usual history
of consecration and disaster ; it was founded by the
monastic order of Eremitani Osservanti in 1290, burnt
down in 1403 in a war between Guelfs and Ghibellines,
and in 1442, after the Augustins then occupying it
were removed for moral reasons and a minor order of
the Eremitani installed, the church was rebuilt. The
only parts now remaining from that date are the façade
and the entrance to the refectory.

The Duomo, which can be seen beside Santa
Maria Maggiore, dates from 1207 but, in its present
form, is quite modern with a dignified if uninspired
interior decoration. Some details in it are worthy of
observation—the " Martyrdom of St. John " by Tiepolo
in the choir circle and the finely carved choir stalls,
the central seat executed by Fantoni, the sculptor of
the beautiful bas-reliefs in the altar of the Virgin in
mourning. The Previtali in the first altar to the left
is discussed in a later chapter.

The great contribution of Bergamo to the architecture of the Renaissance is undoubtedly the church
of Santo Spirito in the lower town, with its somewhat
unprepossessing exterior facing on the square whence
the main road up to the older town departs ; the interior
with the powerful upthrust of column into the arches

supporting the roof and the symmetrical grading of arches to the choir, which seems to bring the whole expression of the church to a single glorious symbol in the high altar, is perhaps the most impressive in Northern Italy. The architect was Pietro Albano aided, as we have already indicated, by Pietro Cleri, and by Caniana, who designed the vaulted roof with its symmetrical spacing of pillar and arch. The church contains some of the most notable works of the Venetian school, Bergognone, Previtali and Lorenzo Lotto. Other churches are notable only for the pictures they contain by those three painters—San Bartolomeo and San Bernardino with their magnificent Lottos, and Sant' Andrea with its Moretto.

* * * * *

The beauty of Old Bergamo lies more in the palaces built along those narrow streets, where even now romance comes forth startlingly in a warm gleam of sun, than in the churches. The shadows between the high walls on either side may obscure some magnificent portal worn with the passage of centuries, or a massive wooden door may open suddenly to unfold a dazzling vision of courtyards surrounded by graceful columns decorated with consummate art, where the sunlight is held in a warm intensity almost like flame beside the cool shadows, or the thin band of azure overhead may be interrupted by an exquisitely wrought iron balcony or a mediæval lantern bracket.

The immense cornice of the Strozzi Palace in Florence, glorified by Arnold Bennett in *Paris Nights*, is repeated here in many a smaller palace with the same un-compromising severity of line and mass, the same expression of defiance and everlasting strength. The rich suggestion of the Via San Giacomo, with its palaces built there by the 15th-century princes, with heavy-barred windows and blurred portals, or the Via Gaetano Donizetti, is something never to be forgotten. The return to the 15th century—atmosphere, architecture, thought—is complete, and the surrender to this past age has in it a profound delight, as at some vision of beauty unexpected and inconceivable.

The Via Bartolomeo Colleoni, with its Palazzo Colleoni, a simply yet massively designed structure in the finest tradition of the Renaissance (the portal in Via Porta Dipinta, with its classical figures being peculiarly suggestive in the expression of the Renaissance spirit), its occasional balconies of wrought iron supported by exquisitely decorated stone arms, and its windows framed in stonework as delicately carved as the woodwork in a cabinet, brings every detail of this beauty to vision, and it is a joy merely to linger beneath those balconies, savouring, exquisite detail by exquisite detail, the wealth of art displayed. The sun touches to radiance the angle of a window, the round of a shoulder, or places a band of gold beneath a cornice, and the warmth of colour gives then to shadow an uncanny life, to appreciation a mystic rapture.

In the Via Gombito, Venice lives again in one palace where traces of frescoes can be seen round windows with Gothic arches, and in the loggia of another palace where shadowy designs break the flatness of the walls between the rows of Corinthian pillars. There are surprisingly beautiful cortili, where a single fountain plays between bare walls with a third wall rising in a wonderful series of *loggie* to the blue sky; across the walls and round the pillars vines may be stretched in a rich contrast of green against warm grey of stone and purple of shadow. In the Via Donizetti there is a continual series of Renaissance palaces, each one as perfect as the other, while the Casa dell' Arciprete puts a seal for quiet impressiveness on all ; it is perfect.

In the Via Tassis, the Seminario presents one magnificent doorway, where the exquisite decoration of the Renaissance, as shown in the lions' heads and the floral designs beneath them, grades harmoniously into the projecting squares of stone broken in their rise to the archway by a massive cornice. The courtyards of the Palazzo Grataroli and the Palazzo Baldini in Via Pignolo, of the Palazzo Colleoni and of the Casa dell' Arciprete, especially the latter, are beautiful examples of Renaissance architecture and show a finer knowledge of proportion than many of the court-yards farther south in Venice and Bologna. The palaces of Bergamo show a distinct similarity, in conception and in execution, to the palaces of Brescia and of Vicenza where, in the latter city, the genius of Palladio has woven the Renaissance motifs into a single beautiful style of his own.

Four palaces remain in the memory through their suggestion of deeper issues, of nobler ambitions : the Palazzo Vecchio, now the Civic Library, in the Piazza Garibaldi ; the ancient Luogo Pio Colleoni in the Via Omonima, with its shadowy frescoes of the 15th century ; the Palazzo Terzi in the Piazzetta Omonima, with its amazing view over the plain of Lombardy ; and the Casa Pesenti in Porta Dipinta, rising above the walls near the Porta San Giacomo.

The Palazzo Vecchio or Palazzo della Ragione in its original form existed prior to 1199 and was supplemented by the Casa dei Consoli, which stood on the site now occupied by the Istituto Tecnico ; in the latter, the judges of the Commune resided, in the former, the

governing body, the Podestà. The ancient Palazzo
was burnt down on June 24, 1513, and the present
edifice erected about 1520. In its simplicity and quiet
beauty of detail, the façade, with its central balcony
and its Gothic windows with vaulted arches and double
columns, shows a certain resemblance to the Broletto of
Brescia and the Palazzo del Comune of Piacenza, but
the architectural proportions are better, the unity of
impression more striking.

The vicissitudes through which it passed under the
Ghibellines, the Visconti and the Venetian Republic
have impressed on it almost a sacred character as of
something which is of the very tissue of the Bergamascan
spirit, a memorial to every fine enthusiasm in Bergamascan history. The staircase, with its inscriptions, brings
the suggestion of historical continuity closer, the Roman
lapide harmonizing with the atmosphere of the place.

The palace now houses the Civic Library, with its
precious MSS. of the 15th century, notable for a 14th-
century codex of the *Laudi* of Jacopone da Todi ;
several illuminated MSS. of the 14th and 15th centuries,
and an album of coloured drawings by Giovannino de
'Grassi, dating from the end of the 14th century. In
the shadowy cloisters beneath the library, which
threatens now to overcome the supporting pillars
through the weight of books, are inscriptions commemorating those who fought in the Wars of Independence against Austria in the 19th century and in
the recent war.

The group of buildings comprising the Palazzo
Ateneo, the Torre Comunale, the Palace of the Istituto
Tecnico (a structure of the beginning of the 17th century, built by Ragnolo on the Palladian model), the
basilica of Santa Maria Maggiore, the Cappella Colleoni

and the Baptistery (a radiantly beautiful work of Giovanni Campilione), forms in itself one of the loveliest and most suggestive asylums of architecture and art in Italy. In the shadow of the basilica, one can dream and be satisfied in dreaming, for there is a harmony in everything, in the sweep of wall against the sky, in the massing of shadow over the square, in the curve of window and sharp rise of arch, a harmony ennobled in peace and radiant in a still beauty.

The present Casa Pesenti has been restored almost entirely from the old palace built by Morgando in 1529 to the order of Da Ponti, a distinguished Bergamascan jurist, and little now remains of the original decoration of the cortile or the portals ; the main lines are still intact, however, and it is still possible to imagine the Renaissance palace as originally conceived. The present structure is remarkable for the five frescoes it contains by a Bergamascan painter of the school of Lorenzo Lotto, representing the legend of St. Julien l'Hospitalier, if we quote the French version of the name in deference to the masterly version in prose of Gustave Flaubert.

More than any other pictorial rendering of St. Julien's legend do the Pesenti frescoes come close to the mysterious vision of Flaubert ; the crudity and intensity of superstitious faith, which make of the St. Julien legend one of the poetical jewels of the Middle Ages and give to it a lasting significance, even as the old French legend of the Châtelaine de Vergi, come directly into the drawing and have entered into the inspiration of the artist.

The St. Julien legend, which found its apotheosis in the masterpiece of Flaubert, was a *pièce de résistance* for the mediæval and early Renaissance poets and

artists; the first definite expression of it in literature, the *Golden Legend* of Jacopo da Varagio prior to
1298, only came after a long period of oral tradition,
when the legend had already formed part of the stock
in trade of the wandering friars.

The legend as inscribed in the Golden Book of Jacopo
states that one day, as Julien was hunting, he came
across a white stag which turned round in its flight
from the hunter and prophesied the murder by Julien
of both his father and mother. Julien, to avoid this
danger, took passage on a ship to foreign lands, became
a warrior in the service of a foreign prince and, in
return for acts of prowess, received from the latter a
castle as well as a châtelaine. Meantime, Julien's
parents sought for him all over the world and arrived
at last as pilgrims at Julien's castle, where they were
recognized by the châtelaine from her husband's description and installed for the night in the matrimonial
chamber. Julien, during his absence, had been effectively goaded by the devil into an insensate jealousy
of his wife and, arriving at dead of night, found his
worst fears verified on entering the matrimonial chamber.
In a fit of rage he beheaded both figures lying in bed
and learnt then, to his horror, their identity. The
remorse which then overcame him forced him as an
exile to found a convent on a lonely island where
pilgrims would be welcomed and cherished. Ultimately God's grace was granted him in a vision and
he could find peace then in the knowledge of ultimate
forgiveness.

The possibilities of this simple story were soon evident to the mediæval story-teller in poetry or in paint;
the idea of a higher power bringing through human
agency something foreordained to pass, the human

character of that conception where filial love could be changed to fear and exile rendered bitter through the thought of a tragic culmination and the final gift of happiness through the boundless grace of God, has even now a strong force of attraction. The legend could form the basis of a colourful story of love and passion ennobled in the strongest emotional instincts and tense with drama. The character of St. Julien is one of the noblest described in mediæval legend.

Three versions—one of the 14th, one of the 15th, and the third of the 16th-century art, to quote the excellent study by Angelo Pinetti in the *Rivista di Bergamo*—should be compared : the frescoes painted in the 14th century, beside the main altar of the cathedral of Trento, where the mediæval simplicity and naïve strength of expression, Giottesque in inspiration, give to the figure of the knight a living force ; the less vivid presentation by B. Gatta in the sacristy of the Collegiate Church at Castiglione Fiorentino, where the landscape contributes to the impression of tragedy and the broad spaces in the Renaissance palace reduce the figures in it to marionettes ; and the frescoes of the Casa Pesenti dating from the early decades of the 16th century.

The tragic suggestion is instinct in every fresco, from the closely detailed version of the hunt, with its mountain landscape, and the nearer view of the hero himself shooting an arrow into the stag in a thickly foliaged landscape, to the finely spaced scene, conceived in the spirit of Carpaccio, where the knight takes ship from a fleet lying at anchor, to the woodland drama where Satan as the stag goads the hero into jealousy of his wife, and, finally, to the last lonely island scene where the sky and sea in a majestic harmony come over

F

the figure in the boat. Few pictures have the imaginative force of those frescoes where the colours have darkened almost to a pure chiaroscuro ; but this grading down of colour tones serves only to emphasize the beauty of the scenes themselves.

As a last vision of all, the traveller should pass from the Piazza Omonima with its gravely beautiful statue into the courtyard of the Palazzo Terzi, where the fourth side is formed of the immense plain of Lombardy and the dazzling glory of the sky. The contrast between the old palace with its flower-wreathed pillars, its early Renaissance sculpture and its Roman amphoræ, and the flooding glory before it—the sea of purple and exquisite blue broken only by church spires glistening in red, and a hillside radiant with vines lifting into the distance within the pale luminance of the sky—has in it all the romance and the attraction of Bergamo, the past in a quiet magnificence of achievement, the present in a wonder of light and colour !

The fountains of Bergamo merit some attention even if none of them reach the beauty and splendour of the Roman fountains ; they preserve, more clearly than the palaces, the true mediæval spirit, both in design and in the quality of art expended on them. Those early fountains, since they acted very largely as washing places for humans as well as for clothes, were generally enclosed in porticos or even within walls ; such as, for example, that of the Fara under the Rocca erected in 1220, one fountain beside Santa Maria Maggiore, another within a courtyard in Via Solata, and the fountain beneath the Ateneo, built in 1342 by Giovanni Maria di Corteregia and Giovanni Corregi, with the arms of the Visconti above. The ancient Pignolo fountain near the façade of San Alessandro della Croce towards the street leading into the Via Mazzone was actually built in 1208, as the inscription shows, while traces of other mediæval fountains can be seen in Via Porta Dipinta, Via Osmano, at Pozzo Bianco.

The Renaissance contributed above all the beautiful fountain of San Pancrazio, a simple basin mounted on a pillar with arms above it in a central group supporting the spraying water—a favourite artistic motif against the mediæval portal of the church with its quaint Madonna and Child—the Delfino fountain in Via Pignolo opposite the Lupi palace, a purely classical theme with a certain vivacity of treatment.

The 18th century, inspired for once by a true artistic vision, saw the construction of the Contarini fountain, now in Piazza Garibaldi, an exquisite group of lions and symbolical human forms, enlivened by the flocks of pigeons which fly round it all day or gather together on the square beside it—a last perfect touch to that beautiful harmony formed by the Palazzo Vecchio and the Istituto Tecnico beside the Torre Comunale. An elaborate fountain, conceived in the usual rococo style, in the Fair ground, dates also from the 18th century and has a certain poetic suggestion through the trees surrounding it, the gleam of water in a silver luminance against the shadowy foliage.

CHAPTER V

BERGAMO AND BRESCIA IN LITERATURE AND ART

THE satirist may well spend a few cynical comments on Bergamo, the home of Arlecchino, the ancestor of those harlequins who provide emotional French artists *de mode* with an exciting, if artificial, motif, and our illustrated journals with Christmas supplements ; but Bergamo has a greater claim to honour than this—through the work of her own poets and scholars, inspired by deeper vision and more disinterested enthusiasm for art and knowledge.

Before discussing the latter, it is worth while casting a glance at Harlequin or Arlecchino, burlesque and vulgar as the *commedia* may have been which made of the figure of Harlequin one of the most interesting in the history of the drama. The classical comedies of the Renaissance, those of Machiavelli and Bibbiena especially, had ceased through sheer monotony of effect to inspire new efforts in their particular class, with the result that the drama itself, as a written composition, became moribund. To this inanimate world of artifice came a world more artificial still, but full of a joyous vitality through artifice, suggesting greater possibilities of laughter and of satirical pleasure.

The new comedy, with its narrow range of characters, Pantaloon, the doctor, Brighella and Harlequin chief among them, dispensed at once with status and with fashion, and came down to the level of even the most proletarian audience. The stately Italian speech of the classical drama became here the pungent and wholly delightful Bergamascan dialect, a living thing and not an abstraction built on choice phraseology ; Arlecchino, with the black face and the bizarre, multi-coloured clothes, remained always the same type speaking the same Bergamascan dialect, but this standardized character, like the characters we now see in the picture-house, appealed to a fundamental instinct in the audience. With no necessity to understand a new character, the audience could see at once in the antics and joyous *mots* of Harlequin some part of itself satirized and caricatured.

The caricature gave complete delight as the history of the Italian comedians in France and Spain discussed by Armand Baschet in his *Comédiens italiens à la Cour de France sous Charles IX, Henri III, Henri IV et Louis XIII* proves, and some of the Bergamascan *comici*, chief among them Alberto Ganassa, enjoyed an international reputation. As a member of the *Compagnia dei Gelosi*, he visited the royal court of France, and was able thereafter, as Beltrame in 1656 says, to amuse Philip II of Spain, a singularly thorny proposition for any comedian, if we can believe Schiller's version of his character, and incidentally to amass a fortune in the true Bergamascan tradition. In 1574, Ganassa formed at Venice an independent Company of the *Confidenti*, which became amalgamated ultimately with the *Gelosi*.

Other Bergamascans had fame in the 16th century, Silvia Roncagli, a special favourite in France and Italy through his representation of the *servante terriblement*

éveillée ; and the latter centuries saw the glorification
of Bartolomeo Savi in the masque of " Pantaleone "
and the " Arlequin Senateur Romain," played in Paris
on October 15, 1760 ; of Alessandro Gnochis, a contemporary of Savi, who made a highly successful Pantaleone
and reached the supreme bliss of a company of his
own ; and, finally, of Atanasio Zannoni, who was
really a Ferrarese but recited the Bergamascan dialect
to perfection. According to Bartoli, he committed the
signal blunder of eliminating the trivial from the
character of Brighella and made him an elegant, fashionable dilettante, able to speak with some knowledge of
the sciences and not a little critical acumen. This
crime may explain the sad end of the author who had
the misfortune to walk into a canal in Venice in 1792
after a night's merry-making, and succumbed to the
shock.

The transition from Harlequin to Donizetti is somewhat abrupt, but, if the burlesque and comic are characteristic of the Bergamascan mentality, the passionate
love of music overshadows everything and is still
decisive for the real study of the development of culture
in Bergamo.

The traveller may see in the lower town beside the
Teatro Donizetti a gracious example of 19th-century
monumental sculpture in the marble group raised as a
memorial to Gaetano Donizetti, Donizetti seated on a
stone seat in the classical style with music, a stately
female figure, striking a lyre before him. Although
less impressive than the memorial to Verdi at Parma,
which has a family resemblance to that immense mass
of stucco commemorating Victor Emmanuel at Rome,
and betrays something of the ostentation inherent in
bad art, the Donizetti monument, against its back-

ground of trees, is striking enough to merit a second glance. The sculptor, F. Jerace, had a certain felicity in conception and execution.

Donizetti, unlike Verdi, is fortunate in his memorials. The monument in the church of Santa Maria Maggiore is a genuine work of art, with an exquisite simplicity and very beautiful delicacy of line ; the feeling of admiration and reverence touched with a sense of pity, almost yearning, brings the figure of Music, sitting there with drooping head and abandoned lyre, into the same plane of art as the Canova monument to the Sobieski in St. Peter's at Rome. The sculptor, Vincenzo Vela, had some strength of vision and emotion instinct in him at the time of conceiving this figure.

A greater monument than either of the Donizetti memorials, if a digression may be permitted, can be seen at the cemetery not far from the town towards Brescia ; the entrance, finished immediately before the war, with its massive Egyptian style and its living groups of figures expressing the full tragedy of death, makes an impression that is never entirely effaced. Against the background of blue hills, golden-purple to the gleam of sun or shimmering to intense blue when the night comes over the Alps, with Old Bergamo silhouetted against the sky above its green terraces of chestnuts, the cemetery seems to hold in itself a quiet, soul-satisfying beauty of association—earth and sky— that imposes a long rapture on the spirit. The sense of harmony, of fitness, is perfect, and through this sentiment the appreciation of detail becomes more intense—the outline of the black cypresses against the faintly gleaming shadow of the distant city, the rustle of a lizard over a stone, the slow lengthening of the shadows in the cloisters.

Something of this pleasure attends the monument to Donizetti in Santa Maria Maggiore, and the musician himself gains by the association.

We may now feel Donizetti to be rather *vieux jeu* in the revived interest in German and Austrian opera, but Donizetti, even as Gluck or Verdi or Rossini, has contributed to music something which we miss at once in the more splendid efforts of his northern contemporaries and successors. It is possible still to recapture the enthusiasm felt by the Italians in the early decades of last century when Donizetti's operas first came on to the stage. With a competent vocalist as the heroine, the performance of "Lucia di Lammermoor" in the Teatro San Carlo of Naples is a rare experience treasured for years. When we heard it in Naples about two years ago, after a small group of Japanese ladies had sung "Madame Butterfly," the impression felt was surprising ; in comparison with the pretty if somewhat flaccid opera of Japan, the Donizetti creation was a full-blooded thing, throbbing with life and passion.

To some, of course, the element of passion can be overdone, and the objection of crudeness has been made against Donizetti. It is difficult to see how extravagance could be avoided in that period of romantic reaction against the self-satisfied classicism of the 18th century, when the enthusiasm for foreign writers caused Manzoni to write the "Promessi Sposi" in an attempt to rival Scott and the musicians, Donizetti and Verdi, derived from Shakespeare, Scott and Byron the subjects of their most famous operas. It is certainly curious to note that, while Italian poetry and prose showed few traces of this foreign element and simply perpetuated the old classicism in a new garb, Italian music took up the romantic challenge at once and launched forth on a period of exuberant production, punctuated by colourful moments of extravagance.

The Romantic epoch in Italian literature escapes definition, but there is no hesitation in defining the romantic movement in music. It is interesting to quote, in this connection, the words of Giuseppe Mazzini. " Donizetti adopted and followed first of all the system of Rossini, not for the sake of study or through lack of inspiration, but through force of conviction influencing an apostle who, choosing one way, does not sacrifice his own individuality. Perhaps, having reached a time when an echo of the old pedantry came to him from the throne where Rossini was seated, he felt that the Rossinian conquest was not enough and that something more vivid, more living was required." The day of complete emancipation had not yet dawned.

Donizetti understood, however, the impetus given to the Italian school by Rossini, and saw before him a creation of life and the beginning of a new epoch. " Donizetti went definitely beyond Rossini and, with full blossoming of his art, would have determined the future course of Italian music ; from ' Zoraide ' to ' Anna Bolena,' from ' Elisir d'Amore ' to the ' Parisina ' and finally to ' Marino Faliero,' to ' Lucia di Lammermoor ' and ' Belisario,' a continual development can be traced." The range of treatment, from the tragic and sublime in " Ann Boleyn " to the gay sparkle of " Love's Elixir," from the almost classical serenity of " Zoraide " to the mysterious and truly Byronesque atmosphere of " Marino Faliero " shows the strength of genius in full stride of development, with much of the beauty and living truth genius alone can give.

The work of Donizetti has an important place in the

history of Italian music, and not least in Bergamascan music as the inscriptions in the musicians' corner in Santa Maria Maggiore and the enthusiastic performances of his operas in the Teatro Donizetti prove. The passionate love of music continues in Bergamo, and the example of Donizetti has been followed in many musical societies devoted to study and composition. Milan and Naples are not alone in the cultivation of modern Italian music, and Bergamo can produce a very fine concert indeed, where every piece has been written and played by contemporary Bergamascan composers.

In literature, Bergamo has no outstanding figure to bring it to the attention of posterity, but, through it, history has always preserved a close connection with the outstanding cultural movements of the time. We have already mentioned Cardinal Longhi, the first great chancellor of the kingdom of Naples in the 13th century, while in the 14th century four members of the Barzizza family gained a position among distinguished Italian Humanists, especially Gasparino, professor of Belles Lettres in the universities of Padova and Pavia, editor of the Institutions of Quintilian and the three books of Cicero's *Rhetoric*. In the 16th century Bernardo Tasso and Torquato Tasso flourished, Bernardo being a native of Bergamo, while Torquato, though born at Sorrento, remained a true Bergamascan in much of his work.

While history has made it unnecessary here to discuss either of the Tassos, it is worth while casting a glance at one little-known Bergamascan of the Renaissance, Pietro Spino, the writer of the immensely detailed biography of Bartolomeo Colleoni, now preserved in the Civic Library, and of many short pieces of verse preserved only in manuscript in several libraries of Northern

Italy. It was said of Spino that he loved study and
books so much that during a serious illness books
more than pillows supported his head, an interesting
characteristic even in that time of enthusiasm for the
arts. Torquato Tasso has dedicated to his memory a
gracious sonnet :

> Spino, leggiadre rime in te fioriro,
> Come rose novelle Amor le colse,
> E si punse cogliendo e si gli dolse,
> Poi disse : ogni tua punta è mio desiro ;
> E col tuo dolce sospirar sospiro,
> E canto col tuo canto ; e dove sciolse
> La dotta lingua il chiaro suono, accolse
> L'alme che ne fur liete e ne invaghiro.[1]

The 17th century records Carlo Azzanica, translator of
Tasso's " Gerusalemme Liberata " into the Bergamascan
dialect.

The internationalization of culture which took place
during the 18th century found a centre in Bergamo
for communication between Switzerland, Germany and
Italy, and the history of the relations of the Swiss
critics, Bodmer and Breitinger, with the Bergamascan
nobleman, Pietro Calepio, is one of the most important
chapters in that broader history devoted to the rise
of the romantic movement in Europe. The Calepian
family had acquired great possessions round Bergamo,
and with the Serassi (one of whom Pietro compiled
an enormous study of Torquato Tasso, still in MSS.
in the Civic Library, and also constructed a tragedy
" Susanna " of some interest even now) the Tiraboschi,

---

[1] Spino, gay rimes blossomed in thee ; Love plucked them
like early roses, pricked himself in plucking and grieved over his
hurt. He said then : every point is my desire and I sigh with
thy sweet sighing and sing with thy song. Wherever the learned
tongue uttered its clear sound, the spirits were joyful and
enraptured with it.

a member of which, Girolamo, was the author of the first genuine history of Italian literature, and other families formed that peculiar aristocracy of which the Bergamascans were devoted admirers.

In a sense, Bergamo still remains self-centred, independent, proud, and keeps those old names which lent it prestige during the 16th, 17th, and 18th centuries. It is justified in doing so, for the Calepios, the Serassis, the Pesentis loved intensely their town and devoted themselves whole-heartedly to its affairs, so much so indeed that the history of the province depends almost wholly on the correspondence and other papers of those families for detail regarding life, custom and trade. They numbered in their members literary men of a distinguished type, not *litterati* by profession but by love, who recorded every detail—philological, historical, geographical, archæological—they found, and strove to keep in the forefront of the culture of their time.

Lorenzo Mascheroni, later in the 18th century (in his " Invito a Lesbia Cidonia," a typically elegant poetic epistle in the approved court style of Pope with, however, a high sense of artistry), Paolina Secco-Sicardo (the Lesbia Cidonia of Mascheroni's poem), in her delicate verses, and Angelo Mai (the seeker after lost classical MSS. and the idol of Giacomo Leopardi), lent to Bergamo some of the distinction that accompanied the more splendid Venice or Rome.

*   *   *   *   *

In art, Bergamo's share in the Italian Renaissance can only be appreciated in conjunction with that of Brescia, since both towns encouraged the same artists and derived part of their glory from the work of artists imported from the Venetian school, Lorenzo Lotto especially, and it is proposed now to examine their work as shown in Bergamo and Brescia together.

Although the division of artists into schools becomes a weariness of the spirit and leads to no conclusions of value since art lives in every production in a greater or less degree, and the intensity of inspiration gives the work of art its force of appeal without reference to origin or model, it is permissible to see in the great artists of Bergamo and Brescia some of the characteristics of one school dependent to some extent on the work of previous masters like the Bellini and Fra Angelico. Lorenzo Lotto, although a Venetian painter, Palmo Vecchio, a Bergamascan resident in Venice, enter into it as well as Moroni, Moretto and Romanino, painters of Brescia.

The essential difference between them and Previtali and Ambrogio da Fossano, the former a Bergamascan, is a difference of conviction and faith : Previtali, nourished at the fountain-head of northern Italian art, Giovanni Bellini, and Bergognone of a later date, preserve some of that passionate earnest, that religious excitement which pulses through Fra Angelico, and their paintings express emotion deeply and truly felt. The drama of the Virgin and Christ had not yet reached the stage of pure convention for them with the decorative scheme carefully planned and the lights exactly adjusted to produce the desired effect ; it was vital, throbbing reality for them, and entered as such into their art.

The example of Bellini was close enough to Previtali at least to keep his work in the great tradition ; Bellinis were fairly numerous in Bergamo and Brescia to provide him with a living standard, and the excellence of the pictures by the great Venetians preserved in those towns can be appreciated to the full even now. The Acca-

demia Carrara at Bergamo has a beautiful Madonna by
Giovanni Bellini of a rare delicacy of execution, serene
and very gracious in expression, the Virgin being placed
against a panel with a Venetian landscape shimmering
behind ; the church of San Alessandro in Brescia
contains an equally beautiful Annunciation by Jacopo
Bellini, with a delicious arabesque of decoration contrasting with the simplicity of emotion shown in the
attitudes of the Madonna and Angel ; and the church
of San Giovanni, a fine " Deposition."

It is well to remember the Bellini in the Accademia
Carrara when viewing the " San Benedetto in Cattedra "
in the Duomo, and the " San Giovanni Battista " in
the church of Santo Spirito, both by Previtali, in
Bergamo. The feeling for a quick emotional effect is
there, carried out with extreme economy of detail ;
there is no desire to introduce a rhythmic harmony of
colour and line, but sufficient symbolism to bring the
teaching of the church into expression. No one can
term Previtali a great painter, although the figure of
John the Baptist is well modelled against the cloudless
immensity of sky, but he is indisputably a sincere
painter with some very beautiful touches of imagination.
The angels spreading out a small canopy along the
top of the throne occupied by Saint Benedict are
deliciously alive.

Ambrogia da Fossano, or Bergognone, as we can see
in the magnificent altar in the church of Santo Spirito
in Bergamo, is an artist of a different calibre. He
shares with Previtali the passionate conviction which
gives to even the smallest detail a suggestive force ;
but in him the emotional impulse has been transfused
entirely into art—complete, sufficient, nobly fulfilled—
while in Previtali this consummation is never reached.

The ancona in Santo Spirito contains a central piece—
the "Madonna throned among Saints," with four lateral
panels showing saints, with a picture above the centre
representing the Holy Father in a cloud of angels. The
harmony achieved in painting and in decoration lends
sweetness and quiet beauty to the masterpiece of
Bergognone ; the Virgin, gazing slightly upwards in a
dreamy profundity of thought, is a living and graciously
beautiful conception.

It is interesting to compare the Virgin in this picture
with the Virgin in the " Annunciation " by Santa Croce,
a Bergamascan artist, in the Accademia Carrara ; the
same conviction inspires both, but in Santa Croce's
work the influence of tradition in the grouping of the
figures weakens the effect. The Santa Croce picture is
interesting also for its representation of a typical lagoon
scene visible through the windows behind the angel.

It may be questioned whether Palma Vecchio, Lorenzo
Lotto, Moretto, Moroni and Romanino can be thrown
together into one group as easily as we suggest, but it
is impossible to overlook some very essential features
that are common to them all. The period of intense
religious conviction with its reverent expression in
paint has totally disappeared for them, and a more
realistic, more vivid period has intervened, where
colour, movement, vivacity, gaiety, rich decoration,
splendid robes draping splendid bodies designing splendid gesture, take the place of simple vision.

With Palma Vecchio, as the opulent " Madonna and
Child with Saints John and Catherine " in the Accademia
Carrara proves, we have abandoned the religious motive
entirely, substituted the wide sweep of colour and
shadow for the painful accumulation of beautiful detail,
each detail conceived as an act of adoration, and returned

to portraiture. Saint Catherine and the Virgin are
well nourished lady-contemporaries of the artist interested in a very human child ; intensity of emotion has
been sacrificed for sleek self-sufficiency and a warm
radiance of colour, very satisfying at first to the senses,
but somewhat cloying after a time.

With Lorenzo Lotto, the opulence of form and colour
practised by Palma Vecchio has been tempered by the
influence of Bellini, and the more scientific grouping of
light and shadow adopted by Giorgione. Lotto has a
greater affinity to Giorgione and Correggio than even
to Palma Vecchio, although consideration of the colour
values in the " Adoration of the Shepherds " in the
Pinacoteca at Brescia might show a resemblance to the
work of the latter. This picture is, in itself, a singularly
beautiful example of the refined art of Lorenzo Lotto ;
the attitude of the Madonna kneeling and gazing down
at the child has been caught in a single instant of life, not
at a moment of adoration for Divinity, but of interest
in a tiny struggling piece of humanity. The child
himself, kicking in the air and playing with a deliciously
sketched lamb, is natural with the vivacity genius alone
can give in portrayal. Even to the shadow over the
cheek, the little figure is perfect.

It is necessary to linger over every detail in a Lotto
picture if only to appreciate to the full the supreme
artistic ability of the man. In the " Adoration of the
Shepherds," the dark background with an ass's head
and shepherd silhouetted, and the foreground where the
faces move out of shadow, show a command of the
resources of light and shade only paralleled by that of
Correggio. Symbolism, simple design conceived in a
simple faith and direct, if crude, representation of
emotion, have yielded here to a suave loveliness with

every resource in full play ; idealism disappears behind a very certain realism.

To accuse Lotto of imitation of Correggio, as some writers have done, is quite unjust to the artist, and the accusation ignores the influence of the time which went to form the artistic character of Correggio as of Lotto ; the age, in its evolution towards the paganism ultimately shown in the whole spirit of the Renaissance, moved from the stage where painting became sub-ordinated to religion to the further stage where painting became desirable as such and art became valued as art alone. It is interesting to quote, in this connection, the words of André Maurel : " Lotto knows the whole science of painting ; this can be seen in the skilful and tender arrangements of light and shade, in the luminous and soft colour adopted by him. This knowledge served a subtle inspiration. His heads have a restful grace peculiar to himself alone ; the placing of the groups, their relation to the central figure, is wonderfully harmonious."

The work of Lotto in the churches of Santo Spirito, San Bernardino, San Bartolomeo in Bergamo, and in the church of San Pietro Martire in Alzano Maggiore, un-doubtedly his most important contribution to the art of his time, gives full opportunity to study and appre-ciate this art. The three pictures in Bergamo, as well as the main altar-piece in Alzano, illustrate the same theme, the "Virgin enthroned with Saints and Angels"; yet the treatment is entirely different, and the only resemblance between the pictures in actual grouping of the figures lies in the convention adopted, the " Virgin on a Throne." Everything else differs not only in gesture, position, but also in lighting effects. The impression of quiet loveliness, movement without the sensation of

G

movement, and ennobled in a rhythm of line and shadow, fine gesture conceived in symmetry but alive at the same time, glorifies them all, and we leave them satisfied as after a feast where beauty has been a living presence.

The Madonna in the picture shown in San Bernardino, shadowed by a canopy held over her by flying angels, a rich note of movement and colour, has the grace and swift elegance of a Madonna by Correggio with more vivacity in gesture ; in Santo Spirito, she is quite frankly the mother with the heavy responsibility of a divine child, so that gesture is more restrained and there is a certain weariness in the attitude of the head; in San Bartolomeo, the energy of youth has returned, and with it a delicious feeling of *insouciance*. In this last picture, the suggestion of satire cannot wholly be avoided ; the attendant saints have a posture akin almost to caricature, and Saint Sebastian is undeniably bored to tears. This effect of humour, faintly suggested in almost every picture by Lotto and responsible for the pleasure they give, comes immediately into expression here with wholly delightful results.

In all three pictures, the grouping, even to the angels playing at the foot of the throne and to the flocks of angels describing rhythmic designs overhead, is perfect, while the adoption of the architectural motif in the San Bartolomeo altar has been tempered with such a judicious grading of light into shade that the Renaissance framework glides imperceptibly into the picture. The art shown in the San Bartolomeo picture brings it into an important place in the history of Italian painting during the Renaissance.

It may have been thought that Lotto has monopolized too much study here, but the Bergamascan altars merit discussion not only for their own sake, since they are

recognized as Lotto's finest achievements, but also for
the clue they give to the art of other Bergamascan and
Brescian painters, especially Moretto and Romanino.

Moretto has contributed one of his most important
works to the church of Sant' Andrea in Bergamo, a
" Madonna enthroned with Saints," the theme of the
Lotto pictures, but little direct comparison can be
made between any one of the Lottos and this picture.
The treatment has become simpler, more direct, more
realistic ; there is no use made of subtle effects of
shade throwing figures into prominence ; the statuesque
has replaced the pictorial and chromatic.

In Lotto, a certain poetical suggestion hovers over
every detail, a veil of mystery which may hide some
wealth of beauty unsuspected, while, in Moretto, the
duty of telling a tale as clearly as possible destroys
suggestion and brings reality stark and vivid before us.
The difference between Lotto and Moretto is the difference between the classical and romantic, between the
concrete and the shadowy.

Moretto has conceived his figures much as a sculptor
would conceive them—solid, true to reality, without a
sparkle, without a single feature out of place. His
genius is eminently plastic but, within the limits thus
imposted, it is singularly impressive ; the " Madonna
and Saints " in Sant' Andrea conveys the same impression
in paint as a Palladian palace in Vicenza in architecture.
The spirit feels before it a sense of rest, of confidence in
something eternally unchangeable, strong with all the
strength of earth and sweet also with the sweetness of
earth.

The ecstasy of Fra Angelico has vanished into a past
never to be recovered, and we have here, instead, the
lush realism of Palma Vecchio, with a full-fed Virgin

portly in gesture, listening heavily to an immaculate Brescian nobleman, while, on the opposite side of the picture, a Brescian beauty stands in a glory of silks beautifully painted. The painter had had a story to narrate, and narrates it here at once with the utmost economy of decoration and characterization. The effect, architecturally right, is direct and uncomplicated —a harmony composed of few elements.

This quality of being able to tell a story and tell it well distinguishes the Brescian painters above all, and we shall find in Romanino a felicity and strength of pictorial narration surpassed only by Veronese. In Moretto, a flavour from the Brescian hills seems at times to have entered into inspiration to redeem his art from too harsh realism. The " Saint Ursula and the Virgins," in the church of San Clemente in Brescia, is a beautiful bouquet of flowers from the hills, exquisite as a dream ; the virgins beneath the banners and the immense cloud-barred sky form, in tender loveliness of expression and attitude, one of the most radiant visions in Italian art. In this case, unity of effect and unity of narration have met in supreme beauty as art. Moretto painted nothing better than this.

The same flower-like beauty characterizes the " Annunciation " in the Pinacoteca, but it has become coarser now and the heart of the painter is not in it ; a warm splendour of colour compensates to some extent the realism of treatment, colour drowning detail and throwing rounded arms, shoulders and faces into statuesque relief.

Brescia has such a wealth of Morettos that it is impossible in this short study to indicate or criticize them all. The churches of San Giovanni Evangelista, of San Clemente, of Santa Maria Calchera, of Santi

Nazario e Celso, the Old Cathedral, the Palazzo Martinengo and the Pinacoteca contain his most notable
pictures, and the days spent in wandering from church
to church, comparing notes of colour and design, live
long in memory simply through the pleasure they give.

As a painter of women, Moretto, as we have already
indicated, excels : the " Herodias " in the Pinacoteca
is a beautiful portrait of a contemporary Brescian lady,
certainly not of the Biblical heroine, but, as such,
commands admiration through faultless technique ; the
" Madonna appearing before a Deaf Mute " in the
Santuario di Paitone, although somewhat lifeless through
the intention of the artist to render immaterial a very
material presence, shows a fine modelling of head and
arms, with long flowing lines of dress harmonizing with
the lines of the hilly background ; the portraits shown
in the frescoes of the Palazzo Martinengo have something
of the firm grace and economy of line to be seen in
Dutch portraits, but, with this, a greater warmth of
colour.   Perhaps his finest picture of stately woman-
hood, and certainly one of his noblest conceptions, is
the " Santa Margherita e Santi " in the church of San
Francesco, with the saint standing in an altar niche in
richly designed robes, almost statuesque in posture.   As
a portraitist, those pictures indicate beyond all doubt
that Moretto would have been as perfect in the genre
as G. B. Moroni, his disciple.

Three pictures illustrate, above all, his capacity for
telling a story effectively : the " Mary Magdalene at
the Feet of Christ " in the church of Santa Maria
Calchera, " The Last Supper " in the church of San
Giovanni Evangelista, and " Saint Cecilia and other
Saints " in the church of San Clemente.   " The Last
Supper " stands out at once through the vivacity of

treatment and the originality of conception. The tradition of Andrea del Sarto or Leonardo da Vinci has no
influence here. Few figures in Italian art have the
force of drawing and expression instinct in the disciple
in front of the table with his back to us. The modelling
is as perfect as anything Moretto ever achieved, while
the gestures and expressions of the other disciples show
a strong sense of the dramatic in the artist.

This dramatic sense comes more into play in the
first picture, " Mary Magdalene at the Feet of Christ,"
which should be compared with the picture of the
same name by Romanino in the church of San Giovanni
Evangelista. The truth and vividness of expression in
the face and attitude of the woman embracing in an
agony the feet of Christ, and in Christ himself, a notable
feature in Moretto's picture, are inadequate in Romanino,
and he has had to depend on subsidiary characters—a
servant bringing in food, and diners discussing important
matters at the end of the table away from Christ—for
dramatic interest.

For Moretto, the Magdalene incident is pure tragedy,
and he conceives it as such ; the whole picture centres
round that anguished figure, and every other incident is
eliminated at this supremely dramatic moment. For
Romanino the incident forms rather an unnecessary
intrusion on a scene already staged in every detail ;
the picture would have been effective without the
figure crouched under the table in a singularly un-
dramatic and uncomfortable position. Moretto's ability
in portraiture can be seen in the " Madonna and St.
Nicholas " in the Pinacoteca, with the two children
kneeling before a precariously situated Madonna,
palpably portraits of the children of a Brescian family.

The dramatic can be seen in Moretto's greatest

picture, the "Assumption of the Virgin," in the old cathedral—the Madonna rising in a glory of angels, while the disciples form an agitated and dramatic group beneath. The architecture of this picture shows almost as complete mastery as the architecture of the Lotto pictures in Bergamo, but there is a sterner force, a deeper suggestion of eternal issues, a more splendid harmony of colour in Moretto ; simplicity and economy of effect have coincided here in great art.

A further "Madonna in Glory" in the church of San Giovanni Evangelista is less effective, although the figures in the foreground are vividly portrayed ; and a third, "Madonna in Glory," in San Clemente, is notable for the modelling of the almost naked figure of St. Jerome. The "Coronation of the Virgin," in the church of Santi Nazario e Celso, is weak, the painter suffering evidently from over-production. As an artist, Moretto lives undoubtedly through his strong feeling for the dramatic, his capacity for telling a story and for his fine portraiture of women as apart from Madonnas. Only three Madonnas are entirely successful : the Madonna in Bergamo, the Madonna in the "Assumption," and the "Madonna and St. Nicholas."

Moretto has sometimes been considered a less imaginative and less powerful artist than Romanino, his contemporary, and we must agree with this assertion when the masterpiece in the Civic Museum at Padua is brought alone into comparison. When, on the other hand, the Brescian pictures enter into criticism, Moretto is definitely superior not only as a colourist but also as an imaginative painter.

None of Romanino's works in Brescia possesses the simple beauty of Moretto's "Saint Ursula and the Virgins," or the dramatic force of the "Assumption of

the Virgin." It is significant that both Moretto and
Romanino should have painted their most perfect works
in towns outside of Brescia, the former in Bergamo
and the latter in Padova, Cremona and Trento ; this,
however, may be attributed to the fact that the force
of rivalry between local artists and strange artists came
into full play when the latter entered (through great
favour or through great art, generally the latter) and
raised the whole level of artistic achievement.

The altar-piece in Padua is undoubtedly one of the
loveliest creations of northern Italian art during the
Renaissance, not only through radiantly beautiful
colouring and vivacity of treatment, but also through
the symmetrical grouping of figure and felicitous adaptation of the architectural motif to the needs of the picture.
The harmony of living expression in the Madonna, the
angels and the saints is remarkable ; quiet adoration,
broken, by delicate touches, into enthusiasm and ecstasy
held in suspense, gives to the group of five figures an
attitude of expectancy very inspiring in suggestion.
The sense of rhythm, of mass yielding harmoniously
into mass, of motif into motif in a single effect of light
and colour brings the picture to a high level of achievement ; the curves of the arches above the Madonna
come through the arrangement of the figures themselves
and conciliate every possible detail emerging from that
harmony. The architectural frame is an essential part
of the whole conception, even as the angels holding a
crown over the Madonna and the delicious angel between
the four saints striking cymbals. The decorative detail
is complete even to the doves in the foreground and
the portraits in the lunettes.

The altar in Padua illustrates the superiority of
Romanino in comparison with Moretto in many essen-

tials—the power to bring a complicated architectural
motif into the spirit of the pictorial conception itself,
to make the Madonna the most beautiful and most
artistically perfect figure in the composition, and to
bring every essential into a rhythmic balance. The
affinity to Lotto can be seen at once, but there is also
an affinity to Moretto in the ability to tell a story vividly
and forcibly.

Romanino's most successful Madonnas are in the
wonderful picture in the church of San Francesco (where
the delicate art of Stefano Lamberti shown in the
framework of intaglio, gilded and carved, of the ancona,
makes a perfect setting), and in the " Presepio " preserved in the Pinacoteca. In the latter, some resemblance, in the attitude of the Madonna, to the picture
by Dürer in the Alte Pinakotek in Munich can be seen,
and the influence of Dürer may have contributed to the
formation of the work of Romanino.

The altar-piece in San Francesco, glorified by the
beautiful figure of the Madonna and Child, suffers here
from a defect which was in Padua an element of strength ;
the grouping of the figures in harmony with the architectural motif, an almost imperceptible factor in the
composition of the latter, has suffered here from deliberate compression ; the artifice has become too
obvious. The control of light and shadow, and the
convention of the angels holding up a canopy show
undoubtedly the example of Lorenzo Lotto.

The capacity for telling a story vividly, with full
dramatic power, becomes evident in the " Feast of
Emmeaus" in the Pinacoteca, and " Mary Magdalene
at the Feet of Christ," already discussed in connection
with a similar picture by Moretto. In the latter, if we
limit consideration to the figures grouped round the

table and neglect the figure crouching under the table, the vivacity of gesture and movement combined with considerable power in still-life painting encourages comparison with Caravaggio ; the handling of shadow and the careful selection of lighting effects to produce unity of dramatic suggestion shows that the influence of Venice has been sufficient to modernize execution and render expression more pictorial, if less decorative. The " Feast of Emmeaus " brings the dramatic into the forefront ; the situation comes at once into vision in a single vivid impression sketched at a moment of vision.

The great frescoes in the cathedral of Cremona, in the Castello Vescovile at Trento, and smaller pictures scattered through the Valle Camonica, as well as the " Mass of St. Apollonius " in the Church of Santa Maria Calchera, complete the contribution of Romanino to the art of the 16th century. In a latter chapter, we shall discuss the pictures scattered through the Valle Camonica.

A disciple of Romanino, Lattanzio Gambara, the painter of the larger nave of the cathedral of Parma, executed, in the Palazzo Averoldi, the Palazzo della Pretura and in many other palaces no longer in existence, frescoes almost of the more ostentatious and more luscious schools of the 17th century, the influence of Correggio combining with reminiscences of Michel Angelo to form a colourful, if somewhat superficial style. The dramatic and the impressionistic, as we can see in the " Presepio " in the church of Saints Faustino and Giovita, suffer from the lack of drawing, from the lack of clear vision imagined intensely and continuously. His inspiration is without staying power.

Contemporary with Gambara, but a disciple of Moretto, G. B. Moroni, a Bergamascan painter, has contributed to northern Italian art a unique series of portraits in the tradition of Titian and Tintoretto, but akin also to the work of Bronzino in the careful, if somewhat sharp, accuracy of drawing. In many essentials, in the handling of light, in the elimination of unnecessary detail, in the effort to get at the heart of his sitter, Moroni is definitely superior to Bronzino ; the influence of Venice gave him a deeper insight into the possibilities of colour and shadow than Brongino ever possessed, and the only painter of the same power and depth in portraiture to whom we may compare him is Tintoretto. The series of portraits in the Accademia Carrara, and especially the " Portrait of an Old Man," is the chief glory of the collection, and the masterly Tintoretto in the Kunsthistorisches Museum in Vienna of the same name can alone be compared to the latter.

The Italian artists had special felicity in portraiture as apart from the more formal studies for religious and historical scenes ; Paris Bordone, Francesco Francia, Titian come immediately to memory, and it may be doubted whether each artist in this own special style did not achieve perfection. In Moroni, some of the realism and hardness of the north have redeemed him from the accusation of plagiarism in style from Titian ; the example of Moretto, with his sure draughtsmanship, his plastic values and his powerful dramatic suggestion, came into the artistic make-up of the Bergamascan painter with results we now admire in the " Navagero " portrait housed in the Brera at Milan, in the two magnificent drawings of Brescian noblemen of the Pinocoteca in Brescia, and in the series at Bergamo.

The mastery shown in all those paintings is remarkable, especially in the expression, poise of the head, and the position of the hands ; Moroni used all the resources of shadow available and the simple blocking of colour to throw the faces and hands into relief. In the " Ritratto d'Ignoto " in Brescia, the black unrelieved mass of the body acts as a setting for the finely poised head and the exquisitely drawn hands.

When Moroni abandoned portraits and entered the field of religious painting, he was wholly unable to avoid imitating Moretto, and nothing of original force remains except, perhaps, the " Last Supper " in the Chiesa Parrocchiale of Romano, a small town on the road from Bergamo to Brescia. The " Assumption " in the Brera at Milan is only an adaptation of Moretto's masterpiece ; the Madonnas in the churches at Parre and Fino del Monte repeat the motifs adopted by Moretto in the picture at Bergamo and the " Trinity " of Albino, as well as the politico of Fiorano, show the combined influence of Lotto and Moretto with no great originality in treatment.

Of the great Venetian school, the school of colour and light as apart from pure form, Titian, Tintoretto, Bordone, Montagna, Veronese, Bergamo possesses in the Accademia Carrara only a few unimportant examples, while Brescia glories in three masterpieces : the " Woman caught in Adultery," in the church of Saint Afra ; the " Resurrection," in the church of Saints Nazario and Celso, both by Titian in his finest period ; and the remarkable " Martyrdom of Saint Afra," in the church of Saint Afra, by Veronese, a companion picture to the " Martyrdom of St. George," in the church of San Giorgio in Verona.

The latter picture may appear, in the grouping of the figures, in the superb colouring and movement of line and mass, superior to the former ; but few of the great Veronese pictures show such nobility of conception or wealth of artistic imagery as the " Martyrdom of Saint Afra " in a public square, with the crowd singing round her and the immense blue cloud-ribbed sky enclosing the whole scene. To find a parallel to it in force and beauty of conception, we must think of the Rubens in the Kunsthistorisches Museum in Vienna, " Ignatius of Loyola Healing the Woman possessed of a Devil." The fine modelling of flesh, the sweep of gesture, the vivid portraiture shown in the main figures are equally good in both; both are on the same plane of great art.

The influence of a totally different school from that of the Bellinis, harsher and cruder, brought the earlier art of Brescia into line with the work of the Lombardian school; Vincenzo Foppa especially, and his disciple Paolo Zoppa, have left in Brescia some typical paintings which are worthy of examination. In the Pinacoteca, Foppa is represented by a painted standard of the Orzinovi family, the Madonna and Child on one side and Saint Sebastian, a favourite subject with him, on the other; by four saints done in fresco in the church of the Carmine, and by the frescoes in the vault of the Averoldi Chapel. None of these paintings represent the art of Foppa at its highest plane of achievement, but they have a certain interest through the light they throw on the artistic level of later 15th-century painting in the provinces outside of Milan.

Foppa has undoubtedly inspired the somewhat flaccid paintings of Paolo Zoppa in the church of San Pietro in Oliveto (" Christ with the Cross "), and in the Pinacoteca (" Christ falling beneath the Cross "), and entered into the work of Ferramola, a contemporary of Moretto. Ferramola shows in his " Madonna in Glory," in the Chiesa delle Grazie, the transition from the harsher spirit of the Milanese painter to the more serene beauty of Moretto, and, in Savoldo, a Brescian painter slightly anterior to Moretto, the period of genuine Brescian art begins. The fusion of influences, Bellini and Foppa, found its culmination in Moretto, Romanino and Moroni.

CHAPTER VI

BRESCIA

BRESCIA, approached from the plain, gives the same fine impression of sun-drenched buildings raised on shadowy hillsides as Bergamo ; the Alps have become less austere and less threatening, and the foothills, moving down into the plain on either side act as a sedative to the traveller more intent perhaps on the luminous beauty of plain disappearing into the sky than on the harsh uplift of mountain shoulder. The contrast of rich colour seen at Bergamo yields here to a hazy purple shot with rose, only broken by the glare of sunlight on a white wall or the flash of water on the mountain side ; the lines of the mountains have become softened and disappear under terrassed vineyards, sink into the plain and rise surprisingly again into small hills wooded with chestnuts, as if the harmony of colour were too uniformly on the one note and some background of shadow were required.

The Valley of the Oglio comes down in a strong blending of form and tone when the sun strikes one side of the valley and moves up the slope, touching each fine edge of rock to flame and outlining every fold and hollow until the sky comes down in a veil of exquisite purple ; the far peaks disappear in the glowing colour, and the mountain walls break up into smaller valleys before Brescia appears, a constant succession of shadowy and illuminated masses drowned in a shimmering haze. Brescia gives the note for that beauty, perhaps a note of too ardent sunshine and glare in the hot summer days when the pavements and the broad streets (broad for Italy) gather up the last traces of heat in the air and throw them back in blinding waves.

From this point of view Brescia is slightly disappointing ; the cool shadows of the chestnuts on the walls of Old Bergamo find no parallel here, although the view over the plain of Lombardy from the Castello, situated on a hill outside the town is as fine as that from Bergamo, and the traveller is forced to choose a cool season rather than venture forth on a journey of exploration in summer or autumn. Brescia, however, always in the shadow of the hills, enjoys much of their suggestion of space and romantic beauty, and it is impossible to forget in the silence of the Piazza del Duomo, where the Broletto seems to have held the centuries in suspense, or in the vivid Piazza del Mercato, with its excited groups of fruit sellers, that the hills have contributed to the formation of Brescian character and Brescia history even as much as in Bergamo or in Vicenza.

The past shades away into the exuberant present : the Roman legionaries find a modern counterpart in the black-shirted Fascisti ; the patient craftsman of the Middle Ages or the 15th-century smith forging armour or sculpturing small ornaments has given way to rolling mills and tube works driven by electricity generated by the rushing waters of the hills ; the town extends its villas and its brilliant streets farther and farther into the plain so that the heart becomes more and more inaccessible. But even with this, Brescia is a treasure store, rich with gems of sculpture, painting and architecture such as we may not find elsewhere in Italy ;

a unique heritage from the past with much of its loveliness still untarnished.

The history of Brescia bears a close parallel to that of Bergamo, largely through the fact that invasion of Lombardy could only be totally achieved through occupation of those two towns almost at the same time. Brescia became identified in the 12th century with the other towns forming the Lombard League, the first real effort to overcome the fatal disunion caused by the communes and mould the scattered elements comprising Lombardy into a united state, self-supporting and self-defensive, and, to a great extent, went through the same periods of disaster and sudden prosperity.

During the Roman Empire, Brescia formed the military centre for the legions operating in Cisalpine Gaul, and was definitely superior to Bergamo and Aquileia in this respect. Under Augustus it received the proud title of *Colonia Augusta Civica* and became noted for the splendour of its public buildings, the Capital situated on the hillside, the Forum surrounded by porticos and palaces and immense votive temples raised to Jupiter, Venus and Minerva, while sumptuous villas were scattered over the nearer hills, the homes of Roman administrators and warriors. The essentially warlike traditions of Roman Brescia formed round the magic words, Fortune, Faith, Victory and Heroism, stamped the Brescian character above all, and we find those traditions preserved intact through the Middle Ages, the Renaissance and even the *Risorgimento*. The Brescians had gained a reputation for dauntless bravery, a courage that weakened only in death, a stern unyielding loyalty untouched by discouragement or dismay.

The waves of barbarians coming down through the Val Camonica and through the Brenner broke first

H

against the walls of Brescia and vented their first fury
on the splendour raised there by the Romans so that
few traces can now be seen of the Roman occupation—
a solitary pillar and architrave of the Forum, an immense
accumulation of ruin left from the Temple of Vespasian,
now used as the Civic Museum for Roman antiquities,
traces of a gateway at Pusterla and fragments of sculpture, bas-reliefs, sarcophagi, the whole ennobled in the
magnificent bronze figure of Victory, one of the finest
achievements of classical sculpture.

The paganism of Rome yielded to the crude, if
passionate Christianity of the earlier centuries, and the
transition became more material than simply a change
of belief; the early Christian church builders became
adept in converting the pagan temples into Christian
shrines; the Capitol disappeared from the Cidnean
Hill, but the Temple of Jupiter was changed into a
church of St. Peter. Theodoric carried out a work of
restoration almost as great as his work at Ravenna,
but the Ostrogothic regime moved southwards and
eastwards and the forces of Byzantium, in turn, made
their impression on the town.

The Lombards, or Longobards, otherwise of little
renown, prospered in Brescia through King Desiderio,
who founded a monastery on the Cidnean Hill, invested
it with vineyards, orchards, wide-spreading lands, and
the accession of Ansilperga, the sister of Desiderio,
to the position of abbess meant further enrichment.
In the Middle Ages, the monastery enjoyed the reputation of being the richest and most powerful in Italy,
where the most illustrious took refuge or donned the
pall; Ermengarda, the rejected spouse of Charlemagne,
lived here and the relics of Saint Julia were laid here,
so that, in the increasing worship of this saint, the

monastery itself became known as Saint Julia. As such
it remained until 1797, when Napoleon suppressed it.

The period between the 8th and 10th centuries is
dark and extremely confused, a nightmarish record of
blood and disaster. The arrival of the millennium,
hailed as the end of the world, meant confirmation of
the Saxon regime in Brescia and the restoration of
nominal independence to the town. Towards the
beginning of the 11th century, the consistent struggle
between the Empire and the Papacy and between the
Empire and the people of Italy gave Brescia its opportunity and the Commune with a city militia and a consul
was established. This period of the Commune, when
Brescia seemed to set a noble example of civic pride
and civic honour to the whole of Italy, became notable,
not so much for the triumphant assertion of civic rights
against the attempted incursions of outlying lords and
against the struggles of seigneurs and ambitious clerics or
for the renaissance of architecture which found expression
in the Old Cathedral, as for the personality of one
single man, Arnaldo, whose statue now stands at the
Porta Venezia silhouetted against the vine-covered hills.

It is difficult for us now to appreciate the importance
of the mission preached by Arnaldo, a mission of equality
and universal fraternity, when we consider the fate
that has overtaken similar missions in recent years.
Arnaldo, like Cola da Rienzi at Roma, dreamed of a
social and religious reform, the restoration of liberty
and of thought, the inculcation of a higher moral
standard, and we can see in the rapt figure on a pedestal
something of the austerity which ennobled the man.

Arnaldo rises above his century by virtue of the
qualities that raised Giordano Bruno ; he was a revo-
lutionary in thought and in ideal rather than in action.

His social commonwealth was largely an improved form of the government then in force in the Brescian commune, where neither pope nor emperor had any say and the citizens were masters of their own destiny.

During the early years of his teaching, the rulers of Brescia found little to censure in him. The accentuation, however, of the doctrine of religious liberty as inseparable from political liberty was taken as a justification for anarchy and rejection of established authority, with the result that the consuls of Brescia, regarding him at last as a demagogue of perilous views, drove him from the city in 1132. The refusal to support recognized authority, religious as well as political implicit in Arnaldo's doctrines, brought Arnaldo against the fanaticism of Saint Bernard, a bitter upholder of the despotic authority of the Church, and the struggle between Arnaldo and vested, if corrupt, authority resolved itself into a struggle with Saint Bernard. When Cola da Rienzi raised the standard of the republic at Rome, Arnaldo went there to raise the morale of the people, and finally met his death in the union of the empire and papacy to quell this revolt against the authority of both church and empire.

The apostle of democracy and justice was even less successful in death than in life; the entire age was unprepared for the change advocated by Arnaldo and the old excesses continued unabated. In this renewed struggle between the empire and the papacy, Brescia, as a member of the Lombard League, fought against Barbarossa, but was forced to yield after the destruction of Milan. Brescia came into favour with Henry VI, and received special privileges as a reward for its assistance in the descent on Sicily.

With the Lombard League, Brescia contributed to

the downfall of Frederick II, the patron of southern Italian poets and troubadours, and entered into a long period of struggle between Guelfs and Ghibellines, the city being in the possession of one party or the other. The city passed into the hands of Francesco della Torre, Charles I and Charles II of Anjou, and, under the wise administration of Berardo Maggi, became architecturally strong, with walls and gates restored, and a new system of irrigation was adopted outside the city. The Guelf leader, Tebaldo Brusato, who succeeded Maggi, closed the gates of the city to Henry VII, who entered it, however, after a long siege, where Brusato was killed. Robert of Naples in 1319, John of Luxemburg in 1330, were in possession of Brescia and the Visconti in 1339 until the death of Gian Galeazzo in 1402.

The regime of the condottieri weighed more heavily on Brescia than on Bergamo, largely through the fact that Brescia lay directly in the path of the condottieri issuing from Milan against Venice or from Venice against Milan, while the main centres for the condottieri, Mantua, Cremona, Piacenza and Parma, had a natural converging point in Brescia. The reign of Pandolfo Malatesta, which lasted for seventeen years (1404-21), was a time of sheer horror for the Brescians and they welcomed the entrance of Carmagnola, who gave it to Maria Visconti and then transferred it to Venice.

The Venetian Republic carried out the same tactics here as in Bergamo, the concession of a large measure of self-government and the encouragement of friendly relations between both towns, in literature, in art, as well as in civic affairs. The conversion of the condottieri into rulers of definite provinces and towns meant ulti-mately disaster for Brescia, and to avoid annexation by Sforza or Piccinino, it became incorporated in the

Venetian Republic. Visconti, after the victory at
Maclodio in 1427, sent Piccinino to take Brescia, and
the siege that ensued is memorable in history for the
fierce resistance of the Brescians under Taddeo d'Este—a
resistance covering a period of more than three years,
when the citizens were reduced to absolute starvation
and were in danger of extermination through plague.
Sforza, descending the Oglio, relieved the town.

The peace of Lodi, in 1454, introduced a period of
recovery, but the cession by Venice of Bergamo and
Brescia to France after the defeat of Vailate, caused
new horrors. Under the French occupation a revolt
took place in Brescia and the town fell into the hands
of a Venetian force under Andrea Gritti and P. Baglioni.
The excessive caution of Gritti allowed warning to be
sent in time to Gaston de Foix with the papal forces at
Bologna. On February 19, 1512, he entered the town,
after having overcome a handful of Brescians under
Avogadro, and put the populace to the sword. Over
sixteen thousand people were destroyed in this infamous
crime. The death of Gaston de Foix at Ravenna forced
the French to retire from Lombardy.

Francis I of France restored Brescia to Venice in 1516,
and it remained thus until the advent of Napoleon.
The history of Brescia during the 16th century is largely
the history of the Republic of Venice now at its highest
period of development, not only in culture, but also in
military and naval strength. In the 17th and 18th
centuries, the growing power of the Church and the influx
of that cosmopolitan spirit which seemed to dominate
the whole of Europe removed much of the glamour from
Brescian history, and it was only in the time of the
French Republic that new life became infused and a
new sense of values introduced. The period from the

beginning of the 19th century to the Risorgimento was a time of readjustment terminating in union in the new Italian state.

The great moments in Brescian history were undoubtedly in the 14th and 15th centuries when architecture and art were shaping out those creations of beauty we now admire and reverence in the palaces, churches and frescoes scattered so richly through the town. The modern mania for industrialization may obscure those things behind new buildings, new pictures, new ideals, but the glory of Brescia is still in the memory of that past achievement, in the work carried out by those artists in stone, in metal and in paint at a time of horror and disaster.

     *   *   *   *   *

Brescia is linked more closely with Ravenna than the history of the city would lead us to believe. The reign of Theodoric and the irruption of the forces of Byzantium made their influence felt on the architecture of Brescia in the 8th century, especially in San Salvatore, the monastery placed on the Cidnean hill. The church in its present condition gives a clear insight into the architecture of that period and resembles very closely the type of the early churches in Ravenna with its three naves and its columns of different styles taken from Roman edifices. The crypt shows in its eight narrow peristyles with forty columns the same accidental characteristics as the basilica above, a mixture of the Roman and Byzantine carried out without regard to cumulative effect ; among the columns representative of rudimentary art, there are beautifully decorated efforts showing the birth of a definite artistic tradition.

In the basilica proper, several of the columns have delicately sculptured capitals worthy of being ranged with the finest capitals in Ravenna ; there are fragments of decorative friezes, peacocks strutting with long tails, finely ribbed foliage, biblical animals and merely gracious interplay of lines, of a rare delicacy in execution. The intimacy of the relation in inspiration and in time with Ravenna can be seen in the Galla Placidia Cross in the Civic Museum with its small medallion showing Galla Placidia and her two children ; the cross is of wood covered with gilded silver sheet and studded all over with precious stones, cameos and antique paste gems, the cameos representing pagan deities and symbols. The cross came into the possession of Desiderio, a present, perhaps, from the Ravennese archbishop Michele.

A later church close by the monastery, Santa Maria del Solario, dates from the 11th century—a quadrangular structure with two stories, the upper one of which is of more value architecturally. The four walls shade off, in this upper story, into eight walls with an arched gallery running round the top which leads up to a central dome. The exterior shows the small blind arches forming a frieze under the cornice, the exquisite little pillars commonly associated with early Byzantine architecture ; the interior is a glory of frescoes painted in the 15th and 16th centuries in the true Brescian tradition of Moretto and Romanino, the Last Supper, the Crucifixion, the Nativity being the most notable frescoes in the octangular walls above, while the four walls below, divided each into three compartments, represent various incidents from the lives of the saints, the Madonna and Child, the Madonna Enthroned and Saint Benedict ascending to Heaven. Of these frescoes, the Madonna and Child and the Madonna Enthroned are beautiful achievements in colour and in drawing, the latter being not unworthy of Moretto himself.

At the time when Arnaldo was fighting his solitary battle against the combined forces of the empire and papacy, the democratic instinct joined to a higher degree of culture found expression in the ancient cathedral of Santa Maria (Duomo Vecchio). Seen from the Piazza del Duomo, it is merely a circular building with the usual small arches under the cornice, more closely resembling a tower for defence than a church—immensely thick walls with small arched windows spaced equally all round. The entrance to the left leading down to the crypt is adorned with a fresco of dubious antiquity, while the interior, with some hint of the model inspiring the architects of the 12th century who had had some direct or imagined vision of the Church of the Holy Sepulchre at Jerusalem, has the gloom of masonry built thickly together without regard to beauty of decoration or exquisite art. The eight trapezoidal pillars supporting the heavy roof and the small galleries along the top as well as the staircase to the tower remind one more of a Norman castle than a church.

With all the passage of centuries Brescia has no church to present of the same architectural splendour as Sant' Anastasia of Verona or the Basilica di Santa Maria Maggiore of Bergamo. The Old Cathedral is approximately of the same period as Santa Maria Maggiore, but the only memorial of the early centuries it presents is the sarcophagus of Bishop Lambertini, a 14th-century prelate, where a crudely sculptured figure lies prone on the top with no resemblance to the prelate as he might have been in life, and the Madonna appears below in a band of church dignitaries of a standardized pattern. The Old Cathedral has its one immortal glory in the Assumption of Moretto. A nobler memorial

can be seen in the tomb in the cathedral, of Bishop
Apollonius, a Renaissance magnate of some weight in
the councils of Brescia and Venice. The three bas-
reliefs showing the ministry of the Bishop live through
the vivid representation of the crowd listening to the
preacher and the skilled grading of the architectural
background into the main sculptural motif. The figures
on each side of the Bishop are finely conceived, almost
in a Roman style.

Passing over the strange little 13th-century church of
San Faustino in Riposo, which has little of artistic
interest to present and is valuable only to historians of
architecture, we may admire the beautiful façade of
the church of San Francesco with its rose-window of
dignified proportions though less magnificent in delicate
magnificence of detail than the ornament gracing the
façade of Sant' Agostino—a successful rose-window in
a country where such an architectural feature presented
insuperable difficulties—and above all, the simply
designed portal with the shadowy fresco. This simple,
yet beautiful portal of the 14th century compares
favourably with the more ornate Renaissance portal of
the church of the Carmine, notable for the wealth of
decoration and the rich arabesque of line and form in
its pillars with their attendant lions.

The architectural gem of Brescia comparable with the
Cappella Colleoni is undoubtedly the *protiro* of Santa
Maria dei Miracoli, where the genius of Gasparo da
Cairano has had full play. The church, or rather *protiro*,
was built in the last decade of the 15th century to
commemorate a miraculous vision of the Madonna,
and became enlarged later on the design of Stefano
Lamberti and San Pellegrino to house a fairly large
congregation. The beauty of the church lies, however,

in the wonderful *protiro* in front of the church proper, where the art of decoration seems to have reached a consummation ; the wealth of floral detail is amazing, but more amazing still is the high artistic value of each detail and of the general effect. The pillars are encrusted with climbing plants frozen there in stone as if nature had grown them there, while the panels above are almost wholly an exquisite brocade design carried out in the most delicate of media, a rhythmic balance of line never once at fault.

The portal of the Chiesa del Christo of the same period illustrates the same decorative beauty, while Santa Maria delle Grazie, with its Romanesque lions, has a less imposing, if more interesting portal with a quaint Madonna and Child above. The church of Sant' Agostino has some beautiful touches of genius to show beside the rose-window—a finely proportioned window above it and two eminently satisfactory lions' heads.

The creation of an asylum of peace in the centre of the town such as we have mentioned as a characteristic of northern Italian cities can be seen also in Brescia, in the Piazza del Duomo, where the series of buildings—the Old Cathedral rising very humbly beside the immense baroque structure of the new cathedral, the Municipal Palace or Broletto, with the church of Sant' Agostino beside it—comes up on one side of the square and shuts out entirely the world of sound and activity. The square itself has a beautiful Roman fountain to break the glare of the sun in the cloudless days and it is possible to saunter from its immobility into one of the many narrow side-streets in the vicinity leading down to the Piazza del Comune, the centre of the city's activities. The Piazza del Duomo encourages meditation and a vague longing to be back in the past of romantic, if painful memories, while the Piazza del Comune causes a swift reversion to the present.

The Broletto was begun after the peace of Costanza in the latter half of the 12th century and reached a conclusion, in great part, about the middle of the 13th century. The tower and the upper loggia with its exquisite triforia and arched quadriforia date from this period. The quadriforia in the courtyard especially, with the allegorical figures of the months forming capitals in the true Romanesque tradition, merit admiration, and the warm brown of the stone round the marble serves almost as a frame for it. The Broletto was continued under Berardo Maggi, and reached a definite conclusion in the 15th century. The change in period caused a change in taste ; the old simplicity yielded here to the knowledge of artifice generated through greater experience in using the artistic medium, with the result that the polychrome triforia appeared, a very beautiful architectural device if more sophisti- cated than the old.

Contemporaneous with the older Broletto, the Torre Pallata, built on the inner ceinture of walls, preserves a certain architectural beauty even through its essentially protective nature ; the unrelieved walls of stone, terminating in the arched battlements so dear to mediæval Italian princes, strike a note of warm colour beyond the narrow range of houses shadowing the busy street.

A greater architectural achievement by modern standards than the Broletto can be seen in the Loggia or Palazzo Municipale, built in the full tide of the Renaissance between 1492 and 1574. Bramante has been considered the original designer ; the lower part up to the balustrade, including the balcony above with its row of small marble pillars, was finished in 1508, Giovanni and Cristoforo dell' Ostello and Jacopo da Verona chiselling out the friezes of the arches and the capitals, Antonio della Porta and perhaps Gaspare da Milano the heads of the Roman emperors in the niches, while Stefano carved in wood the entrance doors below the portico. This part of the palace is, from the point of view of decoration, the most valuable, and betrays the same wealth of fancy as the *protiro* of Santa Maria dei Miracoli, a splendour of execution in stone almost unique in the north of Italy. The heads of the Romans and the classical nudes on the balustrade are vividly and beautifully executed, each a perfect gem of statuary. The upper part, including the bronze roof, with the statues along the upper balustrade, was designed by Sansovino, and modified largely by a commission composed of Palladio, first of all, Gian Antonio Rusconi, and Galeazzo Alessi later. To the sure judgment of Palladio we can attribute the architectural unity achieved.

Palladian, also, is the palace facing the loggia with the clock-tower—an impressive series of arches forming a colonnade—while the Monte di Pietà, on the opposite side of the square, dates from an earlier period. The portico and the loggetta above belong to the early Renaissance in Lombardian architecture and show, in the loggetta especially, the same mastery of decoration as the loggia. The whole square forms an architectural harmony, testifying to the high level of art displayed, and it is a rare pleasure indeed simply to linger in the shadow of the colonnade and watch the sun touching up each beautiful detail in turn, one mass in shadow and the other in a blaze of light.

Brescia is rich in other palaces, the Palazzo Martinengo

with its richly decorated doorway representing the arms of the family, the Palazzo Calzavellia with its vaguely frescoed walls and finely designed entrance, the doorway narrowing above to a biforia divided by slender pillars, supported a richly decorated architrave, both of the Renaissance, while later centuries produced the Palazzo Martinengo Villagna, now in a state of restoration or perhaps disruption, the magnificent Palazzo Cigola with a portal almost exactly the same as that of the Palazzo Colleoni in Old Bergamo, the Palazzo Cocchetti Terzi with its fine iron-work across the lower end of the garden facing on the street, all of the 17th century.

Crowning all on its hill outside the city, the Viscontian Castello seems to preside over the fortunes of the city, a stern but faithful presence, inured to hardship and disaster—the red centuries of the Empire and the condottieri, and the stormy years of the Risorgimento. In architecture, in art, and in sculpture, Brescia has contributed nobly to the Italian heritage, and not least, in one little-known but highly cherished manifestation : small bronzes, armour and chiselled ornaments.

Apart from the beauty of the churches and the frescoes drawn in them by the great Brescian artists, Brescia achieved fame as a centre of the small statuary profession in northern Italy, if we can use this term—that minor form of sculpture in which the Renaissance achieved a perfection only rivalled by that of painting. The palaces of the Renaissance had fostered a demand for small decorative details : door-knockers, ink-wells, chandeliers, bells, lamps, which the sculptor and founder interpreted in his own way. The work of Benvenuto Cellini in silver work is well known, but, apart from him, the Renaissance produced a number of sculptors famous more for their statuettes and small bronzes than for

their more ambitious works; such were, for example,
Giovanni da Bologna, il Riccio, il Moderno, while the
great sculptors, Donatello, Tullio Lombardi among
them, executed occasionally small statues of great
beauty. It has been stated that Donatello, working in
Padua, set the fashion for those minute bronzes which
spread later over the north of Italy, and came finally
as far south as Florence and Rome.

The finest collections of those statuettes and small
bronze decorations are housed at present in the Kunsthistorisches Museum at Vienna, where an impressive array
of masterpieces by Giovanni da Bologna and Moderno
constitutes one of the glories of the collection; in the
Victoria and Albert Museum in London, to quote a
British collection, where Riccio has contributed the
greatest proportion; and in the Museo dell' Età Chris-
tiana in Brescia. The influence of Donatello can be
seen most clearly in a small nude of a clear golden
colour with gracious flowing lines and a delicious sense
of movement, while Tullio Lombardi has contributed
two figures directly imitated from the classical, less
intensely alive than the Bacchus and Diana in Vienna.
The first bronze, representing the Goddess Angerona
uttering the secret name of Rome, has all the severity
of modelling and line of a Roman figure, while the second,
a lady seated on a rock with robes falling from one
finely moulded shoulder, shows greater vivacity in
gesture.

Other figures, recalling the classical, are the Jupiter,
Neptune and Saturn of Alessandro Vittoria, Neptune
being, perhaps, the most vivid realization of all, with
a superbly modelled body and fine bearded head. Jupiter
is less genial, less expressive and shows more conven-
tional decoration, while Saturn, attributed to Vittoria,

has scarcely risen beyond the state of a sketch, full of suggestion but clumsy in the drapery.

The school of Andrea Briosco or Riccio has been responsible for several bronzes of an execution almost as exquisite as that shown by Donatello ; the use of a warm red bronze instead of bright gold, already mentioned as a feature of the Donatello bronzes, quickens up the feeling for decoration and gives more suggestion to the figures themselves. Riccio, with Moderno, may be considered as the outstanding artists using this type of bronze, and the Brescian collection is peculiarly rich in them. Two bells illustrate the art of the former at its best, from the point of view both of decoration and of foundry technique. In the one bell, nudes dance round in a beautifully wreathed canopy of flowers, while an aged philosopher of solemn mien, with chin resting on his hands, personifies the stately wisdom of age above the flowery joy of youth ; in the second bell the floral decoration is more involved but still exquisitely balanced, and small putti, of a delicious grace, supply a living motif. One inkstand, also beautifully executed, represents a horned satyr sitting with legs crossed, with a tiny figure on a sphere beckoning to him—a wholly delightful creation ; a candlestick formed of a female satyr with young satyr beside her shows a strange fusion of classical severity and wayward imagination.

There are two vivid putti playing fiddles, by Niccolo Roccatagliata, both of exquisite workmanship ; a finely conceived Atlas bearing a double candlestick, weighed down apparently with more cares than those attendant on muscular strain—a feeling of lost dignity perhaps ; a delicious series of inkstands of weird forms ; a crocodile with the visage of a satyr, groups of putti

cting as supports, or bulls' heads alternating with heads
of putti and, above all, a fine sculpture of the Venetian
school of the 16th century representing three putti
riding dolphins and supporting at the same time a sea-
shell crowned by an armed warrior.

There are forms and figures of a strangely imaginative quality, all distinguished by that rare decorative
taste which distinguished the Italian Renaissance as
a perfect artistic epoch in history where nothing
could jar against the enjoyment of beauty. Beauty
meant a living thing in the lofty palace as well as
in the small court; in the immense, wall-devouring
fresco as well as in the tiny putto riding a dolphin;
in the stately decoration of a room as well as in
the humble inkstand. It is only now, with a feeling of
reverence, that we can enjoy those little things which,
in themselves, represented artistic problems even as
important as the Perseus of Benvenuto Cellini—small
symbols of a great movement spreading out over every
branch of human activity.

The art of carving in wood found in Stefano Lamberti
a master. The magnificent frames shown in the anconas
in the church of St. John the Evangelist (containing
a "Deposition" of Civerchio) and in the church of San
Francesco (providing a noble accompaniment to Romanino's masterpiece) belong to the most exquisite achievement of the Renaissance in pure decoration. The
wealth of ornamentation is bewildering, but perfect
in every detail, a lace-like splendour carried out in
wood. Other wood carvers who became famous outside
of Brescia were Raffaelle Marone and Lodovico de
Nozi, both of the 16th century; Marone executed the
choir stalls in the church of San Michele in Bosco
at Verona, and assisted in the adornment of the choir

I

and sacristy of Santa Maria degli Organi at Verona ; Nozi carved the doors of the cathedral of Ferrara. A third Brescian, Giuseppi Bulgarini, adorned with foliage, birds and floral wreaths the organ chamber of the church of the Madonna di Tirano, sculptured the two beautiful angels in the Chapel of the Blessed Sacrament at Rovato. Brescia became noted also in the 15th and 16th centuries for highly ornamented armour such as we see now in Vienna. Charles V and Francis I rewarded Serafino da Brescia for his excellent work in tempering and adorning their armour. Plaques and medallions carried out by famous artists of the time —Melioli, Vellano, Riccio, Caradosso, Sperandio and Pisanello—can now be admired in the collection left by Antonio da Brescia.

CHAPTER VII

THE VAL CAMONICA IN HISTORY AND ART

THE Val Camonica is less known, perhaps, than any other in the great valleys opening up a passage for civilization in the Italian Alps, but it possesses, in great part, the beauty of those other valleys with a more intimate suggestion of historical changes and associations—an old civilization partially forgotten grading into the new. Unlike the Val d'Aosta, it has no Carducci to glorify it in verse, no great poetical traditions to cast a glamour over it and hide some of its defects, but there are jewels of beauty in it of as fine a quality as any found farther north or east. The view from the tower of the Gaioni family at Nadro into the immense buttresses of hill, silver streaked with running water or dazzling white in places where the clouds lift and the sunlight falls on banks of snow, or down into the valley where the gradation of exquisite tints from dusky green and purple to the silkiest shade of pale rose transfigures the quaint Alpine villages and brings them at once into harmony with the spirit of the hills, is as fine as anything in Tyrol.

The castle of Breno, one of the last mediæval fortresses in the Alps, is situated on a shoulder of the mountains in what must be one of the most picturesque sites in the whole of Italy. The ruins appear above the vines and groves of the hillside, in an unrelieved stretch of warm grey wall, very effective against the purple and blue of mountain and sky, or dark, in winter or early spring, against the wall of snow stretching from peak to peak across the valley. Few places bear so richly and so nobly the imprint of the centuries as the castle of Breno; the shadows of the towers and ivy-covered walls fall over smooth lawns brilliantly green in the sunshine; the grasshoppers alone break the silence, or the crickets at dusk, and the sky comes to a harmony over all, exquisite as a dream. The valley moves below it into its most radiant colour, mass against mass, mountain slope rising beyond mountain slope, peak tossing cloud to peak until, in the distant gleam of sky and earth, the finely etched lines appear frail and tenuous, no longer of the rock, but of the air. Breno itself, under the steep hills, has something of their inspiring quality, even if, architecturally, no monument of distinction, beyond perhaps the campanile of the church of the Holy Saviour, appears. From the quaintly narrow streets escape to the wider spaces is possible at all times, and the immense harmony of the mountains brings the eternal into perspective.

The Val Camonica is dotted with quiet villages enfolded in the hills, quiet with the quiet of centuries where apparently nothing has stirred since the early inhabitants established there a colony on the outer fringe of civilization, and something of that early peace enters into the spirit of the traveller entering them; Bienno beside the rushing Oglio with its protective church above it, Berzo with its ancient temple located almost in the clouds, Gorzone with its castle raised on a cliff where the hills come straight down into the valley, Erbanno with its campanile rising against a background

IN A VILLAGE OF THE VAL CAMONICA

of bare rock beyond wooded slopes and Edolo under the shadow of Mount Aviolo.

Apart from the beauty of natural setting and the historical interest of the architecture in the Val Camonica, the art lover may spend an exciting time in hunting out the many frescoes painted by Pietro Giovanni da Cemmo towards the end of the 15th century for the churches situated in the valley. Cemmo is not a Moretto or a Romanino by any means, but he is undoubtedly an attractive painter, if only through his complete *naïveté* and his realistic treatment of Biblical character.

Few painters have been so faithful, in delineation, to contemporary standards ; the world that moves in his pictures is the splendid world of the Renaissance, full of rich movement and warm colouring ; every picture appears almost as a scene from a play being acted before our eyes, and the totality of his pictures would seem to be the full scope and the culmination of the play, the Italian world of the 15th century reproduced in every minute detail.

The comparison with the stage goes even farther than this. Cemmo is a remarkably clever scene painter with all the defects of the trade, imperfect anatomy, a tendency to caricature and a somewhat elementary sense of colour values, but, with those defects, some of its direct expression and its capacity for giving at once the pictorial essentials. Cemmo remains practically unknown even in Lombardy since, with the exception of the Val Camonica, the only town containing examples of his work is Brescia, but this obscurity hides many qualities of true art, true vision, inspired by a genuine belief. We can always feel, on viewing a fresco by Cemmo, that his churches, already very close to heaven on the mountains in the full glory of sky and mountain-world, crowned by the clouds and ennobled by the splendour of dawn or sunset, were symbolic for him of heaven itself ; the divine was a living force with him, the inspiration of art came into the ecstasy of belief and the pictorial representation had the force and truth of a heavenly sanction, a glorification of life at the instant of delineation.

Even with this conviction, Cemmo has remained at best ineloquent, without vivid gesture or rich sweep of line and colour ; the difficulty of transfusing the world as he knew it and saw it into the final vision demanded by art, of bringing contemporary life into harmony with that eternal vision of humanity inseparable from his themes, was beyond his power. His madonnas are authentic madonnas of the spirit, but they move in Italian society of the 15th century with every detail complete.

Five villages in the Val Camonica possess examples of the art of Pietro da Cemmo, Annunziata, Esine, Breno, Berzo Inferiore and Bienno, while a number of other villages have frescoes attributed to him. Annunziata and Esine merit a visit, if only for the sake of Cemmo, who has carried out in those villages his most notable work. The Chiesa Parrocchiale of the former glories in an abside entirely covered by beautiful frescoes of the Camunian artist ; the vault comes to a centre in the figure of the Holy Father and Saints surrounded by a cloud of angels who crowd up from the walls in rhythmic masses of pure colour, a fine sensation of movement, while the walls are divided into square medallions representing various scenes from the life of the Virgin, the Birth, the Annunciation, Marriage, Assumption, etc. Ten smaller medallions, showing the figures of saints, are painted round the arch dividing the abside from the other quadrangular part of the presbytery.

Two of the Virgin series are specially interesting, the "Marriage of the Virgin" and the "Assumption"; the former contains some of Cemmo's most successful figures, the Madonna herself being well drawn, while the somewhat lifeless statuary usually conceived by the painter and dressed up to look alive has actually given way here to a vivid representation of life. The figure of St. Joseph bending forward eagerly to place the ring on the Madonna's finger and the audience to the extreme right and extreme left have a certain vivacity of gesture. The sense of rhythm in the angels circling round the shadowy Madonna rising, complete with throne and pedestal, to heaven above a Brescian landscape, and the naïve posture of the angels lifting up the heavy piece of furniture, with every scientific difficulty magically solved, are delicious. The whole church is a memorial to the art of Cemmo, with scarcely a patch of wall left unpainted.

Between the choir and the body of the church there is interposed a wall supported on two pillars which represents Cemmo's most important contribution to the art of his time. The frescoes covering it are divided into thirty-one sections, each of them in a good state of preservation and each devoted to one episode in the life of Jesus. While we may trace in them a genuinely religious intention, they form rather more vivid scenes from the contemporary world, and the large "Crucifixion" in the centre shows a market-place scene, horses and groups of figures complete, with the shadows of Christ and the two robbers only a part of the decoration. The figure, somewhat elongated in leg, which stands in front of the table in the "Last Supper" scene, is striking

in its brilliant note of colour. Some feeling for landscape can be seen in the " Gethsemane " medallion,
while the " Betrayal of Jesus " is a lively piece of *genre*,
where the element of caricature and the grotesque
quickens up the action. The wall in its entirety illustrates the scene-painting ability of Cemmo at its best,
and strikes a definitely modern note ; any one of the
scenes so treated could enter with full honour into the
present realistic school, where an effort has been made
to recapture the direct massing of colour and line
adopted almost instinctively by the early Italians.

At Esine, the walls of the church of Santa Maria
Assunta as well as the vaulted roof of the choir are
covered entirely by frescoes by Cemmo ; the main
subjects of these paintings are, as usual, the Assumption
of the Virgin, the Holy Trinity, the Adoration of the
Magi, Saint Jerome, Saint Francis and the Twelve
Disciples, the Doctors of the Church and the Evangelists.
The Madonna, in the vague colouring of the walls where
much of the sparkle of the original tints has disappeared
in a dim harmony caused by the wear of centuries,
has all the languor and anæmia of the most spiritual of
ladies ; she remains the heroine of the play, illustrated
in a dozen different postures, always with a lifeless
little doll beside her, much as the illustrated papers
seize on the different attitudes of a popular actress to-day.

For Cemmo, however, the actress has a fashion peculiar
to herself, a divine fashion, and there is, even in the
stiff gesture and unyielding folds of the dress, something
of a finer symbolism beyond the fleeting emotion, the
incarnation of a higher faith transmuted into human
life.

The church of the Assumption, with its elaborate
high altar framing an " Assumption " copied by a pupil

from the masterpiece of Moretto, lives in the memory simply through the quiet beauty of form and colour held in the frescoes by Cemmo. It is possible to thrust aside all canons of art in enjoyment of those serried rows of saints which form a nimbus in the vaulted choir round the central figure of Christ, everyone with a standardized face, but every face strangely and potently alive. There is no effort to obtain miracles of perspective ; the figures become elongated as the vault comes over, the robes fall closer round the body and there hovers over the mass of figures something of the passionate intentness of a vision by Blake—a continual upthrust of movement, an uninterrupted strain toward heaven.

At some moments, the passionate strength of expression, especially in some of the figures standing beside the open tomb in the resurrection scene and in the Madonna and Child with the four Evangelists brings the picture into the authentic beauty of true art. Cemmo shows here also a capacity for reproducing carefully contemporary fashions and types with elaborate robes strewn with embroidered flowers.

Apart from the Val Camonica, Bagolino near Monte Gleno preserves, in the vaulted roof of the church of San Rocco, some of the most brilliant pictorial efforts of Pietro da Cemmo, the four Evangelists and the Doctors of the Church, finely decorative and *bien mouvemente* (the figure of St. John being specially gracious) and ennobled in rich luminous colour. The lack of proportion however, and the tendency towards a standard model, in the Madonna above all, with a certain crudity in design and composition are sufficient to keep Cemmo from entering that plane of art where we must place Romanino, his successor in the Val Camonica.

We have already discussed in Brescia some of the more

famous achievements of Romanino, distinguishing his work in many essentials from that of Moretto, but it is a new Romanino that faces us in the Val Camonica, a less restrained, less classical and more impressionistic artist with an exuberance of line and form only seen at intervals in Brescia. There is no picture in the Val Camonica of the same finish and the same luminous perfection of detail as the altar-piece in Padua, the same tranquillity of arrangement or modelling, but there is instead the vivacity and rapid suggestion of a sketch, a sudden vision of beauty disclosed in one rapid sweep of the brush. There is a keen pleasure in the thought of those two artists roaming from church to church along the valley, the one, a disciple recollecting models from a past century and striving to reconcile religious belief with the plain world of fact, and the other, content to adopt the achievement of two centuries, mingle scenes already staged for him according to a strong pictorial imagination drunken with the glowing colour of the Venetians, not sincere entirely, the artist first of all and the devotee afterwards.

Romaninos can be found in practically every important village in the valley, but principally at Esine, Pisogne, Erbanno, Breno, Edolo, Bienno, Borno and Mu. Esine possesses in the Chiesa Parocchiale an interesting Madonna and Child, notable for the expression on the Madonna's face, a well-nourished country maiden, and the fine movement in the figure of St. Peter on the right, a wholly satisfactory creation. The suggestion of mountainous landscape behind gives depth to the picture, and it might well be imagined that the lake among the hills had been copied from the Lago d'Iseo itself.

Erbanno shows Romanino at his best ; the church of

Santa Maria del Restello glories in a magnificent assumption where the quick movement and strength of gesture, almost Michel Angelesque in effect, testify to the dramatic genius of the artist. The figure of the disciple gazing down stupefied to the earth, after being blinded by the vision above, is finely done ; every gesture, every movement of the arm, every turn of the head or body has been brought into unity with the effect of vivid life ; the angels flying round the Madonna are delightfully conceived. The same church has other frescoes, notable for the same wealth of dramatic suggestion, the Decapitation of St. John the Baptist, and an episode from the life of St. George. The figures in the decapitation scene are unfinished, sketchy, but the brilliance of a sketch gives them strength, while Herodias, with the shadowy damsel beside her, is undoubtedly a vivid creation. Another female figure with richly swelling robes and voluptuous suggestion of form, redeems the St. George fresco from artistic failure.

Less successful, if more impressive through the use of the architectural motif, are the frescoes in the church of St. John the Baptist in Edolo ; the mountain landscape behind the Crucifixion at the high altar, where Christ floats in an immensity of cloud-barred sky above vaguely passionate shadows, the three Maries in anguish, gives nobility and beauty to the artistic conception, but this nobility is lacking in that other scene where the Madonna finds comfort in a powerfully arcaded and colonnaded temple. One delicious scene, where the important function of bathing the Divine Child is in progress, dwells in the memory not so much through the force of drawing displayed as through the natural setting. The capacity of Romanino for telling a story without interlude can be seen here.

The parochial church at Breno possesses a Madonna and Child enthroned very similar to the pictures in Brescia, with the same defect of arbitrary disposal of the figures round the central group to form a living frame. The attitudes of both the Madonna and Child are well drawn. Other churches have frescoes to show, mostly in an advanced state of ruin, where only a head or a leg or an arm or a torso emerge strangely from oblivion, but the pictures we have already discussed represent the main contribution of both Romanino and Pietro da Cemmo to the art of the Italian Renaissance, and when we consider even the pictures in the Val Camonica, without referring to Bergamo or Brescia, this contribution is far from negligible.

Romanino is one of the many Italian painters of the later years of the Italian Renaissance whom modern artistic criticism has resurrected from oblivion, placing him, if not on a level with the great Venetians, Mantegna, Cima da Conegliano and Carpaccio, at least in a position only slightly inferior. Romanino, as Moretto, bridges the gap between the Lombardian school proper and the Venetians and, as such, has some of the qualities of both.

The parochial churches of Esine and Breno have two frescoes of a little known artist, Calisto Piazza da Lodi, a contemporary of Romanino, both representing the Deposition ; the figure of Christ is remarkably well done in the Breno picture especially, and the grouping of the figures behind the dead body shows considerable knowledge of expression, aided by judicious employment of light and shade. The work of other artists can also be seen in isolated churches, but Cemmo and Romanino give to all their significance in the history of art.

From art to the frame in which it is displayed is only a short step, and the antiquity of the civilization of the

Val Camonica finds an apter illustration in those architectural memorials of a past century when the Romans penetrated into the farthest regions of Cisalpine Gaul and established there their outposts against the barbarism of the North and the early Christians imported the style of Byzantium into those temples they raised to the divinity of modern civilization.

Few traces can now be seen of the Roman occupation, only a few crude sculptures at Cividate, lying almost neglected in the courtyard of the parochial house, where the richly draped figures are gradually sinking back into the stone from which they once emerged. At the top of San Glisente hill, above the village of Berzo Inferiore, over 6,000 feet among the clouds and accessible only by means of a beautiful winding path through groves of chestnuts, pine woods, and jewel-like pastures dotted with tinkling cattle, the quaint old church of San Glisente appears. San Glisente dug out there a cave of meditation and prayer some time during the 9th century, and on this primitive church, distinguished by Gothic vaulted arches on four red granite pillars, the barrack-like church of a later age was built. It is a pure joy to lie on the grass in front of it on a mellow autumn day, breathing the cool, scented air and drinking in the beauty of sky, mountain and distant valley, a medley of exquisite colours drawn fine as silk beyond a dimming veil of atmosphere ; the cows with their bells and their philosophic herds move slowly between the foreground and the shimmering immensity behind, a sharp silhouette against the world of infinite space.

The Val Camonica glories in two fine examples of Lombardian architecture of the 11th and 12th centuries, the Church of the Redeemer at Capo di Ponte, and the magnificently situated " Antica Pieve di San Siro "

at Cemmo, one of the most imposing churches of the
Italian Alps raised on its sheer cliff on the mountain-
side.   The Church of the Redeemer lies in a more
gracious setting in a hollow of the hills with the trees
grouped round it and the ivy growing thick on the walls
of the abside.   The octagonal dome rising above the
cluster of abside, transepts and naves in a triumphant
culmination has the delicately arcaded windows of the
typical Lombardian campanile, a fine architectural
motif paralleled by the simple, yet harmonious decoration
of the abside.   The interior, divided into three naves
with immense vaulted roofs supported by strong pillars,
has the simple beauty of the age and the beautiful
ornamentation of the capitals, eagles and sheep and
legendary animals in fantastic, yet symmetrical positions,
reminds one irresistibly of the jewel churches of Ravenna.
The wealth of imagination combined with strong decorative effect is on the same level of achievement.

The " Antica Pieve di San Siro," on a hollow in the
sheer cliff above Oglio, where sufficient space to form a
platform for the temple has alone been cleared out
and the façade has become the cliff itself, is undoubtedly
the most inspiring of all the churches in the Val
Camonica.   The pilgrim could climb up the steep hillside
in the early centuries and find in the shadowy court
beside the church where the tree shadows lie peacefully
in a perpetual suggestion of rest, a moment of closer
communion with the Divinity pulsating round him,
and an asylum against the violence and depredations
of the world.

The view from the church is very beautiful, with the
mountains closing up the sky beyond the Oglio, and the
deep-eaved Alpine houses below striking a note of
refuge in the harmony of valley, hill and sky.   The main

portal to the side shows traces of 11th-century sculpture, sculpture almost as fragile as lace with the wear of centuries, the arch of the portal and the two pillars with their quaintly beautiful capitals. At the foot of the pillar to the left, a highly ornamental lion in the true Lombardian tradition, still supports its part of the wall. The abside facing on the valley, in place of the façade, which has been sacrificed, apparently, in the desire to force a passage through the cliffside, preserves the small blind arches common to Romanesque churches, and the campanile towers above all, a square erection perfectly in proportion with biforia at the top, divided by the usual elegant pillars.

The ensemble, although less united than that of the Church of the Redeemer, gives a nobler impression of strength and of undaunted effort, more in tune with the splendour of the hills. The " Antica Pieve " symbolizes more than any other monument of the Val Camonica the spirit we instinctively associate with the mountains, the spirit of simple truth and of beauty distilled from immense power ; it is the mountain temple of the valley.

This feeling becomes intensified on entering ; the choir remains as the 11th century left it, with every quaint architectural feature intact and the crypt below, with its richly decorated pillars and heavy arches, appears almost Roman in design, an early memorial to the Christian faith ; but closer examination of the arched windows and the frieze of stone along the wall, shows that the same architect built the crypt and the church above it. The small pillars with the Corinthian capitals were evidently taken from an ancient classical temple in the neighbourhood and, *faute de mieux*, used as supports for the vaulted roof.

In addition to those two churches, the Val Camonica

has interesting memorials of later centuries to present—
the magnificent portal of the church of San Antonio at
Breno carried out in red marble during the early Renaissance with a wonderful delicacy of style and modelling,
the simpler portal of the church of Santa Maria Annunziata at Bienno with its graceful pillars, the Casa
Ballardini at Erbanno with its doorways of red marble
simply designed in the most gracious ornamental style
of the Renaissance and its upper loggia opening to the
mountain landscape in front. Pisogne has in the church
of Santa Maria della Neve (Our Lady of the Snows) a
richly ornamental work of the Renaissance, with a
finely executed portal surmounted by a quaint marble
statue of the Madonna; a similar portal can be seen
in the church of Santa Maria in the same town.

The beauty of the Val Camonica lies in this association
of the past with the present glory of mountain and
valley; the natural features become mellow in the
remembrance of a civilization that has here traditions
as old and as precious as the traditions of regions farther
south in the heart of Italy, in Sicily and in Tuscany.
The feeling of continuity is less apparent here, where the
Alps dominate all thought and overwhelm the senses in
a magnificent wealth of beauty, than in Tuscany where
the hills are more genial, more friendly, more amenable
to human companionship and human influence; but
the traveller may spend a time of sheer joy in tracing
out through quaint memorials housed in quaint villages
some precious notes of that past world which comes to
expression even now, at unexpected moments, when
the rush of modern industrial life may have changed
some of those features essential to preservation of the
past glory.

CHAPTER VIII

THE ROUTE OF THE ALPS—EDOLO AND TIRANO

THE journey from Brescia to Tirano may be made quite well on foot via Edolo, with frequent stops at the small villages to examine some artistic memorial of the past and appreciate some of the quaint handicraft of the present, but the extension of a small railway up through the Val Camonica has made this method of progression almost unnecessary and robbed the hill people of much of their self-sufficiency. Instead of the richly embroidered dresses and shawls of a previous generation, the traveller may find the latest creation in cotton or silk from Milan, or take away as a local rarity what has been marketed in thousands by a modern factory in Brescia. The artistic memorials of the past still remain comparatively intact, and some of those memorials, as we have seen, are very beautiful indeed.

The process of transformation of the Val Camonica does not end, however, with the introduction of Milanese fashions; an important centre of the iron and steel industry of Italy has been established there, and practically every village of importance from Pisogne north-wards boasts of iron and steel works with motive power supplied by hydro-electric power stations. Those power stations are connected by long pipe lines to reservoirs located up the hillside, and those pipes, especially in the mountains surrounding the Lago d'Iseo, form a distinctive feature of the landscape. The Val d'Angolo, opposite Pisogne, has been changed in appearance through collection of the head waters of the Angolo into an immense reservoir at Monte Gleno, and the once quiet valley is rapidly becoming industrialized.

As far as Darfo, the Lago d'Iseo excepted, the Val Camonica is disappointing to the traveller seeking natural beauty alone, but as a picture of modern industrial Italy striving to utilize every possible natural resource in an effort to overcome the lack of coal, it is more instructive than Milan or Turin. Nature seems at last to have agreed to co-operate with man, and the strange contrast of furnaces blazing against a dim background of mountain testifies to a victory gained after the struggle of centuries. Although, from the æsthetic point of view, this inrush of industrialism into the Val Camonica may mean the progressive substitution of ugliness for beauty, there is an inspiring quality in the actual work of substitution which gives to the valley a strange fascination. The crickets sing in the grass while the forges thunder beside them, and the contrast is piquant indeed.

The Val Camonica is distinguished, however, by having in it the loveliest of all the Italian lakes, the Lago d'Iseo, and only the Königssee near Salzburg, of all the Alpine lakes, approaches it in the sheer perfection of stern cliff mirrored in the calm depths of water. Lugano, Como, Maggiore and Garda may appear infinitely more radiant in beauty than the Lago d'Iseo, but the stretch of flat country intervening between the water and the mountains weakens the effect of sky, hill and blue water with the result that the focus is never quite right. In Iseo the focus is always right, the cliffs shoot down without a break, the San Paolo island in it is an immense bastion of rock where sheer height gives it almost the majesty of a western island of Scotland with a richer suggestion of colour, and the mountains only open up into folds to allow the sunlight to find a deeper shadow and a more vivid reflection.

Apart from the Lago d'Iseo, the Val Camonica has an historical importance inasmuch as it formed the nearest pathway to Switzerland through the Alps; the Brenner, farther east, acted as a direct approach to Tyrol and Germany. From time immemorial, the trade of Switzerland and Italy passed from the Valtellina to the Val Camonica and gave to Brescia and Bergamo an importance equal to that of Verona at the mouth of the Brenner. At Lovere and Pisogne, the trade routes divided on each side of the Lago d'Iseo, one going direct to Bergamo and the other to Brescia. This circumstance explains not only the industrial position of the valley in modern Italy but also some of the characteristics of its inhabitants who, with the Bergamascans, are among the most active and enterprising in the whole Alpine region—Swiss, German, Austrian or Italian.

*   *   *   *   *

First visions of the Lago d'Iseo were impressive. The sun had already dipped behind the hills and there was a reflected light on the buttresses coming down to the edge of the water, dim gold, rose-tinted, contrasting with a milky blue-green of foliage where vineyards and orchards were scattered on the lower slopes. The entrance to the lake was guarded by the heights of the Pizzo dell'Orto, impressive through the sharp mass and abrupt shadow of precipice beside precipice rather than through height, and the sunlight brought into prominence those features, veiling in a tenuous shadow the gentler slopes.

It is only at the lake that the foothills of Brescia are left behind and the Alps begin. The beginning, as mirrored in the calm water of the lake, with the constant succession of mountains on the right, the Pizzo dell'Orto, followed by Monte Rodondone, Monte Armala, Monte Cavrello rising above 6,000 feet to the immense mass of the Dosso Pedalta and grading down to Mont' Agolo above Pisogne, has a beauty almost as varied as that of Tyrol. On the left side of the lake, where the massif lying between the Val Cavallina and the lake itself dips abruptly into the water in a succession of sheer cliff broken only by sudden gashes where streams drop down from the heights behind, the change from rugged strength of hill to calm of water is wonderful indeed.

Iseo is a sunny little town squeezed between the mountains and the lake with all the characteristics of an Italian lake town, quaint buildings ranged along the water front with groups of fishermen resting on the white parapet of the wall before them, flocks of small sailing boats scattered over the near distance and a pier where the lake steamers embark passengers during the summer and autumn months. The peculiar square campanile of the churches of northern Lombardy is repeated here in the main church, and across the water, at Predore, a similar church appears.

The train moves through a series of tunnels with a continual change of picture, so that the whole journey along the lake, especially when the Isola San Paolo appears and throws the farther hills behind it into a dimmer perspective, is rich in vignettes, sometimes of genre : a muleteer driving a picturesque assortment of mule and ox along the narrow lake road, a group of women washing, a crew loading vegetables on a small sloop beside a mouldy wharf, a darkly shadowed crowd standing beside high walls listening to a *venditore ambulante* ; and sometimes of still life : a statue in a garden, richly ornamented villa gates surrounded by ornamental stone-work.

At every station the whole population turned out to meet the descending travellers, the arrival of the train being apparently an event of some importance in the lives of the inhabitants. Existence beside the lake is sufficiently placid to induce keen interest in the varieties of human nature imported from Milan and Brescia. I detected a slightly satirical air in the picturesque group of attendants when a young Milanese lady, attired in the height of Milanese fashion, an extreme version of the Parisian mode, stepped daintily from the smutty compartment where she had been trying without much success to shield her complexion from the constant stream of cinders and coal blown by the engine through the train from one end to another. Being early autumn, not a window or passage-way was closed, and considerable skill was required to reconnoitre a view round the valleys passed by the train. The peach complexion duly elaborated at Milan or Brescia had changed gradually to a pale shade of grey, but the young lady cared little about this since the Italian capacity for resignation to an unavoidable evil is always in full play on occasions like this, and a fashionable robe may harmonize at times quite well with an interesting shading of feature.

Those little scenes at the stations, where something of natural expression became visible and the officials were manifestly proud of their scarlet crowned caps exerting a full dignity of effect, had a delightfully quaint attraction—true *genre* pictures with every detail complete. At Pisogne, at the head of the lake, where the valley of the Oglio forces apart the mountains and there is a broad stretch of marshy green country covered with canes as far as Lovere, the train seemed to unload all its passengers and leave us entirely alone. The passengers, among them a smiling Italian captain resplendent in field uniform and lofty cap, accompanied by a lady almost the exact counterpart of the lady who had descended at a previous station, split up into gesticulating groups, and sauntered off along the high road to the town about half a mile distant in the shadow of the mountains, calmly ignoring the ticket collector who seemed quite contented with this disregard.

The lake itself had become wonderfully beautiful in the frail golden light after sunset, and the gradation from the delicate blue of the farthest mountains, as they rose above the foothills, to the stronger milky purple of the shadowy peaks mirrored in the water beside a flickering illumination, and then to the intense purple of the cliffs across the lake behind the island seemed almost as perfect as a Japanese painting. The highest peaks, where the sheer rock projected above the last clumps of scraggy verdure and absorbed, in a pale rose reflection, the light from the horizon, towered at the end of the valley debouching at Lovere, and the whole stretch from Clusone to the lake edge filled with a tenuous mist mysterious beneath the rosy heights above. The unity of impression was complete, the harmony of colour made more delicate through this faintly luminous mist floating down with the Borlezza river.

The Oglio itself began to lose its reflection in the mist, and the gleam through the willows and poplars on the banks became less vivid.   The mountains stepped back from the valley beyond the Pisogne, but began to rise higher and higher into the sky from Monte Marucolo beyond the shoulder of Monte Muffetto, swung round more and more to the right until they joined at Monte Mattone the immense wall of mountains which culminate at Adamello and the Presanella group.   As the light darkened, the suggestion of mass became stronger, the sudden valleys and clefts, beyond Darfo especially, the sharp heave of rock where the mountains changed direction and presented a bare precipice to the valley and the wall of mountains beyond the river, seemed more and more impressive in shadow.   The little towns, huddling beside their campaniles in an island of smoke, with an occasional gleam of light on water, lost their importance in the landscape and the world presented an unbroken harmony of cane-fields shadowed by the hills.

Occasionally, small groups of figures could be seen in the canes, mysteriously silent and motionless, and a certain statuesque quality was imparted to everything merely through this suggestion.   Even the hoarse little engine, puffing up a gradient of insignificant steepness, formed part of this harmony.   The crickets took a stronger voice, as the sky darkened to a purple-blue and the last gleams died out, until the air was full of their screaming ; every leaf covered apparently a songster, and even the train seemed at times to have been invaded.   The stations had a new significance—havens of silence in a world full of crickets' song, and the

Florentines could have enjoyed here a Gargantuan *Festa dei Grilli*. The poor captives in their tiny wickerwork cages, listless in the full light of the market place of the Tuscan capital, had no relation to the lusty chorus hidden in the canes. This chorus accompanied us until, after a long succession of quiet landscape, illuminated iron works, water power-stations and dimly lighted villages, we surrendered ourselves to the hotel porter at Edolo and climbed the street to the hotel.

In full daylight, the mass of hill represented by Monte Badile, the first buttresses of the Adamello group, Monte Frisazzo and Monte Campello on one side of the Oglio, and Monte Concarena on the other, has a magnificence of colour and form equalled only in its degree by the lower buttresses of the Brenta Alps. Below Monte Campello, there is a jewel lake, like a drop of azure fallen in a hollow of the mountains; a visit to it up the Saviore Valley repays effort. The Saviore Valley constitutes itself the easiest and most direct approach to the Adamello group proper, and one can take at the head of the valley a mule-track which branches at the top of the Salarno pass, one part going to the Lago di Salarno and the other rising abruptly to the shoulders of the Bianco peak. From this point it is possible to attempt the ascent of the Bianco peak itself, the highest part of the Adamello group. The view from the Salarno pass beyond Breno to Monte Presolana, southward over the irregular masses culminating in the hills above Lake Garda and northwards into the overhanging precipices and sheer clefts of the Adamello group is almost as soul-satisfying as the view from the Stelvio pass; the last traces of the plain have disappeared and the eye rests on a heaving sea of mountain peaks rising wonderfully into a cloudless sky, a feast of beauty where repletion is impossible and the magnificence ennobles even as it excites.

In the morning, the sensation of peace was intensified by the vision of mountains rising steeply before the hotel ; one immense flank, forest-covered, seemed to close out the sky as it towered over six thousand feet above. In the early light, each villa was sharp cut in its clearing among the trees, and the belt of glowing sun, as it moved from the top downwards, cut a swath of brilliant gold through the pale olive green, lighted a sparkle on each leaf until the whole landscape shivered in a glory of pure colour.

The town itself, with its Alpine villas, deep-eaved and crowned with quaint chimneys, had an authentic flavour of the hills ; Bazzaro could well have found here a rich series of motifs for his Alpine pictures. Edolo lies at the end of the world, apparently, for the mountains come crowding together round it and Monte Aviolo with Monte Baitone interposes a barrier, 11,000 feet high, against further progress to the east, while the Val Camonica narrows almost to a gorge between steeply sided mountains overhanging a narrow and dangerous road cut in their side. This road is protected at intervals with roofs of stout beams to deflect avalanches into the stream below, so that, in winter, progress is attended by an exhilarating element of risk.

After breakfast in a frescoed room, discussed in some racy detail with our fellow travellers, a young Italian and his wife, who had passed through the district during the war when Edolo had become a military base of importance for the troops operating north of the Adamello group, we climbed into the car and mounted to the square of Edolo.

The sensation of altitude was intensified by the vision immediately in front, so close that the town itself appeared lost in its shadow, of Monte Aviolo rising to a high snow-capped peak to the south in Monte Baitone with the white mass of the Adamello silhouetted behind them against the morning light, dusky purple, frail in tint compared with the sun-gleam on the nearer peaks. Beyond Aviolo the mountain wall continued with a dip down to Monte Pornina, while the Motto Pagano seemed to close up the valley beyond Monno as if the Oglio emerged directly there from the heart of the rock. The encircling chain of mountains was complete and the shadows of peaks on mountain shoulders graded into the light on other peaks until the progression of radiant contrast was done.

The next part of the journey extended from Edolo to Tirano, a somewhat circuitous route by the mainroad, but shortened considerably by taking a mule track to the right about a mile and a half out of Edolo and climbing straight over Monte Padrio, an ascent of about 6,500 feet, somewhat difficult in late autumn and winter. The less romantic traveller can take the motor-bus, as we did, and proceed at the usual breakneck speed adopted by Italian chauffeurs along one side of the valley of the Fiumicello to Colle d'Aprica, and thence to Tirano. The journey along the valley, mounting always, with Monte Aviolo blocking up the landscape behind until Edolo appeared a small splash of colour almost blotted out between the dip of green valley and dim blue mountain infinitely remote, is inspiring in the extreme.

The valley stretched farther and farther beneath as the road wound higher and higher in sudden bends, where we progressed at little more than a walking pace, and straight sections where sudden bursts of speed added to the exhilaration ; the air was very pure, with the pure freshness of early autumn, and the continual change of scene became exciting as Monte Aviolo disappeared farther and farther behind and nearer shoulders projected a shadow over the valley slopes, darkening as the light strengthened, while the waters below had a white gleam in distance, dazzling where the sun came beyond shadow and rested on them. We passed above quaint hamlets huddled together on a mound beside the river, in the sound of rushing water, with heavy eaves throwing a dim light into the narrow streets—a harmony of warm greys and browns beside the pearly greys of the hillside behind—through villages where the sleepy inhabitants emerged from quiet corners and loaded the motor with strange matter : vegetables, fruit, rails, wood, trunks and suitcases.

The animation increased as the morning advanced, the first herds of cattle wandered into the fields, every bell a-tinkle, while watchmen, quietly contemplative beside them, waved a languid hand in greeting to us. The road came to the Colle d'Aprica where the first full view of the valley of the Adda appeared at an immense distance beneath through an atmosphere vibrating with delicate colour. The conductor, a picturesque Italian with a jet-black beard, black moustache and black hat and an inscrutable smile, became obviously more important as the load on the roof increased, and evidently considered the hotel at Colle d'Aprica worthy of a matutinal coffee.

The view from this hotel over a green field dotted with cattle against a background of distant mountain was superb, largely through the sudden contrast between the strong green of the pasture and the shimmering azure purple of the hills. Beyond Colle d'Aprica, an Italian captain, returning to the provincial headquarters at Bergamo, presented us with a strange assortment of deck chairs in wooden crates, camp beds, tents and rugs, sufficient to stock the whole headquarters' staff. This collection had to be taken to the railway passing from Tirano, while the officer would come on at his leisure in a roomy Fiat. The skill shown by the conductor in mounting this mass of material on the roof of the motor amounted to genius, although it added to the complications of existence.

The lurking suspicion that an extra stone on the road would precipitate everything over the hill-side and ensure a somewhat speedier journey to Tirano for his belongings than the captain had designed, gave zest to the enjoyment of the magnificent landscape unfolded beneath. At the Belvedere inn, stigmatized by Baedeker as " simple, but not cheap," although the coffee served to us was excellent and quite cheap, the culmination of the whole journey from Edolo to Tirano was reached when the valley of the Adda lay clear below us for miles, and the Bernina Alps showed above the mountains beyond the river.

There are few points in Italy to compare with this in sheer beauty of vision, the view from the Belvedere at Ravello over the Gulf of Salerno, the picture of the Campagna from Rocca di Pappa or the plains of the Romagna seen from San Marino perhaps, but the majesty of mountain peak and slope with immensely distant recesses holding exquisitely radiant colour, shadow tossed from valley to valley, from peak to peak, is missing from them all.

Wealth of radiant colour distinguishes the valley of

the Adda above all ; the white crests of the Bernina seem
to strike the note for the whole landscape which loses
entirely the dusky green of the valley entering into it
from Colle d'Aprica and forms a harmony of rose and
pearly greys deepening to purple and softening at times
to a milky blue shaded to the most delicate azure where,
in the distance, the last finely etched hills come over the
valley and the sky drapes down on them.   The Adda
itself opens out into a pebbly reach, almost like a shallow
lake, where every gleam of the sun is held and brightened
to single dazzling points of flame.   The mountain
behind us, against the sun, was in dark shadow without
a breath of air to stir the heavy foliage of the woods
and the contrast made the beauty before us more
exquisite.

From the Belvedere, the road began to descend steeply
in hairpin turns where the motor could only find room
to manœuvre without slipping over the side, and after
a long succession of such turns, when the fate of the
captain's luggage hung very precariously in the balance,
we emerged from the woods, crossed over a low bridge
and entered Tresenda, the supply point for the railway
from Tirano.   From this point to Tirano, a few miles
distant, the full contrast between the dark mass of the
hill we had descended and the rich glow of the slopes
on our left, with a wall of blue hills closing up the valley
in the distance, could be appreciated and something
like tranquil enjoyment achieved after the rush and the
excitement of the descent.

The stretch from Edolo to Tirano is surely one of the
noblest in the Italian Alps, and the method of travel—
the motor service supplied by private firms working in
conjunction with the State railways—is undoubtedly to
be preferred to that of private motoring.   The traveller

comes immediately into contact with the life of the region, can appreciate genre studies at every turn and every halt of the road, and is distinctly in a safer position. Lengthy experience only could overcome the difficulties of the road coming down from the Belvedere to the Adda.

At Tirano we met a long procession of worshippers, headed by priests in magnificent scarlet robes, making towards the church of the Madonna di Tirano, a well-known shrine capable of ensuring miraculous cures at certain times of the year. This procession commemorated the day of the Birth of the Virgin. As an indication of local art, the shawls worn by the women in this procession were interesting, intricate patterns of bright colour bordering squares of black, or even covering the whole surface. These patterns formed the only note of vivid colour against unrelieved black, black of hair and of dress, and their variety was bewildering. With this variety, there was not the slightest error in taste in the hundreds of shawls worn by the worshippers, showing the existence of a true natural taste imparted only by the traditions of centuries. The square of the Madonna was filled with slowly circling bands of worshippers entering the church in a rhythmic flow of movement, and the artistic value of this mass of movement, black enlivened only by vivid scarlet, green, gold and purple, against the flaky rose and yellow-white of the church was unique. The church itself, in the reflected light, became ennobled through the colour harmony imposed by the worshippers, and the garishness of rococo decoration, the cheap glitter of the altar, seemed to be swept up in this monotone forming part of a genuine religious ceremonial inspired by a fine evocation.

The portals of the church are notable through the

fine Renaissance decorative work in marble, and the Madonna above the main portal has a freshness of true art, conceived at a period when convention had not yet begun to vitiate belief.

Tirano, the town itself, had all the characteristics of a typical Alpine town, with narrow streets leading some-what surprisingly at times to Renaissance and 17th-century palaces associated with names of church dignitaries, the Pallavicini among others, and at other times to primitive enclosures where all the quaint tendencies of the past seemed to have been concretized, strangely decorated balconies and stairs leading down into yards where industry, from charcoal-burning to shoe-making, is carried on, a single ray of sun providing a casual illumination. In addition to the church, situated about a mile away, the town can boast of a clock-tower of imposing dimensions where the inhabitants of a past century could take refuge. The influx of Swiss travellers from the Poschiavo valley along the Bernina railway has influenced some of the town's activities, so that lunch, for example, was served by a bilingual waitress who tempted us with both German and Italian. The Swiss influence, however, has been unfavourable, and some of the quaint charm of the Alpine town proper has given way to a spirit of bargain-ing not very pleasant at times.

The view from the hillside, among the vineyards, after a quaint street has been mounted with strange *aperçus* into tunnels where dwellings and shops are located, and rich effects of light and shade are obtained against the shafts of sunlight falling into the valley beyond the Madonna di Tirano, is beautiful. The vines rise in a lace-like silhouette against the shimmer of the valleys and the hills. At Tirano, we saw one of the finest

memorials raised to the dead in the war—not a lofty
pillar or statue, but simply young trees planted in a
grove with the name of the soldier commemorated on
each tree. The suggestion of beauty rising from the
memory of the fallen and always increasing in strength
as the years pass until the grove will contain mighty
trees full foliaged, as a natural temple to a fine cause,
has something of Greek novelty and truth, a fit memorial
to the fine taste of the people themselves.

CHAPTER IX

THE ROUTE OF THE ALPS—BORMIO, TRAFOI AND THE ORTLER

FROM Tirano onwards the journey became more fascinating, largely through the suggestion of further penetration into the heart of the Alps where human influence became less and less, and the stark forces of nature rose straight to the vision. The proximity of Switzerland also played a part since the Bernina group came to an end in the lofty peaks bordering the road, Monte Masuccia, Dosso Campiano and beyond the valley of the Grosina, the Cima Redasco, rising over a series of lower heights to the Cima di Piazzi.

The feeling of proximity to some of the noblest mountains in Europe, and the knowledge that further travel would open up new possibilities and add to the memory of beauty a finer wealth of memories more wonderful still, gave to the road an interest and expectation beyond previous experience.

This interest made it possible, perhaps, to enjoy with complete detachment the tactics adopted by our Italian driver, who swept at full speed through villages where the space available between the motor and the walls could be measured in inches. It was literally a case of cutting a path through those villages, and the complete abandon with which every jolting turn was taken

L 145

without previous warning was almost terrifying. The only alternative left for the villagers was either a rush for the nearest opening or a high leap over the motor itself ; this latter was quite impossible even in an age of miracles, for the motor, with its luggage piled on the roof, was almost as high as some of the houses.

Circumstances had evidently instilled in them a capacity for taking up their position in front of a suitable opening so that the work of stepping out of sight could be carried out at once. The change in the aspect of a street on entrance of the motor was positively uncanny ; at one moment there would be a crowd of gesticulating Italians dressed in a picturesque array of mountain fashions, intent on discussion of extremely weighty matters apparently, and at the next moment blank walls would face us with perfect alignment.

Occasionally, however, a small square would open out, and we could admire some vivid *genre* studies, farmers, dressed in a full splendour of colour, selling oxen, or women displaying some of their richest work in embroidery or lace, elaborated during the long summer evenings. It was market day, although Sunday, and the animation of the squares and streets had a very strong attraction, especially for travellers behind us in the motor, four farmers from Tirano, who had each a comment to make on the stock displayed, becoming excited sometimes when a specially fine beast was seen. At this time they would stop the car and enter into a rapid harangue with the exhibitors, showing complete control of gesture.

The pleasure of watching a Neapolitan outlining in the air with expressive hands the happenings of a day is only second to that experienced in watching two Alpine farmers discussing a difference of two lire in price. The traveller from Tirano to Bormio should select some such market day, even if the car driver sweeps through everything, for every detail of the life of the Alpine people is unfolded in a picturesque setting, and the constant background of blue hill ribbed with vineyards lends to every movement a certain symbolical force. The picture is always complete in its frame.

This attraction of background adds beauty to the villages themselves with their campaniles rising above the meadows beside the river Adda. The tranquil beauty of the meadows themselves with their tinkling cows, accompanied always by philosophic herds, whose whole existence lies apparently in absorbing the sunshine and the gleaming colour from the hills, had something immutable in it ; time seemed to have passed over this region leaving it unchanged in its loveliness. The startling white of the churches and campaniles which harmonized with the more luminous background of sky on the plain gave way here to more sober tints, and many of the façades, where some traces of the earlier sculpture of the Renaissance and early 16th century could be seen, were of a dusky green stone, very effective in contrast.

Beyond Grosotto, where the whole population seemed to be gathered in the square round the fountain and the road swept over a bridge adorned with curious sightseers, past a solid mass of stone forming a haven of refuge against invasion in earlier centuries, the valley of the Grosina broke the succession of mountain wall.

One can take the mule track on the right of the Grosina to Fusine and climb on the left to the Pizzo Sassalbo on the border of Switzerland, where a magnificent panorama becomes unfolded; the valley of the Poschiavo, with the lake beneath, and the Bernina group interposing an immense wall of peaks in front with a sudden vision through the Bernina pass to the Engadine. Beyond Fusine, the mule track may be followed along the Grosina, without going off to the left, as far as the Passo di Verva, where the heights fold over steeply from the Sasso di Conca and the Cima di Piazzi, and form a picture of naked grandeur strengthened and ennobled by the vision of the green valley beyond. Descending to the Viola Bormina, the traveller can follow the river in comparative ease to Bormio.

This route is preferable to the more direct route along the Adda, for the communion with nature is more direct; the authentic atmosphere of the Alpine country can be felt at once without thought of modern artificial civilization, and the clouds come down on the hills in a single splendid unity of effect—white cloud and warm grey slopes rising at times to sheer walls, where the sunlight designs patterns of dazzling light above milky blue shadow.

The road into Bormio, however, beneath the Monte Sobretta and the Cima di Piazzi was rich in the reflection from the higher cliffs into the woods below, and the last impression of all when the sunset began to cover up detail in a hazy gold where only shadows appeared in place of the slopes, clefts and walls of the mountains, everything in silhouette, was perfect in suggestion of a majesty only partially revealed. The inspiring force of the Valtellina for a poet like Fogazzaro could be appreciated through this vision alone.

At Bormio, the mountains stepped back and left an open space where the whole group of the Ortler could be appreciated at a true focus. From Bormio, the first direct approach to the Ortler could be undertaken along the Val Furva, where the road ends at Santa Caterina and mule tracks lead over the Passo Zebrù back to the town, or a footpath can be taken over the Ceden Pass beside the Zufall Spitze which terminates ultimately at Goldrein after going through the Martell Valley. This journey, however difficult and arduous it may appear, is one of the most wonderful in the Alps, since the magnificent panorama enjoyed from the Monte Pasquale and the Zufall Spitze does not end with descent on the other side, but yields to a finer sensation of beauty in the passage between the immense buttresses on each side ; the Butzen Spitze rising to the Angelus Spitze on the left and the Venezia Spitze on the right, dipping down beyond the Höchst Roth Spitze, and moving over the Höchste Eggen Spitze to terminate in a last towering height at the Vlatschberg. The valleys of the Martell and the Laas are among the most beautiful in the land, and are only surpassed by the Braulio Valley, as it mounts up to the Stelvio and, after a culmination at the Stelvio pass, where the loftiest heights of beauty seem to have been reached, dips down rapidly to Trafoi.

The people of Bormio, with a true sense of the fitting, have resisted the dangers of innovation threatened with the discovery of mineral springs in the vicinity, and relegated the valetudinarians to a preserve of their own at Bormio Bagni, while the old town remains untouched, with its Alpine flavour intact.

Narrow streets between high walls broken by mysteriously illuminated shops or obscure cafés, where the Bormians eke out existence with cards or spend a melliflous evening over a bottle of wine, discussing rambles over the neighbouring mountains or lamenting scanty harvests ; sudden glimpses of courtyards with a satisfying wealth of romantic detail, wooden balconies tressed with scraggy vines and overlooking fountains of stone where the artistic spirit of the place has found expression in a crude sculpture; an illumined hotel, with the staff standing expectantly at the entrance, the most handsome waitresses first and, above everything, the shadow of Monte Cristallo harshly outlined against a cloudless sky!

Beyond the river, there is a quarter with ancient wooden houses sheltering beneath immense eaves, where the sun throws shadow to the ground below, and the inhabitants form interesting groups of colour, half in and half out of this shadow.

We spent a deliciously languid afternoon on the hillside among long grasses starred with flowers and alive with grasshoppers, breathing the pure mountain air and watching, in perfect ease, the constant change of colour on the hills before us as the clouds passed over, and the light became more luminous with the passing of the hours. The roofs and spires of Bormio beneath us—the valley entering into hollows of the mountains, dusky green into grey-purple gleaming with pale gold where the sunlight rested on the upper ledges and designed every edge and hollow with a deep shadow almost black in tone—the last shoulders of the mountains where the Val di Dentro debouched on the Valle di Sotto—the exquisite interplay of colour in the distance beyond, milky purple shot with every fine tint of rose, blue and green, which made the pool of shadow within the mountains beyond the Bagni Vecchii the darker through contrast—formed an ensemble of a soul-satisfying beauty.

The afternoon grew more luminous, the shadows became less distinct, the light less radiant, and a veil of thin colour seemed to pass over everything, refining contrast, so that the immense pool of shadow behind

the Bagni Vecchii began to gleam with a mysterious
suggestion of tints. The roofs of Bormio struck a more
subdued note of brown, and the upper buttresses of
Monte Cristallo became drowned in a pure rose, very
wonderful against the intensely blue sky. When the
light darkened and the mountains were vaguely black
round the valley, a single glorious vision of the Königsspitze in the distance in a hollow of the nearer hills, pale
pink with purple traces of shadow in the Alpenglühen,
came almost as a consecration of that beauty now
obscured in night. The journey from Bormio to the
Stelvio pass and thence to Trafoi represented a culmination to the entire succession, Bormio a rare incident
in it.

Bormio, for this alone, dwells in the memory among
very precious things. The atmosphere, different from
that of Tirano in its friendly suggestion, makes a stay
delightful indeed, while the standard of service obtaining
in the local hotel is high enough to satisfy even the blasé
tourist. The valetudinarians, who generally contrive
to reduce a town to nervous prostration, have, merci-
fully enough, been banished to Bormio Bagni.

In the morning, after an excellent breakfast of coffee,
butter and rolls, we descended into the yard and took
a place in the motor, closely inspected by a crowd of
the more enterprising inhabitants, who evidently thought
the occasion sufficiently important to rise out of bed
before seven. Our travelling companions were comparatively uninteresting, a group of farmers of the usual
Alpine type, keen of face and rather slower of movement
than the more southern Italians, and a very elegant
young lady, dressed in wonderfully embroidered clothes
palpably made in Milan or Paris, and accompanied by
a bearded gentleman of a certain distinction whom she

addressed as " Zio " (Uncle). Whether the term was correct or not, was a matter of doubt, since he appeared to be a very loving uncle indeed, and the niece had more pleasure in addressing caressing words to him than in absorbing the beauty of the mountains through which we were passing. She seemed, even at the Stelvio pass, to consider the Alps very *vieux jeu* indeed, and kept chattering about Milanese fashions without an interruption ; occasionally she devoted attention to the driver, a swarthy gentleman with reckless eyes, and made him perform the nerve-racking feat (nerve-racking for us !) of driving the motor over a dangerous road beside a continuous precipice and answering her inquiries. Both seemed to be highly delighted with life and talked away with complete abandon. At the Stelvio pass, however, the uncle and niece decided it was *chic* to climb up to the Dreisprachenspitze Hotel and discuss a coffee at ten thousand feet ; it was also *chic* in their estimation to take the path beyond the hotel at Franzenshöhe, and gain a closer view of the Madatscher glacier.

Those two incidents were undoubtedly the only high points in the journey for them. It is quite possible, of course, that constant travel over this route made everything commonplace to them, dulled the first enthusiasm and made economy in sightseeing very desirable. It is more probable, however, that Milanese fashion had prescribed a definite attitude towards mere natural beauty and defined a certain etiquette to be followed. In any case, the uncle and niece contributed immensely to the pleasure of the journey.

At Bormio Bagni, we were detained about thirty minutes until a prospective traveller, a pale-faced lady of uncertain age, had shaken hands with every single

member of the hotel from the boots upwards, had
retrieved her travelling tickets dropped in a corridor
and her handbag also forgotten in her room, and cried
farewell in a voice filled with emotion. As an invalid,
however, she bore up very well indeed, and had no
difficulty in climbing with the uncle and niece to the
hotel at the Stelvio pass, a fairly stiff test at that
altitude of ten thousand feet. The acrobatics of the
car in negotiating steep corners round a mountain wall
left her quite unmoved.

The road from Bormio, after winding up the lower
slopes of the Monte Cristallo and opening up at every
turn further perspectives in the valley of the Adda
and the Val di Dentro now clearly defined in the transparent atmosphere of morning, swept round the face
of Cristallo and entered into the Braulio Valley. The
immense mass of the Ortler group threw up a wild
series of peaks, moving across the sky to the Geisler-
spitze, where the serrations became less violent and a
smoothly sloping wall came round towards the Stelvio—
the Ebenferner rising from the main crest of the Ortler
Alps to form with the Madatscherferner two mighty
buttresses.

Across the River Braulio, a mere rushing torrent
between walls of bare rock, where only lichens relieve
the uniformity of dazzling grey-gold rock, and add a
note of pale green colour deepening to bloodstone in the
moist shadows beside the water, the Pedenollo mountain,
followed by Monte Radisca and Monte Braulio, interpose
a frowning wall between the valley and the sky. At
some points the mountain rises sheer above the sparkling
water in a smooth wall, where only the sun can rest,
and presents a mass of warm colour almost painfully
brilliant to the sight ; every little fissure or crack becomes

etched out in black, and the hollows between those walls are filled with a solid blue shadow almost as impenetrable to vision as the rock itself.

Higher up, the stark monotony of colour breaks into a gleaming wilderness of gleams and shadows where the surface ceases to be pitilessly barren, and presents ledges and cracks where a pale vegetation can grow. Above this, again, the buttresses of the single peaks begin to separate. The wall disappears in a series of broad serrations where streaks of snow add a dazzling white to the rose-purple, and the blue sky between the hollows of the crest darkens to purple in contrast.

The valley of the Braulio is notable through this naked beauty of colour where everything is sacrificed to one overwhelming effect ; the majesty of the hills comes very close to appreciation, and the eye never tires of surveying every single detail in that effect, every etched shadow being treasured in the memory of a unique experience. There are certainly few valleys in the high Alps with the same suggestion of relentless force, of savage independence from the wear of centuries.

The road wound at intervals through tunnels, for no natural roadway is found here, and a path had to be levelled out of the sheer face of the Cristallo mountain, and each tunnel framed, at its exit, a single radiant picture, as if the whole spirit of the landscape became concentrated here in single moments of vision. The perpetual danger of avalanches had forced the road-makers to build protective roofs of massive timber where the boulders could be deflected into the gully beneath.

The experience of driving through a tunnel in the midst of a herd of cattle should be recommended only to chauffeurs of strong nerves and a good vocabulary ;

our driver had both, as a heated discussion between him
and the cattle driver showed to our full satisfaction.

Beyond the Monte Radisca, the road climbed in a
serpentine fashion for more than a mile, disclosing newer
and more radiant views of the valley behind with a
frail shadow of distant peaks, and finally entered on a
flat meadow country almost as green and smooth as
a lawn. We stopped for some time at the Cantoniera
beyond the Rocca del Braulio, and some of the party
went on to a quaint old church immediately in front,
notable evidently for its pious associations.

The contrast between the savage beauty of the valley
and the tranquil loveliness of this meadow country was
grateful indeed ; the hills had a softer note of harmony through association, and the green colour of the
foreground continued up the lower slopes and gradually
shaded into the grey-purple above. The beauty now
before us was a beauty of fine shading and rhythmic
lines ; the mighty chorus had softened down here to a
single note of wonderment, tenuous and subdued in the
folds of the hills.

Beyond the Cantoniera, the meadow country began
gradually to yield to a landscape even wilder than the
valley we had left ; the symphony, after dying down
to a moment of still rapture, was opening out to the
last great movement of all where, in the mighty volume
of sound, the final glory of inspiration would come and
as suddenly fall again to silence.

It was at this moment that we saw the first definite
traces of the war—long lines of barbed wire stretching
in black lines from one side of the valley to the other,
with the hollow of a trench outlined against the uniform
grey colour. Those defences were almost as perfect
as when first placed, and no effort had been made to

clear any part of them away. Along the crest of the
Pizzo Umbrail, a mountain almost ten thousand feet
high, the dark lines stretched, in a place where a fly
might have difficulty in staying, and the white snow
beneath them showed relentlessly each turn in direction.
It was obvious, from this circumstance alone, that no
very determined fighting had ever taken place in this
region ; the landscape itself made extended operations
impossible, and the imitation of a fly on the ceiling
could be attempted without fear of disaster. The
Pizzo Umbrail showed exactly how close the imitation
could be. At isolated spots, groups of dug-outs could
be seen, still in good condition, and the mountain-side,
especially towards Monte Scorluzzo, seemed to be pitted
with them ; they formed, undoubtedly, divisional or
battalion headquarters for the troops operating in the
trenches in front.

On the left, the Umbrail pass opened up suddenly,
yielding a fine perspective of distant valleys and peaks
drowned in a pearly luminance ; the descent from the
pass was very steep beyond the first half mile or so,
and the country seemed to stretch almost beneath the
pass itself, a curious sensation of space to the traveller.
This constituted the most direct approach into Switzerland, and the trenches on the crest of Umbrail were
obviously intended to prevent retreat beyond the
frontier.

After sudden windings, the road came at last to the
highest point of all, the Stelvio pass, and the full glory of
the Alpine world became unfolded before us. The Ortler,
with the Madatscher glacier, stretched along the sky
in front beyond the Trafoi Valley, and at the end
of the valley in the far distance the serrated wall of
the Ötztaler Alps bounded the vision ; behind us, the

COMING DOWN FROM THE STELVIO
THE ORTLER IN FULL VIEW

whole mountain world of Switzerland stretched in countless peaks to the sky, and the valley of the Braulio
added a note of subdued green colour to this splendour
of purples and warm greys.

It was impossible to appreciate in its full magnificence
this panorama of countless peaks snow-crested and
hollowed into shadow by the sun, a sea of crests glittering
and flashing in a radiant colour softened to the palest
purple by distance, until the last rows of peaks were as
silken shadows against an immense shimmering background of sky.

The Ebenferner came down in sharp slopes to the
river beyond the war-swept ruins of the Franz Joseph
Hotel, and it was by this dark mass of rock in shadow
from the sunlight that the beauty of colour tossed from
peak to peak in the morning light could be measured.
The vision became lost otherwise in space, and nothing
seemed to lie between the sky and earth but this
amazing sea of mountains, where life itself was held in
suspense—the ennoblement of earth in a blaze of glory
to the sky !

With that beauty, there was a feeling of trust and of
kindliness, even in the sharp ledges of the Madatscher
glacier viewed at close quarters from Franzenshöhe,
and nothing could entirely dispel that feeling, not even
the barbed wire and the squalid dug-outs of the Stelvio
slopes where all the foulness of war seems to have been
perpetuated.

The road from Stelvio to Trafoi descends four
thousand feet in less than nine miles, and the first
section of this descent, for three thousand feet sheer
down the slope of the Stelvio in a series of hairpin bends
and stretches, must form one of the most exciting
journeys in Europe. Seen from below, the road appears

like an exaggerated oscillogram against the dark colour of the mountain-side, and it is scarcely credible that vehicles of any kind could risk it. Our driver, true to type, kept a very high average of speed, showing uncanny skill in slewing the motor round within less than an inch of disaster; sometimes, however, he was unable to save that space and had to reverse before taking the turn in safety. A constant succession of gushes of speed alternating with a slow creeping round the turns made this part of the journey exhilarating in the extreme, a unique pleasure, if somewhat trying to the nerves of the ladies. Our lady passengers, by the simple expedient of closing their eyes at each critical moment and opening them again for a moment when the crisis was past, took the journey with apparent equanimity. We passed a motor also descending, inch by inch, at a slow foot-space. The driver had evidently less mathematical knowledge of the possibilities of the road. From our experience, it was evident that the descent must be negotiated rapidly or not at all; by the time we had swooped round the last corner and were jubilantly on the way towards Franzenshöhe, the former had negotiated two turns, or rather less than a tenth of the total descent.

Beyond Franzenshöhe, the road dipped down between pine forests, until at the Weisser Knott Inn we emerged from them and came again into full vision of the Ortler, this time immensely above us against the sky. The feeling of equality experienced to some extent at the Stelvio gave way here to admiration of sheer mass, an enormous barrier of rock closing out the world.

At Trafoi, where we sampled the products of the first authentic Austrian cuisine, this sensation of immense power became strengthened, but with it a keener sense of kindliness and peace. It was only at Trafoi that the Ortler could be appreciated in its true nobility of mass and contour—an immense wall stretched across the world where the sun lay in broad bands of white flame of a dazzling purity, touched and starred with blazing points of light where a fine edge on the glacier caught the radiance, and the sharp lines of snow broke off into crystals. The contrast between the mountains and the quiet beauty of the fields beneath where the haymakers were gathering up the last of the harvest, and the cows were moving slowly from meadow to meadow accompanied by music from their own bells, had in it something of the eternal. The changes of government and struggles of nations were of no significance beside the changeless harmony of green field, dark mountain snow-crested, and faintly clouded sky. There are few places in Southern Tyrol that inspire so richly the feeling of rest after struggle, the sense of a triumphant culmination to a long period of storm and disaster ; the mass of the Ortler, more impressive in this alone than even Adamello and the Bernina, speaks more of resignation and peace than of struggle. The whole landscape from Trafoi to the Stelvio and Bormio has this suggestion of profound peace, of reconciliation and harmony. Time seems to have brushed off all ugliness and softened harshness so that the hills alone preserve the noble and eternal beauty praised by Hölderlin : " Lebendig sie, die Immerjugendlichen ! "

CHAPTER X

THE CASTLES OF SOUTHERN TYROL

THE romance and beauty of Southern Tyrol has already been described with varying success by innumerable essayists and travellers, from the æsthete delicately picking a way through the memorials of the past to the professional *vulgarisateur* dishing up each savoury item in due order. It is difficult now to embark on a course that could by any stretch of the imagination be termed original, but even the most jejune performance has in it some note of value, some echo of an appreciation that goes deeper than words and touches on the very spirit of the writer, and those authentic notes are always valuable, valuable for the impressionistic traveller intent on confirming what he has already anticipated in spirit, and valuable, above all, for those who, brought face to face with an unexpected beauty, treasure that memory to themselves and seek in others some of the enthusiasm that possessed them.

Southern Tyrol is peculiarly rich in these associations, not so much through sheer splendour of natural beauty as through the interlinking of history with the present memorial ; the castle designs a fine harmony of form and colour against the sky, and the traveller may content himself with that vision alone, but he may also see in it the achievement of past centuries coming to expression before him, and, content to thrust aside for the moment all appreciation of natural loveliness, visualize a shadowy procession rising before him from the dimness of the centuries, knights and poets and legendary heroes, each in his setting of romance, ennobled through recollection alone.

The forces of history lie close to the surface in Southern Tyrol, and it takes little effort to disclose them and even to watch them in action now. From time immemorial, the Etschland has formed, with its glorious orchards and vine-groves filling up the valleys and flooding round the lower slopes of the hills, the earthly paradise of the nations round it, the Germans, the Bavarians, the Slavs and the Italians ; the struggle for its possession, continuing throughout the centuries with only slight interruptions, until now, when the most unlikely nation of all, Italy, has entered into domination, has left behind shadowy records which only the monuments still existing can show.

Historically, Southern Tyrol lives in a strangely beautiful tapestry woven by innumerable incidents of warfare and of peace when the arts came into the service of the gods of battle and excited heroic enterprises or, content with more gentle conquests, glorified love and the sweeter pleasures of life. The early culture of the German races found in that region its most perfect expression ; the Etschland was for the German race what Provence was for France, a home of artistic radiance and joy, where love had an authentic note in poetry and something of the serenity of Greece found expression.

Walther von der Vogelweide and the Minnesinger were poets of Tyrol first of all, and we have even now a certain joy in tracing from castle to castle what might have been the life of those mediæval troubadours ; the

M

heroic legends which arose from the Nibelungenlied
and centred round the figure of Dietrich von Bern,
a knight of an amazingly mercurial disposition, were
legends of Tyrol, and many of them belong to the
most precious collections of tales handed down from
the past.

The association of legends with definite places, the
tale of King Laurin, chief of the fairy kingdom, with
the peak of the same name in the Rosengarten group,
and of poets with definite places, Walther with the
town of Bolzano, and the Minnesingers and in more
recent times, Victor von Scheffel, with Schloss Runkelstein, lends to the whole region a peculiarly intimate
appeal.

The evocation of history seems to have less difficulties
there than anywhere else, and one can lie on the hillside above Merano, listening almost through the clear
air to ghostly music from ghostly instruments, the
Minnesinger of the past making merry in the town below.
The intimacy of appeal deepens with the years ; every
line, every silhouetted mass in the gracious mountain
world vibrates with the suggestion of visions to come,
the armies of the past marching in a purple glory out
of the shimmering distance, and the gods striding hugely
from rose-tipped peak to rose-tipped peak.

It is impossible to forget those things in a castle like
the Schloss Maretsch, especially towards evening when
the hills lose their folds and become misty blue veils
dropping between the vision and the infinite, and the
vineyards disappear into that harmony of exquisite
colour. The stage has been set in a rich glory, every
decorative element brought into place and nothing now
remains but the play itself. The sense of expectancy
becomes more and more intense until we can almost see

against the shadows of the hills, the sweep and gesture of mighty combatants struggling for possession of the world.

The difference between the castles of Southern Tyrol and the fortresses erected in Lombardy by the Sforza, the Visconti and the Scaligers becomes evident at once when we consider the traditions of good cheer and joyful literary contests attached to the Tyrolese castles. The Italian potentates established a centre at Milan, Verona and Cremona, where full license could be given to festivities and the cultivation of the arts, and scattered fortresses in the more remote districts to act as regional defence headquarters. The function of the castle, as the Sforza conceived it, was to be impregnable, and the closer the resemblance to a mass of rock, unrelieved by decoration or window apertures, the better the fortress. The ruins at Riva and Castello Tenno, the fortress of Malcesine and the Scaliger stronghold at Sirmione are as sinister and as menacing as the Norman keeps of France; not a single touch of ornament relieves the blank monotony of dark grey stone wall.

The Lombardian castle was conceived essentially as a refuge for soldiers, and not as a place of sojourn for the prince himself. When we come northwards up the Brenner to Rovereto and Trento this characteristic disappears; the Castel del Buon Consiglio looks down on the palaces of Trento almost as a kindly presence, the dwelling-place of the lord of the city himself, where festivities could pass the nights away and the arts had a living strength. The castle of the Trentino was a residence first of all for the ruling prince and secondarily a fortress; it was built to be inhabited by beings on a higher plane of culture than rude soldiery. A similar inhabitable and friendly air distinguishes the castles of the Sarca region, especially at Toblino, and shows the transition from Lombardy to the Etschland.

In the Etschland the change is complete. At no time did the whole region come under the absolute control of one ruler as in Lombardy ; the small prince erected his own dwelling-place, which was at the same time his castle, and the only approach we have to the Castel Sforzesco at Milan is the Burg at Merano with its auxiliary and more strongly defensive fortress in Schloss Tyrol. The Tyrolese castle, if we consider the Schloss Pallaus at Brixen or the Schloss Lebenberg at Merano or the Schloss Runkelstein, was eminently inhabitable, and an extremely pleasant place indeed to reside in, with richly furnished, well-lit rooms, surrounded by orchards and vine-groves acting as a beautiful pedestal of living colour to the building towering above.

Some of the earlier castles, like the Reiffenstein at Sterzing or the Strassburg at Gossensass, which acted in the early centuries as a dam to the Northern invaders coming over the Brenner, preserved some of the characteristics of the Norman keep, but the rich mountain landscape, carpeted in the valleys with white and rose when the apple and pear orchards were in bloom, robbed them of their gloom and made them almost inviting in aspect. The Strassburg, originally an earthen Slav fort with a wooden tower overlooking the whole valley, presents a series of walls without a break in their unrelieved grey, the inner courtyards providing light for the rooms, but the circle of pine trees clustered round it takes away much of its harshness, and brings it into harmony with the landscape ; the Reiffenstein, on a low mound full in the centre of a green valley among the snow-tipped mountains, occupies one of the loveliest sites in Tyrol with the green pastures, flock starred, unfolded round it, and the meadows beside the river gleaming with sunlight and radiant with flowers.

The Schloss Gufidaun, near Klausen, becomes trans-figured when seen through a veil of cherry blossom strewn over the orchards climbing up the hillside round it ; the square ugly block of masonry lightens, and takes on the appearance of a dream castle, placed there only as a final artistic motif to the blossoming trees beneath.

The affable, well-cultivated residence comes into its full splendour in the Schloss Pallaus at Brixen where the mountains seem to close out the sky above, and the clouds wreathed round their shoulders hang precariously almost as a canopy above the castle itself ; the trees are grouped symmetrically round it, pines and oaks, while the grassy meadows between, green as emerald, form a quiet contrast with the pale rose-grey of the castle walls. The suggestion of struggle, of defiance through the centuries has disappeared here in an air of suavity, a cultivated self-sufficiency.

The Tyrolese showed positively genius in their choice of sites for erecting their castle-dwellings ; the most beautiful pictures of the Etschland can be seen from them alone, and it is always advisable to choose the nearest castle when a panorama of mountain and valley is to be enjoyed.

The south, with its cypresses and poplars, lends a peculiar distinction to the Eisack Valley and to the Trostburg at Waidbrück raised on its foliage-shaded rock, as if rock and castle formed one structure, in colour and in line, the yellow grey walls and red roofs blending harmoniously into the grey-green bushes hanging down the cliff-side beneath. The Trostburg has in it something of the inspiring upthrust of the

Gothic church, every line rising immediately towards the sky. It has a more inspiring suggestion, however, in the fact that it stands near the reputed side of the Vogelweiderhof, the dwelling-place of Walther von der Vogelweide. Walther, although a songster of the 12th century, is undoubtedly the greatest living poet of Tyrol ; the Tyrolese character, its strength, its daring independence, its passionate loyalty and its overweening egoism, comes into expression in his poetry as no other national character has been expressed ; there is the breadth of the hills and something of their sweetness, nature and love, the spring of flowers and the rapture of youth. One verse shows this quality of sweetness above all :

> So die bluomen uz dem grase deringent,
> Same sie lachen gegen der spilenden sunnen,
> in einem meien an den morgen fruo,
> und diu kleinen vogellin wol singent
> in ir besten wise die sie kunnen,
> waz wunne mac sich da genozen zuo ! [1]

the love of nature, the beauty of the Tyrolese landscape with its flowers and birds.

The castle may give to the village its one abiding significance, and may symbolize a whole landscape, the work of man coming into line with the eternal glory of the hills ; the castle overlooking Klausen huddled at its foot beside the river raises the village into a fuller dignity and brings it into the purpose of the mountains ; the mission of the village becomes the mission of the hills, a conciliation of all things in the final beauty. The vision of the three castles beyond the meadows at

[1] When the flowers spring from the grass, smiling to the brilliant sun on an early May morning and the little birds sing in full-throated joy, what happiness can equal that !

Sand in Taufers, where the shrine by the path seems to grade without a check into the stern grey walls of the castles, and hence into the white and purple of the mountains, comes as something inevitable even as the mountains themselves or the clouds. Nature had moulded them all.

The artistic or religious message of a whole commune may have avoided the churches and shrines, as we now see them, and found expression in the galleries of the castle on the hillside, in the courtyard or in the frescoes on a ceiling ; the castle on the hillside near Lienz in the Pustertal has in it beautiful frescoes of the 15th century, perfectly preserved—the crucified Christ held in the arms of God, painted on the vault over the altar, which has, in turn, an exquisitely drawn Madonna and Child, while the wall behind is divided into compartments each representing a saint. The frescoes at Lienz find a parallel in many other castles in the Etschland, in Schloss Tyrol, and in Schloss Runkelstein especially.

For sheer beauty of position, the Schloss Karneid and the Sigmundskron at Bolzano must be considered the most impressive castles in Southern Tyrol. The Schloss Karneid, on its pedestal of lofty cliff, weather-scarred, rising in warm grey pillars of bare rock above a clinging forest of pines bathed in a luminous mist from the rushing waters below, might well be a castle of romance, imagined only and quite beyond the limits of reality, a vision of a poet's brain. The sensation felt on looking down into the immense gulf beneath where the sun forms a continually changing rainbow through the mist, and the pines lose shape in the dim glory of colour is almost a sensation of unlimited space, fearful in retrospect.

The Etsch flowing from Merano encircles a peninsula
of rock at the end of the valley before it enters into
Bolzano, and this rock comes to a steep promontory
opposite Bolzano itself ; Sigmundskron is perched precariously at the very cliff edge and forms for the
Bolzaners a link between the distant mountains and
the rushing Etsch beside them, a silhouette of dome and
wall and tower against the evening sky. It seems to
hold in it the spirit of the mountain world, a spirit of
trust and of defiance against the wear of the centuries
framed in a stern beauty of colour and of form. The
builders knew instinctively what would harmonize with
the magnificent hilly landscape round them.

Bolzano and Merano have, however, in addition to
those, the two noblest castles of the whole Tyrol, Schloss
Runkelstein at Bolzano and Schloss Tyrol at Merano,
while the Schloss Planta, a friendly ivy-coloured building
with a fine view of the Ortler group, and especially the
snow-capped Königsspitze, is also a cherished possession
of the latter district. Schloss Runkelstein lives in
history as the Minnesinger castle, the home of the early
troubadours of Tyrol, and everything even now has
something of that past glamour when the Rosengarten,
gleaming in a thousand points of flame in the clear
distance, symbolized the hero of all epics, Dietrich von
Bern.

Schloss Runkelstein, throned on its cliff above wildly
struggling bushes and sudden clumps of flowers, where
a fruit-tree scatters blossom over wild roses and
accessible through a path dating, in its solid workmanship, from Roman times, is undoubtedly one of the jewels
of Tyrol—the haunt of the Minnesingers, the sacred
shrine of the romantic poets of 19th-century Germany.
We can still enter the portals in the full glow of the

sun, stand in that quiet court with its soft harmonies of grey and dusky green, touched to flame as the autumn foliage of the trees in the yard comes into sudden contrast with the ivy cloaking the walls, and feel something of the thrill of discovery when the quaint frescoes along the walls under the overhanging brown-tiled eaves appear.

These frescoes are symbolical of the spirit which inspired the early Tyrolese patrons of the arts, small local Mæcenas determined on acquiring fame through poetry if the more gaudy fame of war and conquest were denied to them in their small domains. The whole course of the legend of Tristan and Isolde, the tragic story of passion and illicit love that thrilled the Middle Ages, pulsated through the epic of Gottfried von Strassburg, and has since become a favourite subject for poetic speculation, with Swinburne and Matthew Arnold, and, for musical drama, in Wagner's opera.

The unknown artist who covered those quiet walls in the 15th century, in the sound of the Talfer rushing down over an impetuous waterfall into the gloomy Sarntal ravine and in the shadow of the immense blue hills raising sun-tipped heads to the sky, must have felt some inspiration welling up in him from the beauty around him. The vision from the castle wall down the sheer cliff of porphyry into the echoing valley with a full-flooding colour over everything, and over the town of Bolzano on the other side, with its shadowy colonnades and its quaint houses always vibrating to the sound of rushing water, must have entered into the painting of those figures ranged so stiffly round the walls.

The three famous giants, Fasold and Fasner among them, and the three famous swords, the Balmung held in the hands of Siegfried and Eckesacks with its proud possessor, Dietrich von Bern, with a third unknown sword and knight form an introduction to two other frescoed groups, the three lovers of history and the arts and sciences, astronomy, mathematics, philosophy and other nightmares dear to the mediæval scholar.

The walls round the court have been graced with those frescoes devoted to inevitable preliminaries ; the artist knew the value of atmosphere, the creation of a sympathetic attitude, before embarking on the main theme, and the curious mixture of natural beauty expressed in colour and sound—war and blood symbolized in Siegfried and Dietrich, love and lust in the three lovers, science and culture in the figures drawn stiffly to represent them to the physical eye and the naïve suggestion of legend, old as the world, in the three giants—inspires in imagination something of that colourful tragedy which ennobles the drama of Tristan and Isolde for all time.

The tale itself lives in the walls of the summer-house, the windows of which afford a completely satisfactory vision of an abyss as dark as the Romantics ever conceived, in a medley of slim figures painted in fine delicate greys and greens and browns, smoothed over by the passage of time into a dream-like harmony. The painter, with true conscientiousness, decided to record every possible detail in the eventful drama, but found himself confronted with the apparently insuperable problem of packing an immense number of characters and incidents into an exiguous wall space.

Even if he, as a good artist, may have felt that one single scene of passion given in a rich sweep of colour and line would be worth a thousand figures packed tightly together, the Mæcenas employing him, the Master of Vintl, would have demanded good value for his money. The artist compromised by elongating the bodies, placing the arms close by the sides and measuring off each incident without a break from the incident portrayed before. The result of this canning is extraordinary ; ships and characters, king and people, forests, wild beasts, sea, perspective, atmosphere are all crushed together in a strange combination of line and colour. The painter, to use a different simile, has thrown all his goods into the window at once.

The figures stand erect with arms close to the side, as if a hollow had been made in their bodies to hold them ; unnecessary additions like the sea and ships, and an odd stretch of landscape are clipped down to the minimum to give the painter room to make King Mark, Tristan and Isolde, a full head higher than the rest of mankind, each with his or her name inscribed above. The effect is of a field of poppies growing thickly together, every poppy of the same shape and colour. The ladies have been invested with perpetual youth, the youth of a girl of fifteen summers, and the men have not yet grown out of their beardless boyhood ; they all have round, unwinking eyes staring fixedly across the years, and their long, peaked shoes seem to have a snaky quality. The modistes of to-day, who believe so enthusiastically in slim figures and exiguous limbs, might well model their illustrations of fashion on those figures hung all in a row with not a protruding member anywhere.

The quaint beauty of the early days of art breathe almost like incense from those frescoes ; their unconscious and inevitable futurism is not the painful result of a carefully groomed attitude to art and life, but the frank simplicity of innocence. The golden years have thrown a glamour over them, and we see them now through a mist of recollection :

Cheer, cheer thy dogs into the brake,
O Hunter ! and without a fear
Thy golden-tassell'd bugle blow,
And through the glades thy pastime take !
For thou wilt rouse no sleepers here.
For these thou seest are unmov'd ;
Cold, cold as those who liv'd and lov'd
A thousand years ago.

With those words, Matthew Arnold ends the second part of his " Tristram and Iseult." There are no glades and no huntsmen in the Runkelstein pictures, but the years rest lightly and vividly on them, warmed in remembrance.

The journey of Tristan to Ireland, and the marriage of King Mark, the treachery of the wicked Melot and the distrust of the sorrowful old king, the miraculous spring of Tristan from his bed to that of sweet Isolde and back again, for the ground between was strewn with ashes to betray to King Mark any communion between the lovers, are portrayed with patient crafts-manship. The scene where Isolde is embraced by Tristan disguised as a beggar, and that later trial picture where Isolde swears to the bishop that, beyond King Mark and the beggar, no man has ever held her in his arms, a sufficiently satisfactory evidence of fidelity to King Mark, if not to Isolde herself, and last of all, Tristan and Isolde wandering alone, abandoned in the wood, in hardship and in death—the artist has imagined them all as best he could, with the same immobility of feature, the same elongated bodies, the same moon-like visages as described in the ancient text.

The beauty of Schloss Runkelstein lives through this suggestion of passionately human issues, of a drama that renews its youth eternally, and is eternally exciting in us something of that vague yearning, that dim lyrical ecstasy which dwells in the frescoed Tristram and Iseult. The Minnesingers still invest their castle with a splendour of remembrance :

> Wer immer ins sonnige Etschland fährt,
> Halt 'Einkehr in diesen Räumen,
> Und ist ihm eine Isolde beschert,
> Mag er von ihr hier träumen.[1]

For the romantic poet Von Scheffel, Isolde was a living presence, a radiant figure in his dreams and we, even now, feel also something of that intimate appeal, that tragedy coming to our hearts through the silences of the years.

Galsworthy in his *Villa Rubein* gives a fleeting impression of the latter days of Castle Runkelstein : " Schloss Runkelstein—grey, blind, strengthless—still keeps the valleys. The windows which once, like eyes, watched men and horses creeping through the snow, braved the splutter of guns and the gleam of torches, are now holes for the birds to nest in. Tangled creepers have spread to the very summits of the walls. In the keep, instead of grim men in armour, there is a wooden board recording the history of the castle and instructing visitors on the subject of refreshment. Only at night, when the cold moon blanches everything, the castle stands like the grim ghost of its old self, high above the river."

The path to the Schloss Tyrol, where the whole history of Tyrol has found an embodiment, and the Romanesque portals betray the artistic Renaissance that seems to have swept over Europe in the 12th and 13th centuries, is surely one of the most beautiful in the world. The valley of the Adige lies unfolded as

---

[1] Whoever fares into the sunny Etschland and comes to those halls, if an Isolde holds him, he may dream of her here.

far as Bolzano to the south and Schlanders to the west, with the Ortler group gleaming behind the lower range —the Hochjoch, Hochwand and Rontscher to the south-west, just a trace of jewelled glaciers and frail shadows of peaks. The colours move from shoulder to shoulder of the hills as the clouds float down and hover for an instant in a palpitating mist of white and purple ; the full clusters of the grapes deepen the green of the vineyards and intensify the blue of distance and the pink clefts in the mountain-side glow intensely, almost like blood, when the gleam is reflected in their shadow.

The castle on its pedestal of tree-covered cliff breaking into a steep white face below the tower, where the light of the snowy peaks behind seems to have rested for a moment before disappearing into infinite space, sets a crown on the beautiful town beneath, and acts as a coign of vantage for surveying the whole course of the Adige until the tenuous blue of the Rosengarten chain strikes across the nearer mountain world and raises the vision into the faintly clouded sky. Schloss Brunnenberg falls away beneath into the shadows although, seen from the road up beyond Gratsch, it appears the most significant element in the landscape, and we are isolated in the midst of the past, memories crowding on memories, bitter-sweet at times, but never melancholy, the thought of the revenge taken by history on those who thought to dictate the future of the civilized world.

For the Counts of Tyrol in the 12th, 13th and 14th centuries were not merely local princes content with prosperous fiefs, rollicking in wine from the vineyards of Merano, the Tyrolese prototypes of the King of Thule consecrating life in a golden beaker, but

CASTLE TYROL

sserted a position of equality in the chancelleries with
the most powerful rulers of Europe. They were justified
in asserting their independence and their equality, since
the key to the fair land of Italy, the desire and ambition
of every ruler north of the Alps, lay in Tyrol, and Tyrol
itself, approachable only through the Brenner and the
Pustertal, could easily be made impenetrable.

The balance of power had become in Tyrol a practical
policy before the theory came into the minds of
European monarchs, a balance between encroachment
from Austria on the east and Bavaria on the north ;
the routes to Innsbrück were comparatively open and
invasion was practicable as far as it, but the rich towns
in the heart of the mountains, Merano and Bolzano,
remained untouched. The Counts of Tyrol developed
a talent almost as pretty as that of their Italian com-
peers at Venice, Milan or Genoa, for preserving a balance
between two enemy powers and successfully bleeding
both. The moment when Bavaria and Austria could
combine meant disaster for Tyrol, and we can attribute
the loss of Tyrolese independence in the 14th century,
not so much to the Habsburg succession after the death
of Margaret Pocket-Mouth (Maultasch) in 1363, as to the
inefficiency of the later Counts of Tyrol themselves.
The theory of close diplomatic balancing, and the ability
to manœuvre at once and skilfully towards rupture of
opposing forces had died a natural death in the
degeneration to a life of lust and extravagance.

Schloss Tyrol brings those shadowy memories of past
history, those shadowy *arazzi*, where the splendours and
movement of a past world are drawn in a frail colour,
into vision and the beauty of the mountains grades
into that imaginary beauty—a rich association. The
old spirit of independence has not died in Tyrol with

the passing of the centuries. The native of Merano
looking up at Schloss Tyrol, cannot forget that thi
solitary castle raised on a cliff above the town represent:
the real focus of Tyrolese history ; the Counts of Tyro
were the royal princes of the mountains before the
Habsburgs came into power, and the beauty of that past
some indications of which can be seen in the armou:
displayed in the Kunsthistorisches Museum at Vienna
is always reality to him. Merano and the Schloss Tyro
come to him as essentials of his own spirit, and hi
pride in the historical development of Tyrol is stil
perhaps the most salient feature in his character. Th
forces of tradition vibrate in the air, and speak to him
from the castles and the mountains ; culture, education
art, literature, have combined to produce a mentality
more closely akin to the German than the Italian ; the
early Tyrolese paintings and sculpture grade directly
into the frescoes and sculpture we see in Nuremberg
and Würzburg, certainly not in the churches of Trent
and Verona.

The Schloss Tyrol owes its present condition to a work
of considerable restoration undertaken at a time whe:
a local peasant had begun to use it as building material
at a time when, in the struggle for independence agains
the French invaders in 1809, Andreas Hofer and
Hormayr consecrated it as the symbol for all time o
the Tyrolese spirit, the Tyrol of the early centuries now
gloriously resurrected. This act of consecration chased
away effectively the local builder, and led finally to
complete restoration. The Roman tower, the knight'
hall with its beautiful Romanesque portal, the Zodiac
and the beasts of the Apocrypha ranged round finely
sculptured pillars and arches done in the time of Walthe:
von der Vogelweide can be seen now as they were seve:

centuries ago ; the chapel contains memorials from time immemorial and frescoes from the 13th and 14th centuries, while the upper room has still in some of the windows the finely sculptured pillars of the original castle.

The castles of the Southern Tyrol are the natural decoration of the beautiful mountain-land, not through the savage splendour of the Castello Sforzesco in Milan or the Castello of Brescia, monuments to the administrative genius of the condottieri who, of an origin even as obscure as the princes of Tyrol, founded noble cities and encouraged international trade, but through the intimate connection they have with their surroundings. The princes of Tyrol, small lords with confined ambitions, moved in the narrow orbit of their mountain territory and desired little more. Their main object in life was to live as richly and as coarsely as their supplies would allow. Their castles were their dwellings and nothing more ; nature, in the shape of unscalable cliffs and yawning chasms, gave to them more complete protection than a thousand legionaries ; the mountain peaks traced their church towers in the sky, and the clouds were the tapestry on which their faith was wrought.

At the time when Sigismund, Count of Tyrol, built the Burg at Merano (1450), Sigismund Malatesta was building the temple at Rimini and the Medici, the Riccardi Palace at Florence ; of all three the Burg, the least ostentatious, the lowliest—but now, when we stand in the courtyard and gaze up through the vineyards at the snow-capped mountains, glorious in the sunlight, we feel that no human palace could ever have the beauty of that natural palace and that the Burg, lowly as it may appear, came closer to the spirit of the

N

mountains than the Malatesta Temple to the spirit of
the plain. The sense of fitness persists, and the
standards we would adopt in criticizing the more
splendid achievements of the south give way at once
to the intimate appeal of castle and mountain joined
in a single vision of beauty.

CHAPTER XI

THE HEART OF TYROL: MERANO AND BOLZANO

THE two cities of Bolzano and Merano have always a strange fascination merely through historical association, and innumerable pilgrims who have journeyed to this Mecca of the Alps have left on record their impressions of their mellow beauty and warm, full-blooded life. It would appear presumptuous now to add a further record of impression and feelings to that continuous narrative which has evolved for generations; but they are impressions which cannot be reproduced, and they are peculiar to the traveller himself. Some of those may have an æsthetic and psychological interest rather than a purely historical; they have not the splendour of a great reputation behind them, but they may serve to show how one spirit may react, however humbly, to a beauty that is renewed from year to year, becoming richer and mellower with the passage of the years.

From time immemorial, the fertile valley in the heart of the mountains, bounded on the west by Merano and on the east by Bolzano, has been the envy of the surrounding countries; the history of this part of Tyrol is largely the history of international relations, inspired by invasion of armies from the north and even occasionally from the south, and by the constant movement of trade between Germany and Italy. The two cities are symbolical, each in its peculiar degree, of this shaping process : Merano, the capital of Tyrol and the centre of the court life of the Counts of Tyrol, has in it something of the atmosphere we would expect in a centre of culture rather than of trade. The invaders from the north and the west found a resting-place in that beautiful recess of the hills, secure from danger and with only one flank to protect. Merano was the strategic centre, the resting-place, the home of gaiety and pleasure, undisturbed by thoughts of im-mediate danger. We find the aristocracy spreading out to the hillsides among the pine-trees round the capital, and there is even now, with that splendour risen almost to a state of legend, something of the *insouciance* and lightness of a Latin city. Bolzano, on the other hand, had also a strategic importance, but it never could be held for any length of time against opposing bands. It lies in the centre of four converging valleys and strikes the great international highway of the Brenner. The mediæval invaders, even as the Romans, decided that Bolzano had more value for them as an international town than as a purely personal possession ; influenced perhaps by the early pioneers and traders, they were willing to grant it immunity from any attempt at an-nexation which a successful campaign in the Tyrol would bring with it. The Empire, in its struggle with the Papacy and in its continual desire to gain possession of the fair land of Italy, sent waves of soldiers down the Brenner, and occasionally those waves spread out over the whole valley from Merano to Bolzano, but drained away rapidly as the main current flowed beyond Trento and swept into the Venetian plain. No local tyrant could ever hope to hold Bolzano even for a day against such a flood, and so we find this pleasant city of the Tyrol specializing early as a commercial and banking centre rather than as a court centre. The counts of Tyrol derived from it the wherewithal to pay for their pleasures at Merano ; Bolzano was the constant source of wealth to the overlords of that rich country.

Apart from historical associations, the heart of Tyrol has a wealth of natural beauty quite different from that of the Dolomites or of Trento ; it is beauty flavoured with memories of the past, and rich in its suggestion of human activities and associations. With this natural beauty there is a force of tradition, the mystery of art and the splendour of legend coming to expression in the most unexpected places.

The beauty of Tyrol and the Dolomites is a beauty of colour accompanied by strangely contorted forms— the glowing Alps, a majestic blue shadow against a cloudless sky, touched with a delicate rose-purple in the shoulders turned to the sun, peak after peak rising wonderfully in a haze of pure colour above vineyards, and quaint towers each on its vaguely emerald hill.

Bolzano is huddled under the stern hills so confidingly that there is a feeling of friendship in those towering heights, as if one could stretch a hand over the house-tops and, touching them, unhook the moon from the faintly clouded sky. In the square stands Walther von der Vogelweide, a darkly shadowed figure with flowing robes on a simple yet beautiful pedestal—Walther whose fierce call for independence rings through the long silence of the past and trembles always in the heart of those who, having read his poetry and known the pure artistic emotion of the man, wish also for that fierce independence and that stark hold on life. Now the base of the statue itself has been defiled with crudely painted

Italian national colours, a worthy example of the reverence felt by the new regime for some of the memorials dearest to the inhabitants of the Southern Tyrol.[1]

The town is full of the echoes of past things—the legends of King Laurin, the King of the Elves, who lived in the peak named after him and in the Rosengarten, the loftiest group in the Dolomites, visible in its full glory just behind the Eisack Valley. In the morning it was a pleasure to gaze at the Titschen hill which filled up the sky entirely. When dawn broke it was all a-shiver with pale grey and green lights, milky-blue in shadow ; then, as the light strengthened in the sky, it changed to a delicately lovely rose above and a paler purple shot with grey beneath, dark amethyst in the clefts and hollows. When the sunlight came clear across the hills, the glory of milky blue-purple and gold was startling, wonderful in its softness and voluptuous radiance. In the full morning, the light picked out the green foliage against dark shadow and gave a harder rose to the projecting buttresses, with a softer shade of pale purple-brown in the half light. The highest peak, the Rothwand, shone vaguely in a velvety green through the enveloping sky, where every beautiful colour seemed to be enfolded and drowned to sleep.

Nothing could be more peaceful, more exquisitely gracious than the quaint red-tiled roofs of the town with their tiled chimneys, the lace-like tower of the 14th-century church hovering above a roof of green majolica, the memorials inset in the walls, and the overhanging stories supported by richly carved beams. The

[1] This chapter was written in the autumn of 1923. Since then the statue has been restored to its original state without the Italian colours.

double association—the mediæval legends and the
mediæval poetry with its finest embodiment in Walther,
with the more savage records of the War of Independence
against the French in 1809—can be seen in the tombs
outside the church, the slightly defaced knight on the
wall and the memorial to Peter Mayr, the Lieutenant of
Andreas Hofer.

The square in Bolzano has always an interesting
throng passing through it, and the whole population
assembles in the cafés towards nightfall, so that the
splendour of the sunset becomes almost a symbolical
background to the gaiety below. The constant sound
of music, almost Viennese in quality, with the glare of
the café shining out full on the square, thins out
into mystery at the foot of the walls of the old church,
standing in a strange shadow of its own between
the vivid purple and blue of the mountains, and the
bright gleam of the light on the square.

From our Pensione window in Gries, beyond the noisy
waters of the Adige, we could gaze on a landscape of
idyllic beauty ; the valley lay open before us almost to
the mountainous approaches of Merano—on the left the
Mendola group with the Virgl coming full over Bolzano
and closing out the valley of the Adige, the island of
rock in the centre of the valley with the Sigmundskron
castle at the highest cliff edge, and behind this, finely
etched against the sky, the fantastic peaks of the range
of hills forming part of the Ortler group. Beyond
Bolzano the decorative background was supplied by the
most spectacular peaks in the Dolomites, the Rosengarten, rising in a strange medley of colour behind the
solid block of the Schlern. On the extreme left the
wings of the stage were supplied by the Ritten, so that
the full glory of the mountain wall was disclosed in all

its dramatic strength. In the early morning we could watch the distant hills emerging softly and exquisitely from the haze to become silhouetted against the pale green sky, the plain taking shape round the dark island of rock, while the Sigmundskron gradually lost its dark outline and became merged in the prevailing note of dusky green, shot through with metallic purple. On each side of the island, the white mist would lie in bands with a faint gleam through them occasionally where the sun rested on water and the shadowy splendour of the Mendola would begin to disintegrate, the pine trees breaking the uniform tone of colour. There was alway a tenderness in that landscape, especially in the distance where the Gantkofel and the Hofbichel dip down almost to the plain edge and the hills rise again at Tisens, closing up the valley with an aura of lower peaks drowned in a haze of colour. There was nothing profoundly impressive in that picture, but it was satisfying, simply through the suggestion of fine detail waiting to be unfolded, and the Sigmundskron, with the white gleam of water beneath it, gave a meaning to it all, the beginning of a dramatic theme. On the left this suggestive quality disappeared and we had, instead, the sharply defined pillars and towers and massive battlements of the Rosengarten rising clear above the rich green of the valley. At times the clouds would come over in solid masses and the mountain wall would appear cold and gloomy against them ; the lower clouds would brush the Schlern with trailing swathes, through which the dark bulk of the mountain would appear impressive enough but repellent.

The Rosengarten has a more suggestive beauty at those repellent moments than in the other moments when the sunlight drops down on it from a cloudless sky, and every edge, every crest and every column glows intensely in a strong rose-grey gleam, not colour but illumination. Bolzano lives for those last exalting moments, when the afterglow comes creeping over the mountains and rests on the Rosengarten in a sheer conflagration, a dazzling wonder of golden-rose with shadowy streaks of purple. At that time only the fantastic mass of the Rosengarten counts in the dramatic theme ; it is a last defiant exit from a world grown dark and lifeless.

The contrast between those two aspects—the vague tenderness of the mountains leading to Merano, and the dramatic effectiveness of the Rosengarten—supplies a clue to the real difference between the Etschland and the Dolomites ; in the one there is a wealth of poetry and of suggestion, the human note always sounding faintly in the distance, and in the other there is a strong perfection of beauty where every detail is outlined with absolute certainty of touch, but with no intimate appeal. Before the vaguer beauty of the Etschland, there is a feeling of intimacy and trust, but in the Dolomites nothing deeper than admiration ever takes place.

Merano has no wealth of architectural memorials or frescoed walls or picturesque fountains to present to the traveller—simply a beautiful city nestling in the heart of the Alps, sun-filled, open to the sky, very gracious with its colonnades and with its rushing waters, the orchards clustered thickly round it, and the vine-terraces ranged on the lower slopes of the hills. Its beauty made it once the refuge of the blase aristocracy of Vienna, come here to enjoy music and drink the waters in the Kursaal, a fashionable *va-et-vient* along the promenade, notable for dazzling toilettes and inimitable swagger, especially when the highly-decorated beaux of

the Austrian army tried out the effect of a new uniform
or a new style of moustache curled to a turn. Much of
that glory has departed now with the departure of the
Austrian regime, and something of the real life of Merano
has taken its place ; the ladies still pass in splendour
before the white Kursaal and exhibit their mondaine
elegance before the grey turmoil of the Passer river,
but the social extravagances and the careful social
observances due to rank have almost disappeared.

The haughty duchess of Vienna, with every gesture
rigidly controlled to accord with prescribed regulations,
has given way to the demi-mondaine of Milan, interested
in merely human things without paying obeisance to
the society gods ; the idol of race fades away before
the idol of wealth ; Vienna or Munich has only now the
former, while Milan has the latter. Instead of the
swaggering cavalry officer of a crack Austrian regiment,
groups of Bersaglieri pass with nodding plumes in full
arrogance of possession, or insolent subalterns from an
infantry depôt in the neighbourhood, immaculate in
tight uniforms and high caps, cast an appraising eye,
en passant, on the samples of feminine charm scattered
over the seats in front of the bandstand or drifting along
the promenade in exiguous costume. The Italian
officer of those days must have acquired a pretty education in curves and rhythmic lines. Merano, in the
three years after the Italian annexation of the Southern
Tyrol, was practically stagnant socially, at a loss to
discriminate between old visitors now departed and
new visitors inflicted on it. Should it abide by tradition
and turn a cold shoulder to the conquering race ?

The Italians solved the problem for her by quartering
a heavy military force on Bolzano and Merano, much
heavier than the original Austrian, and the capital is

MERANO

only now recovering from this involuntary change. The old cosmopolitan atmosphere, where the usual international rulers of society exerted a benevolent dictatorship and regulated to a nicety the various degrees of *bon ton*, valetudinarians combining a diseased imagination with a love of artifice and formal decoration, the search after a good digestion coinciding extraordinarily well with a fashion parade, yielded almost overnight to an atmosphere of conquest, and Italian conquest of all things. The Italian regime has now passed its time of greatest triumph, in spite of *decreti leggi* and other legislative nightmares, and once more the cosmopolitan atmosphere threatens to predominate.

The bandstand in front of the Kursaal emits music now, not from Milanese orchestras, but from picked orchestras of Vienna and Salzburg ; the Mozart festivals in the latter town are reproduced at Merano, to the immense delight of those *rentiers* who come down from the *pensioni* in Obermais and the hills behind, and the old German pieces are inexorably pushing out the Italian. The regime may be rendered pure Italian, but it is difficult to Italianize culture, and especially music, when the prosperity of a town demands entertainment for visitors from every country in Europe. One can imagine the café director gazing mournfully at the serried rows of white chairs and tables, not a soul visible near them, and across at the Italian band discoursing approved music, and thinking of an end to all things.

The Italian occupation confused the issues in an extraordinary fashion, and convalescence was scarcely as rapid as expected, so that, even now, the Kursaal appears vaguely out of tune, and the great hotels across the river strike a note of distrust and, to some extent, of disillusionment. It is a shock to find an official guardian of the law, strictly Italian now, who has never heard of the *Rennweg* and knows it only under some barbarous Italian name. There is not even the consolation of seeing the explanatory " già Rennweg " under the new title. This circumstance explains the feeling of *gêne*, of discomfort, now experienced in Merano. One expects a complete metamorphosis which has only occurred in patches.

The Kursaal may, one day, change into an Italian cathedral, complete with altars and officiating priests. The traveller must now think out the whole situation and decide what it is to be—the old Tyrol or the new Italian province with its Italian capital he is visiting. A distinctly uncomfortable position for the traveller come here precisely to avoid thinking ! The cosmopolitan atmosphere can be breathed, as always under any occupation, in the great hotels over the river which present at night-time glittering façades reflected in golden pillars in the water ; but an hotel is insufficient pabulum for a full-grown man in search of pleasure, and so, he comes straight up against the problem.

The simplest course would be to select a castle on the hills and forget Merano in the cloudy beauty of the mountains, which nothing human can effect, wander over the Ortler Alps or the Mutt Spitze, and simply revel in the beauty of nature alone. But Merano and history would be neglected in this way, and it is doubtful whether the same flavour would be given by the mountains bereft of their human associations. It is difficult to avoid the cosmopolitan devil entirely as one remarkable experience we had on the path up to Castle Tyrol proves. Not content with flooding the Southern Tyrol with soldiers, Italy has committed the one

unpardonable crime of allowing cinema fiends to exploit
it in the search after new pictorial motifs.

We had sauntered from Gratsch over the winding road
to Schloss Thurstein, a picturesque mass of stone, on a
beautiful, vague day with broad splashes of sunlight
alternating with shadow, and continued along the narrow
footpath, when we saw behind us a party of cinema-
actors carefully touched up to resemble nothing human.
The hero, dressed in breeches of a startling check-
pattern, orange leggings and boots, a black waistcoat
and grey, belted coat with a brown fur collar. His
face was of the usual sensuous actor type—heavy,
dark-blue chin with thick, rouge-tinted lips, a long,
straight, wide-nostrilled nose, wide-staring eyes with
brown pupils and brilliant whites, carefully framed in
bluish paint to make them appear wider than reality,
a broad, pinkish-purple brow beneath oily masses of
smooth black hair. This remarkable combination was
crowned by a light-fawn Viennese broad-brim of a
recherché pattern. The general effect was blinding and
blotted out very thoroughly the delicate loveliness of the
sun-filled valley beneath.

He had two ladies with him : one, a coarse-featured
vulgar heroine, with thick lips excessively red and little
white pimples under the eyes which even paint could not
hide. She had sweated a little *en route*, and an infinite
number of little runnels broke the smooth surface of
rouge hiding her cheeks. With a little encouragement
she would have been in the same position as Lady
Wishfort, " errantly flayed, like an old peeled wall."
She seemed to be dressed solely in an orange scarf of
silk draping her head, a heavy blue-green coat, and fawn
kid boots laced down the side. At one time, during the
climb, one boot got loose and we enjoyed the spectacle

of a magnificent lady trailing a mass of leather about, looking for a lace, and swearing like a dragoon. Apart from these accessories, nothing else was visible except a light grey camisole just visible across the breast. Her greatest pre-occupation was in holding on the coat and whatever lay beneath. I had the uncomfortable feeling that, if by any chance she were forced to release her hold, the whole unwieldy mass of clothing would fall down, disclosing an Eve in fawn-coloured boots.

The second lady was quite beautiful, but distinctly commonplace in dress—a light-grey, close-fitting costume and the usual laced boots, an enormous fur and a wobbly hat. Her features, thrown into startling relief by the make-up, were vivacious, her voice musical, and her seductive glances at the hero were delicious. The operator kept clicking merrily and, at one flat space of grass open to the radiant mountain landscape, they performed a dance. At this dance the first lady's boot became undone and she was photographed thus, stalking about. The second lady grew tired half-way on the road to Castle Tyrol and, in a tearful voice, refused to go farther—the sun was so dreadfully hot. Then we had a delicious scene where the hero persuaded her to go just a few yards farther. At the Schloss, the ancient caretaker turned not a hair but seemed, on the contrary, to take huge delight in elaborating every detail in the inner decoration of the castle capable of intensifying the boredom of his audience.

For us, the castle had no meaning that day, and the landscape became resolved into three farcical characters satirizing, in their very presence, the spirit of the mountains. The modern world with a vengeance !— at a place where the whole purpose of life seems to be a return to the world of the past. We would not,

however, have missed the fun for any æsthetic considera-
tions, and enjoyed the scene from the castle the follow-
ing day, when no picturesque hero from Los Angeles
was present, and only a well-nourished Bavarian with a
well-nourished wife gave animation to the landscape.
The unexpected may happen now at Merano at any
time, and the traveller must cast behind any æsthetic
superiority he feels, content to rejoice in the exuberance
of life in a world of rare beauty.

CHAPTER XII

THE DOLOMITES

THE Dolomites have a magical suggestion even to the most coarse-grained realist, since the admiration of centuries lingers, and it would be a determined *littérateur* who could set out again on a voyage of exploration, hoping to surpass the work of his predecessors in the genre. The best one can hope to give is simply a record of impressions, fugitive perhaps, ill-defined and colourless, and trust from this that the work of evocation will be completed in the imagination.

There has been a tendency to adopt a questioning attitude towards mountain scenery, which is already well known, and find in it something unsatisfactory, obvious and even *démodé*. That attitude is difficult to understand in the splendour of the Alps, especially in the wealth of colour and form presented by the Rosengarten, Latemar and Monte Marmolata, and I, at least, can only attribute it to the desire for exclusiveness, for severance from the possible trend of fashion in travel. We may wish to keep that feast to ourselves and grow sated in a unique experience, the world left behind us and only the mountains and skies before us, but at best such a feeling only betrays misconception of the real nobility and splendour of the hills.

The time is past for ethics of the mountain land as declaimed by Ruskin in torrential prose, the quieter

genius of an Edouard Rod comes closer to the modern
spirit ; but no education in beauty, no careful inculcation
of æsthetics can equal one moment of contemplation
beside the Karersee, when the pillars and towers of
Latemar are strained to an immeasurably delicate
emerald in the still blue water, or a single short climb
round the lower slopes of the Rosengarten from the
Karer pass, when the mountain blocks come magically
together to form the abside of an immense Gothic
cathedral.

Those are moments of vision—single, intense, com-
pelling—and they inspire something deeper than mere
admiration ; they throw unexpected gleams on things
that were hidden beyond reach, faint ecstasies, faint
stirrings towards a deeper sense of being. The Dolomites
have this power of revelation to a greater degree than
any other part of the Alps—not through historical
tradition or association, but through sheer unexpected-
ness ; the wind, the sun, the clouds may change a whole
landscape and transform a serenely smiling world of
mountain peaks into a shadowy menace, fantastic in
form and overwhelming in suggestion.

The regular slopes and harmonious lines of the Western
Alps have disappeared and given way here to lofty
columns, unbroken cliff walls, hollows cut through the
rock for thousands of feet, solitary peaks rising without
a break sheer into the sky, bare crags weathered to
every blazing tint of rose and pearl grey ; the resistance
to the centuries has been bitter and bitter the mighty
fragments that remain. They have maintained their
independence and their strength defiantly, and now
stand forth, incorruptible, inconquerable—the pillars of
an immense cathedral consecrated by history. Beauty
flutters round them in the cloudlight and in the sun,

o

but they are stronger than suggestion ; every line, every mass comes forth clear to vision, gaunt and unshaken !

In the days of the grand *tour*, the Dolomites presented a fascinating problem—the delightful uncertainty of a journey into the unknown, beset with difficulties and suggestive of adventure. The bolder spirits looked on it as a worthy finish to the leisurely stroll through France and Switzerland, and embarked on the enterprise with a feeling that the memory of dark mountain roads, sheer cliffs and fathomless valleys would serve to spice the more florid days in store at Venice. The Dolomites formed a decorative border to the main theme of carnival : mountain walls and palace façades, mountain lakes, heaven-kissed, were a noble counterpart to calm lagoons reflecting the magnificence of Venice ; the strain of the high peaks could melt away to the sound of music in the ballroom of a *procuratessa*, the clear wine of the solitudes thicken to the perfume-scented air of a magnificent drawing-room.

It is doubtful whether the travellers of those days, even to the time of Ruskin, took the Alps seriously ; they formed an unavoidable interruption in the procession from capital to capital, from festivity to festivity ; their bouquets of Alpine flowers held in a rich vessel of green meadow and snow-streaked mountain wall, could scarcely compare with the more *recherché* displays farther south. The flowery meadows of the Karer pass, ablaze with colour in the spring and early summer days, appeared unfinished, crude, beside the smooth lawns of the Boboli gardens at Florence, and we find Browning, for example, musing at Florence and Sorrento when his whole genius needed the harsher and purer atmosphere of the mountains.

The Dolomites have still to find their poet or their acolyte with the enthusiasm of Ruskin. Perhaps it is better so. We could spare purple passages for the quiet contemplation of beauty undiluted, forming in the silence our own images and bringing together in recollection all those unseizable impressions into a single moment of vision. The preparation of the mind to seize impressions before the impressions are born, is perhaps the greatest futility of all ; how many travellers have found their enjoyment of Venice ruined through the conflict of recollection inspired by literary romancing and the actual scene unfolded before them !

The Dolomites have been pictured in many canvases (a view of the Monte Nuvolau, by Sidney Lee, at the 1924 Royal Academy, a fine example), and the Rosengarten must appear a distant relation to many connoisseurs, part of their garden formed of choice pieces from all the world ; but the memory of a picture is less penetrating than the memory of a few set phrases, a few magnificent sentences. " A chorus ending from Euripides " lingers after the splendour of the play has disappeared. That is perhaps the great merit of a journey through them—a straight meeting, a direct confrontation, with every sense clear to the impression and the authentic note of admiration !

Even with this, a passage in Meredith's *Amazing Marriage* haunts Tyrol and Dolomites for me like a shadowy refrain, a subtle music bringing a rarer suggestion to the mountain glory. The passage describes a morning in the Carinthian Alps to the east of Tyrol, deeper into Austria, but it gives the key, as no other passage I know, to the spirit of the mountains and may form an opening to the fuller spectacle of the Dolomites.

" Dawn in the mountain-land is a meeting of many

friends. The pinnacle, the forest-head, the latschen-tufted mound, rock-bastion and defiant cliff and giant of the triple peak, were in view, clearly lined for a common recognition, but all mere figures of solid gloom, unfeatured and bloomless. Another minute and they had flung off their mail and changed to various, indented, intricate, succinct in ridge, scar and channel ; and they had all a look of watchfulness that made them one company. The smell of rock waters and roots of herb and moss grew keen, air became a wind that raised the breast high to breathe it ; an uplifting coolness pervaded the heights. . . . Peaks of ashen hue and pale dry red and pale sulphur pushed up, straight, forked, twisted, naked, striking their minds with an indeterminate ghostliness of Indian, so strange they were in shape and colouring. These sharp points were the first to greet them between the blue and green. A depression of the pass to the left gave sight of the points of black fir forest below, round the girths of the barren shafts. Mountain blocks appeared pushing up in front, and a mountain wall and woods on it, and mountains in the distance, and cliffs riven with falls of water that were silver skeins, down lower to meadows, villages and spires, and lower finally to the whole valley of the foaming river, field and river seeming in imagination rolled out from the hand of the heading mountain."

Meredith's vision of the Alps finds its one sure confirmation in the journey through the Dolomites, past Latemar and the Rosengarten down to Canazei, and again over the Pordoi pass to Pieve di Livinallongo, and thence over the last mountain saddle at Falzarego to Cortina d'Ampezzo, and his description could apply to almost every corner of the route.

*　　　*　　　*　　　*　　　*

The earlier travellers required a full week or more to reach Cortina from Bolzano and covered the journey by stages well recognized : the first stage, from Bolzano through the Eggenthal to the Karer pass, with its congeries of hotels ; the second stage, thence along the Vigo di Fassa to Campitello and Canazei ; the third stage, the dangerous ascent to the Pordoi pass, where the easefulness of the Fassa valley was very thoroughly banished, and a temporary halt made at Arabba before the longer rest at Andraz ; the fourth stage, along the Andraz valley to the Falzarego pass between the immense masses of the Tofana and Nuvolau, whence the shadowy wall of Sorapis looming over the Mecca of the Alps could be seen ; and the last glorious descent to Cortina, the end of danger and of struggle. From Cortina to Pieve di Cadore or north to Toblach and the Pustertal, the road presented few terrors. Cortina represented a meeting-place, a centre of enjoyment and sport, prior to the descent on Venice via Pieve di Cadore, Belluno and Treviso, or the longer journey east via Toblach, Lienz and Klagenfurt to Vienna, or the cold route west and north to Innsbrück and Munich via Bruneck and the Brenner.

The war destroyed the exclusiveness of the Dolomites and opened them up, to their deepest recesses, to motor traffic, so that the strenuous days of old are now gone, and it is only by an effort of imagination that the difficulties of the journey to earlier travellers can be appreciated. Perhaps in the shadows, when the clouds have gathered heavily over the mountains and the sun has gone down in a flurry of crimson and dull grey, something of the fear, some breath from the past inspiring courage and high-souled endeavour comes to us even now and the menace of the hills becomes very real.

The Alps have been brought closer to us; the bare walls of the Tofana lose part of their sullen majesty when we remember that lines of troops fought shoulder to shoulder over those apparently inaccessible heights; remoteness and reserve have been shed, and the splendour stands naked before us; but, even so, the splendour remains, and with it the keen joy of the lofty spaces, vivid, incommunicable.

*   *   *   *   *

It is impossible to describe, detail by detail, the wonderland of the Dolomites, and we must be content with a few vignettes, a few pictures culled hastily from the magnificence placed before us. Perhaps the finest *vue d'ensemble* can be obtained from the Vigiljoch at Merano, or from Oberbozen on the Ritten, while the Rosengarten can be appreciated from the Virgl above Bolzano. Perspective is necessary to appreciation and the view from the Vigiljoch does this.

In the pearl-grey sky, where a gleam lies waiting to flash on a glacier or snow-tipped ridge, the Dolomites stretch along in one immense wall, impenetrable and yet frail in shadow through the luminous distance: beneath them and closer to us, the humpbacked Ritten with its dense fur of pines, where only a bare patch of meadow appears at wide intervals like a wound; and, nearer still, the more abrupt hills on either side of the Sarnthal, filled with opaque blue shadow touched on a sharp cliff edge to a brilliant rose. The black pines of the hillside on which we are standing serve to throw that immense rocky landscape into the distance, to render more ethereal still the fine purple wall stretching across the world.

On the left, the Sella stretches with its flashing

snow-platforms and its massive head one unrelieved block of colour, then the solid peak of the Marmolata, one scintillating glacier riven by purple clefts where the buttresses come up to support that silver shield. The hollow between the Marmolata and the Rosengarten group is filled up by the smooth block of the Schlern, lying like an immense whale across the landscape, one solitary peak jutting out like a tooth ; the Schlern, closer to the foreground, is of a duskier purple with faint suggestions of green, and its buttresses gleam distantly in a milky blue shadow.

Beyond the Schlern, rendered more exquisite through contrast, rise, like a filigree of lace on the border of the sky, the richly fantastic peaks of the Rosengarten, tossing from pillar to pillar, from one exquisite peak to another exquisite peak, the glory of frail colour— silver of glacier and snowfield, azure of highest shadow, dim purple of deepest cleft, rose and pearl grey of rocky face, dusky purple, almost green, of the shoulders turned away from the sun. Against the mysterious gleam-filled sky, the procession of mountain shoulders, glaciers and peaks, with its culmination in the Rosengarten itself, was etched very delicately but very sharply, and the last shadow-covered slopes towards the blazing mass of Latemar stood out clear-cut as if to form a worthy contrast to the sun-filled magnificence before them.

Latemar, carved and riven to a many-pillared temple dedicated to the Goddess of Light, scarred with flame and touched to a diamond brilliance on the walls where the snow lingered, had in it the full warmth of the sun ; beside it, the Sella, Marmolata and the Rosengarten were mere shadows deriving their radiance from the glory reflected, and the landscape became duskier in contrast as if to bring everything to a harmony of consecration.

To taste to the full the picturesque quality of the Dolomites, the traveller should begin with that climb to the Vigiljoch, especially on a clear, sunny day in spring or early autumn; he can look behind at the brooding mass of the Ortler and, with it in his memory, turn round and gaze at the mountain splendour before him. From the Vigiljoch he can then proceed to Bolzano and travel up the mountain railway to Oberbozen, a swelling plateau visible in the foreground from the Vigiljoch and three thousand feet above Bolzano.

The sensation is quite different here; at Merano, the sense of detachment lent its own distant fascination to contemplation, but here the urge is more insistent—the urge to move onward and enter at once into that splendour through the mysterious portals now opening through the Eggenthal. At Oberbozen, in the midst of quiet pastures and windless forests opening occasionally to quaint farmsteads and immaculate churches, the feeling of struggle, of defiance, of life in the mountains lying in front is very real, and it is no longer remote, detached appreciation, but a real desire to share in that life, to breathe that spirit of defiance.

The landscape round Oberbozen, from Maria Himmelfahrt to Klobenstein, has something of the quiet self-possession the romantic painters of Germany depicted, an idyllic simplicity only slightly artificial—quaintly timbered farm-houses in the shadows of the pines, where the tinkling of cattle bells echoes continually, silent, deep-rutted paths winding through flowery meadows and past smooth green pastures to the edge of the sky, where they seem to glide into the unknown.

There are cool valleys and thinly flooding streams, dense blocks of pines and open spaces richly aglow in the sunlight ; there are strange corners where the forest opens out and discloses an immense perspective of mountains and distant valleys veiled in a luminous haze of distance, exquisitely blue and exquisitely unreal within the dark frame of the trees.

The Ritten is a mass of rock in a sea of reefs, with islands rising in a gleaming magnificence between the mist of the hollows and the clear blue of the sky, and the beauty of that landscape lies exactly in the feeling of expectancy the paths through the forests and over the meadows inspire. Beyond the narrow confines there is a suggestion of illimitable distance ; beyond the solid colour of the foreground, the jewel tints of glaciers resting at the edge of the sky over a world of peaks and hollows.

The journey from Bolzano up the hillside, with the Etschland lying open to the view beneath, from the rich valley between Merano and Bolzano to the mysterious shadows of the Mendola, with the nearer hills beyond the Eisack disclosed in every fold and cleft, a dusky green deepening to blue in the hollows, with the earthen pyramids rising on the hillside beneath like organ pipes, is dazzling in sheer brilliance of light and colour ; the whole world flames in the sunlight and casts a triumphant reflection to the sky.

The more thorough pilgrim may journey through the coolness to Klobenstein, deeper into the meadow and forest land and nearer to the solid mass of the Schlern lying like a barrier of menace between the Eisack Valley and the Dolomites proper ; the more adventurous pilgrim will disperse with the ascent to the Ritten altogether and, going up the Tierser Valley, attack the Schlern itself. As great pleasure, however, can be felt at Oberbozen, sitting at coffee in the hotel grounds in full view of the Dolomites with the immense mass of the Schlern towering in heavy majesty to the left, behind it, the Langkofel and the Sella, and on the right the full splendour of the Rosengarten, of Latemar and the last fantastic peaks of the Dolomites. The jewel quality of colour, the fine etching of line against the sky admired at the Vigiljoch, gives way here to a more definite impression of power and of strength. The mountains have moved into the world of reality from the world of vision.

The justification of the ascent to the Ritten does not lie in this, however, but in the single perfect view of the gateway into the Dolomites through the Eggenthal. There are few finer passages in the poem of the Alps than this ; the mountains come crowding together, cliff against cliff, block against block, until the valley seems to be threatened with destruction, and the immense barrier lying beside it between the higher walls becomes dwarfed and overshadowed—a menacing but incredibly beautiful grouping of forces to guard against intrusion into the sacred world of the Dolomites beyond. The gateway of the Dolomites is an example of nature, the architect, on the grand scale.

More intimate glimpses of the Rosengarten alone beyond the Eisack Valley can be obtained from the Virgl, and of the nearer peaks from the Titschen, where the whole Etschland becomes unfolded, with its castles and quiet villages beside the rushing Adige, or from the quaint St. Cyprian hamlet in the Tierser Valley, where the landscape glows in the light thrown by the cliff walls grown, through the effect of nearness, to lofty screens closing out the sky. St. Cyprian lives in the

TOFANA AND THE AMPEZZO ALPS FROM THE PORDOI PASS

glory of that single mountain peak ; it is the single dominant motif beside which everything shades off into insignificance.

*   *   *   *   *

Instead of describing painfully, detail by detail, the block of mountains lying between Bolzano and Pieve di Cadore, and describing how the more spectacular peaks of the Dolomites can be climbed, we might adopt a less remarkable method of progression and simply devote attention to the journey through the Dolomites as we experienced it. There is an immense literature devoted to the most difficult climbs in the Dolomites ; there are legends innumerable of alpenstock heroes blessed with the capacity to climb up chimneys hundreds of feet high and perform breathless feats over the mountain walls. The pages of the *Alpine Journal*, for example, are a continuous testimony to deeds of prowess, very inspiring in their kind (I remember a description by Geoffrey Winthorp Young of an afternoon and early evening spent in the communion of the hills, which might well be true of a similar afternoon and evening spent in the Dolomites), but the less enterprising traveller will prefer to see his mountains in the proper perspective and leave the details to imagination.

In previous years we climbed conscientiously some of the more spectacular peaks, but, beyond the first amazing vision of mountains spreading like a storm-tossed sea below, the traveller gazing up from the meadows beneath has a finer sensation of beauty and of strength. The road through the Dolomites has the picturesque quality more completely developed than almost any other route in Europe. There is a continual succession of pictures always changing in form and colour as the road winds higher up the mountain pass or beside rushing torrents and deep valleys.

*   *   *   *   *

We set out from the square at Bolzano on a clear, sunny morning of early autumn ; there was a fine gleam on everything, and the pigeons circling round the statue of Walther von der Vogelweide seemed to leave trails of light behind them. Our fellow passengers belonged to the Tyrolese and Southern German type. Judging from the somewhat crestfallen countenance of a bulky Teuton who sat immediately in front of me, the long journey through the morning without any stops for liquid refreshment was distinctly tedious. He might have enjoyed life better in the Harz or in the Fränkischer Schweiz, where the ramble through the forests and over the gently sloping hills is of the comfortable type, an inn at every hundred yards' distance. In the Dolomites something more magnificent than an inn must be met, and only at infrequent intervals where the mountain passes rest for a moment before dipping down again into the valleys. The Tyrolese were evidently bent on enjoying the crisp mountain air and the beauty of the mountains themselves, and they kept up a running commentary on every single fragment of rock that appeared within their frame of vision. They had evidently committed the landscape to heart and we only required to lie back and listen without consulting maps.

The first stage in the journey lies through the gloomy Eggenthal, with its entrance guarded by the picturesque and inspiring Castle Karneid, a typical stronghold of Southern Tyrol, built for strength rather than for beauty. It is perched on an almost inaccessible pinnacle of rock, with the rushing waters of two streams casting a white radiance in the shadows beneath before they join together to form the Eisack which surges through Bolzano. The Eggenthal has not the grip or the direct menace of the Partnachklamm which leads up to the Zugspitze, for the road is not forced out of the side of the mountain and is only occasionally overhung by the cliff walls, but there is a continual succession of radiant pictures done in three colours only—the rich milky purple of the valley, with a narrow band of golden green where the sun comes over one wall and rests for a moment on the wall beyond, and above it all the clear, unhesitating blue of the sky. The shadows differ in shape, the valley widens out to allow an island clump of trees to take the sun, but the colours remain the same and they are beautiful through this simplicity alone—a colour symphony on three notes. About a mile from Welschnöfen, which has now assumed the barbarous Italian name of Nuova Levante, the valley begins to open out and sinks down into gentle slopes, pine-covered with occasional meadows, where the cows keep up a constant music of bells. The first vision of the Rosengarten appears, a finely etched silver background to the gleaming colour of quiet meadow, dark forest and swirling stream. There is nothing impressive, but something quietly decorative in the picture— simply a piece of silver placed there to give point to the decoration.

Beyond Welschnöfen the road begins to mount slowly up between the pines, becomes cold in the shadows, and, after sweeping through an area of broad meadows, enters definitely on the ascent to the Karersee. The Latemar comes more and more insistently into vision, its walls rise more and more steeply above the pine-covered landscape and they gleam with stronger flashes of colour in the sunlight, every wrinkle on the bare surfaces, every notch of shadow, every splash of sun standing out prominently from a background of dazzling grey-purple. The Rosengarten on the other side begins to lose its familiar form as the buttresses supporting the main masses of rock come more prominently into vision, and the fantastic pillars and towers of the Vajolettürme move back into obscurity, merging from vivid lights and solid blocks of shadow, into the shimmering purple of the distance. There is a highly cultured tone about the landscape, the jade green of the meadows contrasting irreproachably with the bloodstone tints of the pine groves, where the sun picks out unexpectedly golden patches ; even the shrines by the wayside look as if they had been carefully dusted and polished, and the Crucified Figure inside appears almost gay at times.

As we rise higher and higher up the mountain-side the valley of the Adige becomes visible in the distance, just a faint haze of milky blue, and beyond it the scintilating masses of the Ortler, which seem to grade into the nearer mountains without interruption, a world of peaks stretching away to the limitless distance. For miles we mount through the pine forests, with sudden glimpses of rocky walls and sheer overhanging cliffs, until we reach the jewel lake of Karer lying flawless like an emerald dropped into the hollow of the woods from the clouds. Although the Karersee has become the *jeu d'esprit* of Alpine travellers intent on putting together at least one purple passage in the narrative of their adventures, it is impossible to overlook the beauty of this simple mountain scene, so perfectly achieved, so exquisitely coloured with not a marring touch anywhere.

The threatening cliffs and pinnacles, snow-crested, of Latemar rising above their shroud of snow and glacier are mellowed in the still waters of the lake to every delicate shade of green, deepening to blue in the shadows, and a slight brushing wind may draw across that reflection a fine bar of silver resting between shore and shore. Between the mountain and the lake stretches a broad band of pine forest and the colour succession, glittering purple, dark green and emerald, is a remarkable *tour de force* in decoration.

Beyond the Karersee the road enters into quiet meadow uplands where the cows are at pasture, cropping alternately the Alpine flowers and grass. There is no interruption in the sweep of the landscape right to the foot of the Rosengarten, and the single pines which dot the meadows, evidently placed there by nature to allow the budding artist to obtain an easily acquired effect of distance, lead the eye insensibly to the immense walls which rise up between the meadows and the clouds to close out the world. The round block of the Rosengarten, poised like a solid giant among its sharper satellites, disappears here through the turn in the track which brings its shoulders into line, and the full splendour of that central mass becomes more impressive as we move round.

It is generally considered *de rigueur* to sojourn at the Karersee Hotel, a very splendid structure indeed, placed right in the heart of the landscape ; but we were more modest and dined instead at the Hotel Latemar, a remarkable creation in red and green about a mile farther along. It is certainly one of the mysteries of mountain life—the capacity shown by those *alberghi* placed in the clouds to supply luncheons which would bear comparison with the best achievements of a restaurant in Paris. The only objection the more æsthetically minded of the pilgrims to the Dolomites may have is to their existence in the landscape at all ; they have certainly the capacity for making sublimity appear slightly out of fashion. It is difficult to enthuse over the magnificent world of mountains if the immediate foreground is taken up by an eminently respectable hotel, and it is disheartening to think of aged spinsters enjoying the same spectacle of beauty from the balconies of the Karersee Hotel. Afternoon tea has certainly a unique flavour when taken in full view of the Latemar ; the aroma of weak tea blends very agreeably with the stronger perfume of the pines.

The road descends beyond the Passo di Costalunga in intricate coils and the back of the Rosengarten group becomes more definite. The Rosengarten loses its individuality and disappears behind the frowning masses of the Dirupi di Larsec ; the landscape becomes a monotony of tortured mountain masses, torn and twisted into every fantastic attitude, breaking into wide gashes filled with a bluish purple shadow beneath startling rose-pink lights ; the mountain walls rise up sheer, without a single graceful curve, straight into the sky, and they appear almost as immense needles forcing a way through a blue silk curtain. The road keeps in full view of the Rosengarten as far as Campitello, where the lower hills close up the landscape and the eye is drawn to the less fantastic Langkofel group.

The view up the Vajolet Valley between the twin colossi of the Ciampedie Hütte and the Dirupi di Larsec to the frowning walls at the end, where the Vajolet Towers rise like a screen of a single uniform colour, is surely one of the most inspiring in the Alps. To the right of the track, there is a constant succession of less

spectacular peaks filling up the view with a rich splendour
of green valley and pine-clad mountain slope, where
the colours flicker and gleam with the changing clouds
above and the sunlight appears in a sleepy radiance.
Every line and every corner have an exquisite quality,
perfectly finished vignettes, thumbnail sketches all
forming together a mosaic of a rare beauty.

When we come down to Vigo di Fassa, the harshness
of the mountain walls becomes tempered by the feeling
of human association—the quaint churches in the
picturesque Alpine villages, the narrow patches of
tillage, the struggling orchards and even the unexpected
magnificence of an inn, with its romantic group of satellites. At this stage the mountains have stepped back
to give the landscape a pastoral and idyllic quality,
very refreshing after the strenuous moments mounting
up the Karer pass. Campitello comes at the end of a
string of villages lying in a cosy corner of the hills,
complete with meadows and quiet pine woods and dusty
roads, with an orchestral accompaniment from the Fassa
river. In the near distance, however, there is a promise
of greater magnificence to come, and at Canazei, where
the traveller, if he is sensible, remains a few days to
explore the Marmolata and the Sella, the mountains
come down in a solid dark mass, unrelieved and almost
menacing in suggestion. Canazei is a very modern
effort in Alpine villages, boasts of an enterprising art
club and equally enterprising beggars ; it can still claim
an international clientele and is a distinctly attractive
village, tucked away among the shadows of the hills.

From Canazei the long ascent to the Pordoi pass
begins—the most desolate and perhaps the most majestic
pass of all the Alps. The road winds slowly and painfully through pine forests that have been thinned during

P

the war, and the splendour of the Fassa Valley becomes
unfolded, a harmony of delicate colour fading away from
the clear green of the foreground to the most exquisite
shadows in the distance, where the Rosengarten rises
like a ghost out of the shimmer. After a few miles,
the first mountain shoulder is reached, the Fassa Valley
disappears, and we are confronted with the symmetrical
mass of the Langkofel, rising with its three peaks from
gently undulating grass-covered slopes, and full in front
can see the enormous gleaming wall of the Sella—an
impasto done in one uniform colour of pale rose-grey.
The proper method to appreciate the Sella is to compare
it with the more graceful Langkofel and contrast the
shadowy blocks of colour, where the sunlight quivers
and flashes in a strange medley of tints, with the unrelieved dazzle of the Sella. Seen from Canazei the
mountain rises like a many-pillared Greek temple or
like an enormous sky-scraper built according to the
new zoning laws, where the whole structure is stepped
back to form a series of towers leading to a central
tower. The snow has gathered on each shelf and forms
a glacier roof of an incredibly fine texture, when the
twilight comes over the valley and the afterglow rests
on the highest peaks.

Among the Dolomites three mountain blocks stand
forth very solidly to the vision—the Sella, the Marmolata
and Sorapis; they impress through sheer bulk; they
form a splendid drapery in one colour between the sky
and the pine forests below, and their beauty is perhaps
more satisfying through this simplicity than the fantastic
vagaries of the Monte Cristallo or the Croda da Lago.
The Pordoi pass has no pretence to silvan magnificence;
it rises slowly but surely through a wilderness of grey
rubble, broken only at rare intervals by a last desperate

clump of grass. The hotels, which once graced its summit, now stand like skeletons, windowless and roofless, ignoble relics of the past war.

One enterprising Italian has established a hotel at this cold summit, capable of exuding a little coffee under pressure, and we certainly required some heating agent to counteract the chill. The Sella steps back and allows a single peak, the Pordoi, to come forward and claim the pass, and it seems to act as a chill and draughty corridor, concentrating all the winds of the mountain peaks on that single gloomy platform, where only a lion-hearted mule could find sustenance. On the other side of the pass, however, the view changes entirely, and with it the welcome of the landscape. We have left behind us the cold slopes and look down on sunny pastures stretching gracefully away down the valley, with an occasional Alpine hamlet giving point to the gently rhythmic curves where the landscape folds over and spreads out again, almost like a cloak. Although the view from the Pordoi has not the stern, somewhat ponderous gravity of the picture disclosed from the Ostertaghütte, it has a finer unity of colour and is a very good example of exquisitely sure gradation from golden green in the foreground to dusky green in the middle distance, where the pine forests are thickly assembled, to the more tenuous grey-purple of the nearer mountain shoulders which form the Col di Lana, and then to the dazzling and infinitely delicate glow of the Tofana which barely emerges from the purple shimmer of the sky.

The road has a family resemblance in its hairpin turns and many windings to the Stelvio, but it is much more suave and has nothing really menacing about it ; its curves have almost a fanciful suggestion as they sweep down into the valley, carefully encircling single clumps of pine-trees. The Buchenstein Valley has a more attractive quality than even the Fassa Valley; its hamlets, especially Arabba, Pieve and Andraz, have a slightly more cultured look and are distinctly more prosperous in suggestion. There is always expectation of the marvellous unfolding beyond the next turn in the landscape, and this air of expectancy gives a peculiar charm, even to the meagre splendour of Arabba. We are now among the giants of the Dolomites—Sella, Tofana, the Ampezzo mountains, the Col di Lana, Nuvolau and the Civetta, the glory of Cadore. The Civetta provides at Pieve a singularly perfect mountain symphony—a steep valley, pine-clad, rising fold by fold in a single colour gradation to its last fine consummation in the sun-drenched mountain behind. Civetta appears like an immense jewel placed on a pedestal of green emerald, and there are certainly few places in Cadore which can give so luminous a vision. The Civetta requires some stage manipulation to be interesting, since there is nothing remarkably fantastic in its formation and the steep shoulders rise up in parallel ridges exactly spaced out to an uninspiring central mass. It is certainly worth while resting at Pieve sufficient time to go up the valley of the Cordevole to Lake Alleghe, which can be seen from Pieve in an intense note of light. The village of Alleghe at the foot of Civetta is certainly one of the most beautiful and one of the most pleasant in the Alps.

Beyond Pieve, the road turns up the thickly wooded valley of Andraz and rises very steadily towards the Falzarego pass, the last obstacle confronting the pilgrim to Cortina. In the valley below all traces of the war had apparently disappeared, but here we come again to the theatre of war, ruined hotels, farm-houses and occasional cemeteries with their pathetic crosses. The last section of the road, where it leaves the pine woods and merges into a bare world of rock, was rebuilt and widened during the war and is now one of the finest roads in the Alps. The view from the upper stretches into the valley behind towards Civetta and the mountains of Cadore gains in magnificence through the effect of distance ; the harsh cliffs rising on the right and culminating in Nuvolau render more tenuous the distant greys, purples and blues. The top of the pass between the cloud-capped Nuvolau and the cloud-swathed Cima di Falzarego, which stands as a sentinel guarding the last approach to the shadowy Tofana behind, comes as a last act to the dramatic theme already unfolded, and it has all the qualities of a last act—wonder at the consummation now reached, with a strange memory of what has gone before.

*   *   *   *   *

On the chill corridor of the Alps between the vaguely majestic bulk of the Tofana on one side, where the sun cast an uncertain gleam above cloudy masses, and the brilliant, sun-drenched mountain dike stretching from Nuvolau to Croda da Lago, the traveller goes in a state of wonder rising almost to exultation as the colours deepen towards sunset. He has come from a land of fantastic forms, fingers of mountain designing a richly decorative border to the sky—the fringe of a blue curtain—to a land where the sky drapes down over the high towers into the valleys, suffuses with a pearly radiance the remotest shadows lying between the mountains in the last recesses of the valleys, clothes immense blocks like the Tofana in a vague majesty more effective than the clear-cut symmetry of lofty peaks against a limpid background of sky could give, and brings to a single harmony of fine colour the varied features of that crested world enclosing Cortina.

It was dusk when we descended from the hotel along the straight road, and the failing light had already moved up out of the grassy meadows dotted with cattle and the black clumps of pine forest to rest in an exquisite glory of pale purple and rose on the quaint towers of the Cinque Torri, on the solitary Nuvolau, rising like a dog's tooth, and on the splendid isolation of the Croda da Lago, which comes almost as a final touch to that wilderness of contorted and wildly passionate mountain forms. The characteristic of that landscape above Cortina is exactly this note of passion which, subdued and almost hidden in the clear light of midday, comes out startlingly in the twilight and grows intense when the last purple glow dwells on the highest peaks.

Tofana had a ghostlike quality, the dark mass rising to a dim grey of cloud and above it, infinitely remote, to a frail shimmer of sunlight reflected in a delicate rose on the mountain walls—tenuous almost as a dream. Below, the twilight had gathered together the strongest and most velvety dark blues and purples in its palette, mixed them together and cast them over the Ampezzo Valley, so that between the pale green of the sky and the dark colour below, Pomagagnon, Cristallo and Sorapis floated in a brilliant rose-purple, very luminous and very unreal. A deep sea full-sailed with the noblest creations of the Dolomites !

Night after night, the same glory appears. The Ampezzo Valley darkens to a blue sea, Pomagagnon flames to orange and finally to a purple inconceivably luminous ; behind it, the Cristallo gleams forth, the

Antelao, the Sorapis and the Croda da Lago take up the splendour and the night closes down with a last triumphant display of mountain glory! There is a beauty in Cortina through this alone—the decorative motif dwells in the memory and gives a suggestive force to every detail.

Cortina stands at the parting of the ways; the road may go north-west over the Sella to Bruneck and the opening of the Pustertal, north through the Ampezzo Valley to Toblach and the full splendour of the Pustertal, or east beneath the Piz Popena and the Cristallo to Tre Croci and Auronzo, and thence to Pieve di Cadore, the northern end of the great road along the Piave to Belluno, Feltre and Venice. It represents a meeting-place of Alpine wanderers, and of the more sophisticated set that prefers to forgo the expensive social amenities of St. Moritz and enjoy winter sports less decorated with social stars. Cortina, from time immemorial, has been a strategic centre, and functioned as such during the last war, coming early within the destructive range of the guns. The road from the Falzarego pass over meadows and through ragged pine forests bears with it the memorials of conflict—the ragged, shell-torn forests themselves, deserted hamlets reduced to a mass of rubble, an occasional network of trenches and a solitary villa, roofless and windowless.

The Cortina we now see suffered almost as much as San Martino di Castrozza, but the force of recuperation has been so strong that everything looks almost as untouched and as well-established as before; the sparkle is perhaps brighter through the introduction of the Italian element in place of the more stolid Austrian, but the fine air, the exquisite trimness and the purity of colour remain. The unhappiness and the ill-disguised feeling of alienation with the existing regime which complicate existence in Bolzano or Merano or even Toblach have yielded here to a quiet enthusiasm ; Italy has been the spiritual mother of the Cortinesi even as much as Austria is the spiritual mother of Merano and Bolzano, and Italy only a hated step-mother.

Cortina lives a gay, self-centred life of its own, a continual *scène de théâtre* played against the background of the hills. The Italian fondness for a square is here indulged with its provision of cafés ; the church raises a single barock spire above the single street, and the hotels have been placed at intervals down this street so that the night pilgrim can march in the splendour of one continual restaurant. On one secluded upland, the aristocracy has built its family of hotels and *pensioni*, but the introduction of English and French snobbery has not been complete enough yet to ruin the wholly delightful character of the town. Life can be lived here very quietly and very wonderfully, with the constant invitation of the hills and the sedate rapture of strolling through fairyland meadows, pine clumps and up shadowy valleys, with the sunlight dwelling on the bare walls above.

Cortina inspires an idyllic mood, especially in the early autumn, when the mellow tones of the landscape grade into the dark browns of the quaintly timbered houses ; the brooks and the spouting wells have a more subdued music, and the sky comes quietly and vaguely over all ; there is no futility in dream and no unhappiness in thought—simply a warm glow of being.

The town is conceived in warm browns and pearly greys, an eminently satisfactory combination, and one scene, especially, showed how picturesque it could be. In the early morning a funeral procession followed the

CRODA DA LAGO FROM THE CORTINA ROAD

coffin through the street to the church, where the priests should perform the last services ; almost the entire female population joined in this procession, clothed without exception in black with the picturesque appurtenances of the Tyrolese costume. Only an Israels or a Daumier could have done justice to those faces, etched and coloured by the strong mountain air ; the constantly circulating line of mourners, jet black against the pearly grey of the buildings and the streets, had a splendour of pure contrast—the symbolism and strangely artistic force of a poet's vision !

The mountain landscape round Cortina has an inexhaustible variety and an inexhaustible beauty ; Cristallo, Sorapis and the Croda da Lago are a world in themselves, only less magnificent than Tofana with its immense buttresses and cloud-wreathed shoulders. Cristallo seen from the Dürrensee, a shallow, storm-tossed mountain lake bordered by shaggy pines, has a rare quality of uplift, an urge towards the sky more insistent above the waters of the lake than that of Latemar above the Karersee ; the Dürrensee on a calm, clear day can be a flawless jewel of turquoise, where the stern slopes of the Cristallo are inverted, tier by tier, glacier by glacier, swooping towards an immaculate heaven.

Sorapis, a solid mass of rock impressive through sheer bulk, is moulded to symmetry behind and stands, an Egyptian temple with two mighty pylons and a cloud-brushed capital, in lonely grandeur beyond the Misurina See. It has a Sphinx beauty, something unchangeable, impassive, fully matured—a creation of art built to a perfect symmetry. There are few pictures more inspiring than Sorapis rising above the waters of the Misurina Lake. The Croda da Lago has a more graceful presence and comes as a last touch to a mountain harmony already assembled ; the Reichenberger See lies on its shoulder full to the sky with only a faint shadow on it from the highest slopes ; it is held almost like a silver goblet to the sky and lies on the mountain-top in a cool isolation.

The Dolomites are specially fortunate in their lakes ; the great peaks have their mirrors to double magnificence and the series of lakes conjures up visions of an everlasting splendour—the Karersee, Dürrensee, Misurina See, the Toblacher See, the Lago di Colbricon, the Reichenberger See and the Lago di Alleghe ; they are the jewels on the throned peaks, the mirror of high towers piercing the sky. The Dolomites should be appreciated, not from the lonely heights of Tofana or from the frowning precipices of Latemar, but from the pine-bordered shores of those lakes where the majesty of the hills comes very close to vision.

Cortina gives the key to many of the noblest creations in the mountain world, and the whole region between the Pustertal and the Val d'Ansiei with the Ampezzo Valley, the Drei Zinnen (Tre Cime di Laveredo), the Hohe Gaisl, Monte Piano (where some of the bloodiest fighting of the war took place), Monte Cadini, Cima Undici, Einser Kofl, appears in a single splendour where every mountain falls naturally into place. The road from Cortina to Tre Croci moves from splendour to splendour as the Piz Popena and the Cristallo are unfolded and the Marmarole move into vision from the depths of Cadore ; at Misurina, the Sorapis is reflected in austere majesty in one arm of the lake and the Tre Cime di Lavaredo on the other, with each stern peak outlined, while the less fantastic Monte Cadini fills up the gap between. The Marmarole become more prominent, as Cristallo and Sorapis yield to more distant groups, less imposing in form, and take up the whole of the landscape until at Auronzo, the glory fades away and foothills emerge in the near distance.

Beyond Auronzo, Cadore with its thickly wooded valleys and rolling hills appears and only the Marmarole remain, the pride of Pieve and Cadore. The valley of the Piave has its own inspiring quality, through the force of historical association even as much as through natural beauty, and the traveller, passing through those thoroughly Italian villages sprinkled so thickly along the route, feels that the culture of Venice is near, and that the land of Titian will soon be disclosed in all its wonder to him.

CHAPTER XIII

CADORE—THE LAND OF TITIAN

AFTER the somewhat grotesque beauty of the Dolomites, with their strangely contorted mountain forms and vivid colour contrasts, where harmony is achieved through grouping of colours almost daring in conception, even to a modern artist—the more cultured and more suave beauty of Cadore comes home at once to the imagination.

It might be considered as a necessary part of initiation into the whole spirit and atmosphere of this mountain country, the close and intimate knowledge of the work of that genius who has given to almost every detail in the landscape something of its majesty —Titian.

It has generally been conceded that impressions formed during childhood have a direct influence even on the creations of after years, and one cannot willingly forget that, in the midst of those richly beautiful valleys, those quiet harmonies of vague colour, where the harshness of contrast has been shaded off through the effect of distance, a distinctive note of inspiration was struck which even the splendour and vivid culture of Venice could not wholly destroy. In Palma Vecchio we can see something of the warm luxuriousness of the landscape round Bergamo, and the low hills stretching at the edge of the plain of Lombardy, from Brescia to Treviso, and the Florentines, for example, have each their distinctive type of landscape to reproduce. No one could possibly mistake Botticelli for a painter of Lombardy, merely through the simple, quaint hillsides behind the personages in the dramas he depicts. The trees are highly polished, well browned and well nurtured, and every little fold of earth is as green as an emerald beneath a pure sky. In Titian as in Palma Vecchio and other Venetians, we have abandoned the jewel landscape and entered into a less perfect world of mass rather than of fine contour. In no painter is this feeling of mass in the landscape more intense than in Titian. It is only necessary to look at the " Jupiter and Antiope " at the Louvre, " Sacred and Profane Love" in the Galleria Borghese, to see how effectively this new conception of the landscape contributes to the strength and vividness of the central action.

It might be thought that in this use of a new motif Titian was only giving expression to what might be considered a change in fashion ; the whole tendency of the later Renaissance, influenced by Michel Angelo and Leonardo da Vinci, was towards unity, simplicity and strength of action, with an insistence on mass rather than on accumulation of detail, and Titian may have only been tracing one further stretch in the path of evolution from the simple lines of the early Giottesque painters to the powerfully suggested artifice of the 17th-century painters. It is only necessary to visit Cadore to thrust aside this idea. The one impression which remains from contemplation of the landscape is one of mass, and the feeling of intimacy disappears behind admiration of blocks of colour placed in harmonious succession of values, rising against the sky from the mountains, and designing richly varied effects in the valleys.

There is no fatigue felt in contemplation of this succession of colour masses, since detail becomes blurred behind a fine mist, which deepens to intense blue in the last folds of the valleys and lightens to silvery radiance on the higher slopes of the hills. The sun only rests in flame on the finest edges of cliff, sheer against the sky. From that lofty point it filters down to the valleys, losing more and more of its crudity, until only a faint splash of old gold on a roof or on a grove of chestnuts shows that the full glory of light has not been entirely shut out. That forms the one fine attraction of Cadore ; in the midst of quiet, unobtrusive colour masses, a single flashing point of colour emerges, giving to every fold and every corner a gleam of suggestion. It is the last quickening touch of the artist to the finished landscape.

The same impression is felt on viewing a Titian, where the figures act in the midst of a broad landscape. The colour masses are spaced off in harmony from the foreground to the tree silhouetted against the sky, and this harmony of tone is quickened by a sudden flash of colour, warm brown almost orange, rising from a dusky green-purple, and a sudden flash of gold on a rock face behind a dark silhouette of trees. It is impossible not to see the influence of Cadore in even the most hurried sketch of Titian.

* * * * *

Pieve di Cadore is a distinctly friendly little town, perched on the hillside beneath a very satisfactory fort, which after several centuries of restful monotony had a few exciting moments during the war, when the

Austrian attack in the Trentino threatened to weaken the whole Italian position. Pieve has very carefully obliterated all traces of that exciting time, and has made even a rusty old cannon on the hillside as unobtrusive as it possibly could.

Now we can sit on the grass at the foot of the walls and enjoy the radiant landscape beneath, the smooth green valley with its occasional vineyards and maize fields rising in soft folds to the Marmarole mountains, which take up the dusky green of the fields, deepen it with dark purple shadows of the pine groves reaching up their flanks, warm it to a reddish purple with dashes of milky blue in the higher shoulders, and in the *crevasses*, and finally, with a last triumphant flourish of deeply serrated peaks, throw it into the blue of the sky. The transition is complete, and has a mysterious quality even in the perfect grading of tones ; the white road, winding lazily from Domegge round the side of the hill down to Calalzo, and thence with a single determined stretch into Pieve itself, only makes the green more inviting and brightens up the purple of the high mountain slopes. It is singularly pleasant simply to lie on that hillside, with only a multitude of grasshoppers to keep you company, and watch the fine changes that take place in the tints of the Marmarole as the sun grows less strong and the first tinges of shadow appear in the sky.

Pieve has evidently a great admiration for its setting in the shadow of the Marmarole, but, even at its best, the Marmarole has a certain monotony of a Dolomite substitute made almost respectably *bourgeois*. Memories of the Rosengarten and Latemar with their lofty columns and sheer cliff faces tend to weaken the effect of the mountain wall behind Pieve. In the Marmarole we leave detail behind, and see at once the effect of mass without any special symmetry. More interest attaches to the less portentous hills on the left, the Croda Dilego, rising to the Monte Montanello with a last peak at Monte Cridola over 8,000 feet high, not so much through variety of detail as through the splendid sweep of the hill slope, pine clad right to the sky. It rises up directly from the rock-strewn, milky-green waters of the Piave, without a moment's hesitation, majestic in its very directness. Against this background every detail in the landscape stands out in relief as if the mountain slope formed a dark sky behind them ; the foothills and the isolated mounds of earth which seemed to have been thrust up by accident in the middle of the valley have a strangely remote suggestion through this alone. The grass has a deeper green and the pine-trees a more formal grace.

Pieve stands on the edge of a flat shelf overlooking a steep slope which goes down through gardens of flowers and vineyards to a shallow valley, very cool in the summer with its water and heavy foliaged chest-nuts. Lying along the bottom part of this valley is the strangely picturesque village, Sottocastello, with a complete collection of old wooden houses, not a single spar of dark wood marring the quaint beauty of those century-old structures. Pieve has all the characteristics of an Italian town, but Sottocastello brings us back at once into the mountain village, swept by the winter storms and lashed by the heavy rains. Its deep eaves overshadow strangely carved wooden balconies, where groups of old ladies with picturesque faces and children gossip and chatter the whole day through. It is strange that in those mountain villages there is no transitional period between young children and old dames; it looks almost as if the children become old dames in an afternoon; they certainly blend very well together. The men are probably in the court behind playing cards in the shadows. Sottocastello also boasts of a deity of a specially ripe flavour—one of the filthiest and most pertinaceous old beggars in Europe. Pieve on the hill above can boast a singularly fine statue of Titian, but only a genius in the art of sculpture could do justice to this beggar.

The hotel in which we lodged, with the flattering title of Albergo Progresso, faces the square where the statue of Titian stands; but some of the quaint beauty which once distinguished this corner, rich in memories, has been weakened through the erection of a square tower to replace the tower that was destroyed by the Austrians during the war. The present tower is an exact replica, but it is appallingly new, and it will take the Pievians several generations to live it down. At certain hours in the day the population debouches on the square, circulates round the statue of Titian in groups of black, contrasting vividly with the glaring white of the street and the faded yellow of the buildings. Then there is a public performance by the more musical members of the group, the tables in front of the hotel sound to the clink of glasses, and a vociferous multitude invades the café immediately opposite. At the hottest parts of the day this group fades quietly and gently away, and the square becomes deserted, with a few pigeons left in sole command. At night-time the groups gather again in masses of rich shadow beneath a marvellously purple sky, and there is a constant murmur of dance music mixed with an undercurrent of sound composed of many things, shuffling of feet, swishing of clothes, an occasional laugh and an insistent rattle of glasses.

Q

Pieve is at once the friendliest and the most romantic little town in the whole of Cadore, simply through this mingling of certain characteristics with an atmosphere which has still some of the rare quality of the high Alps. The church, which is round the corner from the square, has a number of paintings by Cesare Vecellio and one painting by Orazio, both brothers of Titian, and in certain of the houses in Pieve are a number of sketches attributed nominally to Titian himself. The main glory of Pieve, however, is exactly Pieve.

We spent an afternoon beyond Sottocastello in the warm sunlight, mellow with autumn gold. Below Sotto-castello, the valley rises again over a hunchback of land crowned with pines, and dips down suddenly to a deeper valley through which the Piave flows, a sheer cliff two hundred feet high terminating the descent. We scrambled down some of this slope to get closer into the magnificence of the landscape lying in front of us ; there was nothing living in that grassy hillside with its shrubs and wild rose bushes, only an occasional flutter of a wing and a swift scurry of a rabbit dipping out of sight.

From the lower end of the slope we could look right down into the valley of the Piave beyond Perarolo on the one side and Caralte on the other. The smooth progression of the valley from the dusky foreground to the immeasurably pale shadows of the distant hills against the sky was broken by an island of rock, full in the centre of the landscape. The river swept round in a flurry of water, almost Dresden blue in tint with sudden splashes of green, and disappeared in a cleft of shadow formed by the dark green of the island, con-trasting with the mistier blue of the mountain wall behind. On the other side, the green meadow stretched

PIEVE DI CADORE

THE BIRTHPLACE OF TITIAN

between the island and the mountain wall; on this
meadow was built the village of Caralte, with its stucco
walls and church spire designing a fine gleam of pale
colour against the shadow thrown by the island. Beyond
this island, the mountain slopes formed a succession of
walls of colour grading, with a sudden splash of
dazzling flame where the sun struck a smooth cliff
edge, fine shade by fine shade, into the infinite splendour
of the sky.

There are few scenes in the Alps of a beauty so
satisfying as this, and Pieve is ennobled merely through
this vision into a wealth of rare magnificence of form
and exquisite harmonies of colour.

The road from Pieve to Belluno is a very fine example
of Austrian engineering, especially in the first four miles,
where it goes through Tai and winds down to Perarolo
along the sheer face of the cliff. The view from the
heights above Perarolo, down over the misty valley
with its surging river below, over the quiet village, with
its broad stretches of logs drifted down from the hillsides and its scattered orchards, is almost as beautiful
as that we have already described. The suggestion of
romance is very keen, simply through the combination
of rich greens and golds and pinks.

*　　　*　　　*　　　*　　　*

The railway from Pieve moves precariously below the
road and occasionally branches out into a station visited
infrequently by peasants dressed in the usual dull shade
of black with dark brown weather-beaten faces. Beyond
Perarolo it skirts a cliff beside the Piave, and after one
glorious view of Monte Antelao blocking up, with a rich
background of misty blue, the dusky green slopes of
the valley, we entered into a long, varied series of fine,

detailed pictures shadowed against the background of wooded hillside, with the broad-flowing creamy-blue water between. An occasional small village huddled in a confusion of brown roofs and equally brown shadows between the cliff face and the surging water—a single deserted church, with its tower etched sharply against the dusky foliage of the pines behind—a sudden swing-back of the mountain to allow a stretch of meadow, intensely green, to soften the harshness of the mountain forms, and sometimes at the end of those meadows, silhouetted against the vague blue of the distance, a quaint Italian hamlet would appear in picturesque masses of colour beneath sparse pine groves.

There are few parts of the Italian Alps with so varied and yet so friendly genre pictures as the valley of the Piave, especially in the upper reaches, only a few miles from Perarolo ; below Longarone the dead hand of industrialism has intervened, and at the end of the valleys, when the road winds round the mountain slope, we can see the churches still as beautiful as ever, but beside them the outlines of factories with singularly repellent smoke-stacks. In the Val Camonica, where beauty is not so concentrated as in the Piave, it is possible to bring the factory, chimney and all, into the landscape simply through relegating it to a corner of the vision and leaving it there, while the eye enjoys what is left. Along the Piave, however, the mountains come so close to the river-side that the horizon is restricted and enjoyment lies in contemplation of rich detail—the fine tints of the water gleaming through every shadow.

A few miles from Belluno, we leave at once the hills and come into full sight of the plain, the plain full of the weary magnificence of colour we see at Brescia ;

the river has broadened out into sandy flats of a pleasant colour in the sun, and the once surging floods thin out into streaks of silver, dazzling in effect against the heat-drenched haze of the distance. The change from the cool shades of the hills, where everything has a certain romantic suggestion, to the more matter-of-fact brilliance of the plain country is very striking, and may be responsible for the slight feeling of disappointment which occurs when we enter Belluno.

If Sottocastello glories in a remarkable example of the mendicant class, Belluno has a remarkably perfect example of the Prussian official in its station, and his sole function is to make the tradition as imposing as possible. Preservation of dignity is perhaps the only function of importance left to him in that land of sleepy incompetence. The difference between Pieve and Belluno is simply the difference between friendliness and *joie de vivre* on the one hand, and listlessness and *paresse* on the other. Every year is repeated the awakening of Rip van Winkle ; the inhabitants take their turns at awakening for an afternoon and then go to sleep for about a century. The most ancient thing about Belluno is undoubtedly an old square tower built towards the end of the 12th century, but the inhabitants themselves run it a close second. The harmony between the people and their surroundings is complete, and they regard as almost sacrilege any effort to inspire anything like activity in them before the afternoon siesta is over. We found that the town museum could not be visited before the afternoon, owing to the fact that the custodian was still enjoying his well-earned repose. At Belluno they work on the excellent principle of preserving their most beautiful memories of the past even from human eyes.

Joking apart, however, there are some very beautiful things in Belluno, especially the Palazzo dei Rettori, where the influence of Venice can be seen in the combination of Gothic and Renaissance in the façade. The harmony of the decoration has been weakened by the busts inserted between the windows, so that the fine lines of the arcaded windows themselves lose some of their effect. The central balcony, however, is a triumph of pure decoration in stone. Beside it stands the old square tower dating from the 12th century, and a little farther to the right is the Palazzo dei Giuristi, of no great significance architecturally, but notable as being the sleeping-place of the custodian nominally supposed to be in charge of the museum housed within those walls.

The chief beauty of Belluno lies in its position on a low hill above the Piave, and there is something of the thrill of discovery felt on viewing the silhouette of the town against the distant shadow of the mountains. The streets are narrow, with almost continuous arcades, with a constant succession of old palaces where the walls are still beautified by little details of architectural decoration—a richly carved stone balcony, an occasional stretch of wrought-iron decoration across windows, a coat of arms, and even in some places a vague shadow of a fresco. The streets open out suddenly from the sunless shadows into moss-grown squares with mouldy fountains rich in their suggestion of decay consummated by the work of centuries.

There is a very satisfactory fountain of this type in the Cathedral square. The cathedral itself has a beautifully proportioned bell-tower, dating from the best barock period, and contains some very fine sculptures of the saints by Andrea Schiavoni, while there are good examples of the northern Venetian art represented by Cesare Vecellio, brother of Titian, Jacopo Bassano and Palma Il Giovane ; the crypt contains a polittico by the only Bellunese painter of note, Simon da Cosiche, somewhat crude in execution, although the inspiration has genuine strength behind it.

The artist, intent on recording fine contrast of brilliant sunshine and dark shadow, will find Belluno a pure joy, although the smell of mouldy cheese seems to form part of the atmosphere.   It is certainly impossible to escape it.   Some streets have timbered houses and quaint chimneys, with an occasional statue placed in a niche, which give the flavour of the Middle Ages intact.   Our last impression of the town seemed to contain in itself the essence of everything we felt in wandering through. We found quite by chance a very fine hotel indeed with a shadowed restaurant, cool and spotless, with a Napoleonic waiter complete in every gesture. This hotel is evidently the haunt of the Rip van Winkles of Belluno, and a delightful place it is if one is disposed to spend three hours over every meal ; any effort to hasten events meets with a solid wall of indifference and even distress. We found it an exciting experi- ence trying to hasten through lunch at a sufficient rate to avoid spending the afternoon there. Belluno has not the friendly liveliness of Pieve, but it has nevertheless a picturesque quality which grows in the memory.

The landscape from Belluno to Feltre has all the characteristics of the plain of Venetia, with foothills to keep the horizon from disappearing entirely ; the shadows become merged in a uniform heat haze and the Piave, after having broadened out at Belluno, draws together again, and glides off to the east, so that Feltre is several miles away from the river bed, and the wanderer looking out of the hotel window at morning sees in the distance a low wall of mist, with occasional streaks of silver through it where the surface of the river comes bare to the sun.

Feltre itself has recovered from the somnolence of Belluno, and glories in a specially virulent type of official. The atmosphere of this old-world town has more of the genuinely historical in it than any other part of Cadore ; there is a suggestion of past glory almost as vivid as that we feel in Brescia or Bergamo. The upper town, with its single street rising steeply between Renaissance palaces with their frescoed walls and heavy cornices, is one of the most perfect examples of historical pre- servation in northern Italy. We feel no longer that this is artifice, but that those palaces, with their walls painted in warm colour or in grisaille, have not been preserved specially for the traveller, but have remained naturally so—the very texture of the history and life of Feltre.

Feltre glories in a single street opening out into a lovely square ennobled by the statue of Vittorino da Feltre, who must have been the Italian prototype of Browning's "Grammarian"—the stern, unrelaxing forti- tude of the latter toned down in this Venetian humanist to something more gracious and attractive. Even Brown- ing's " Grammarian," however, was not less daring in the pursuit, and in the teaching of knowledge than Vittorino, and one of the most gracious chapters in the whole of the Renaissance, when every chapter had its own wealth of beauty and fine gesture, is that of this scholar from Feltre gathering round him at Mantua a band of students from all parts of Europe, supported and encouraged by him, under the enlightened patronage of Lionello d'Este, and sent forth again with a sure grounding in the highest culture of his time.

Vittorino comes closest to the ideal conception of a man with a mission, a mission not to instil any narrow religious dogma, but to bring out everything that was best and more lasting in the mental and spiritual enthusiasms of his generation, and we find those students coming eagerly to that academy at Mantua, owned and dominated by one man, with the same whole-heartedness as they came to Padua earlier in the century.

The Feltrians have placed the statue in a quiet square, where the only sound is of water falling into a broad fountain, which was there in his time, with its wall of Renaissance decoration, coats of arms and scroll-work. It is possible that Vittorino may have derived much of his vision and his singleness of purpose from that quiet moss-grown square, dominated on the one side by an old bell-tower rising above a grey cluster of buildings, deep eaved with shadowy frescoes, and on the other, by the massive structure of the theatre, conceived in true Palladian style, with lozenged pillars, square capitals, and a finely decorated cornice throwing a faint shadow over a blank surface of wall, where the sunshine designs a fine pattern of warm brown and golden light. In this theatre, Goldoni produced his first plays at the beginning of the 18th century, and the success achieved in Feltre may have laid the foundations for the future fame of this greatest comedy writer of Italy.

The sense of the past is very strong in that quiet refuge, and we can feel again something of that fine devotion to culture which made of Vittorino one of the outstanding spirits of his time ; there is a feeling of something that goes beyond mere local interests or traditions, something of that international friendliness and devotion to the pursuit of knowledge which gives to the Renaissance its unique savour among the great developments of the human mind. There is always a pleasure in thinking of that meeting between the young cleric from the north, Nikolas von Kues, with a whole world of study in front of him and the teacher who had already explored most of that world. Nikolas von Kues dabbles in humanistic law, unearths a series of comedies by Plautus unknown before, goes to Rome to see some of them acted and incidentally to gain a name as a religious diplomat, and then returns north to Brizen, in the very heart of Tyrol, to apply to the elaboration of philosophic and religious speculation the method taught by Vittorino.

This memory hangs round old Feltre almost like an incense ; even the frescoes on the walls represent Vittorino as often as they represent the *lares et penates* of the Feltrian nobleman. There is a wealth of fine detail in every palace in Feltre's single street, the iron work in front of a window, an occasional door-knocker, a massive wooden door with two rampant lions of a refreshing originality where the wood has cracked with age, a sudden statue in a corner and a lunette hidden behind a porcelain Madonna and Child. Through a stately gateway, stately even now in the menace of decay, we descend into the newer town that has grown round the older town above.

Feltre is also remembered in history through the work of Pietro Luzzo, called Morto da Feltre, whose frescoes are scattered over Cadore, and whose main function in life was to decorate the outer walls of many of those old palaces which are still the glory of the old town. The cathedral, although the façade has been modernized and ruined accordingly, has still one or two chapels dating from the 15th century, and there is at least one good painting by Bassano. Apart from the old town, the lower and newer town has its own special attraction, although at midday, when the flies are buzzing and the fruiterers display singularly unattractive peaches and plums sheltered beneath string nets of a distinctly dubious tint, it takes strong courage to concentrate on romance and still keep a good appetite.

Modern Feltre has many of the delightful characteristics of Rimini ; the female section of the population divides its time equally between the washing-stands beside the river, which trickles into the Piave three miles farther down, and the cafés. It is probably a mistake to talk of cafés in Feltre, since one-half of the main street is taken up by one single establishment, which goes on repeating itself from section to section, each in a different style of architecture, graded possibly to suit different social conventions. At its present rate of progress, this café should be able to wrest from the café of Padua the glory of being the largest coffee-retailing establishment in the north of Italy. At certain hours of the evening the population mixes, but during the rest of the day the ladies are in the ascendant and the consumption of fly-blown cakes is truly marvellous.

The hotels and restaurants generally believe in the principle of full public inspection of their cooking arrangements, so that one can order a chicken in the dining hall and then stroll round the corner to see the victim being treated in a kitchen, which would make a useful piece of decoration for a scene in " Faust." The Feltrians are convinced that the picturesque always adds flavour to the finest culinary creations, like a landscape to a pastoral, and they have certainly brought the combination to a very fine pitch of excellence. You can estimate with some accuracy from a casual view in the kitchen what parts of the chicken are going to be tender and what parts unnaturally fresh.

Our last recollection of Feltre was singularly fine ; from the square, where the statue of Vittorino da Feltre stands, there is a double flight of stairs leading up to a church, and past that church to a long grassy slope, where the whole mountainous landscape becomes unfolded in all its wealth of colour and form. We sat there beneath the ancient walls of the castle watching vaguely an active peasant woman raking the green grass into piles ready for transport to the picturesque old farm below. The good lady had taken her family with her, evidently as part of the day's routine, and the combination seemed to work quite well, even the baby on a shawl having a fitting sense of values.

There was a pale shimmer in the air as if the sun had been drowned in a haze of its own creation, and the pale blue of the distances seemed to be powdered with a fine golden-dust, the pine-clad slopes of the mountains dipping down from a mellow splendour of colour into a milky blue of shadow where every detail was lost. There were no lofty peaks in that landscape, only blunted masses of hill, pine-covered on the higher slopes, with level patches of vineyards beneath ; the blending of colour from the shadowy grey-green of the fields to the delicate purple outline of the higher shoulders was perfect, and gave to that whole landscape a unity of impression more striking than the barbaric luxuriance of the Dolomites farther north.

Feltre seems to lie on an undulating stretch of plain like a green basin surrounded by the hills, and the Piave moves along slowly in the distance to break through the last barrier of mountains lying between it and the immense plain of Lombardy.

There are bitter memories in Feltre of the struggle which took place there in that last group of hills during the most critical days of the war. Only twelve miles south of it rises Monte Grappa, and farther along to the west the Asiago plateau, two of the bloodiest theatres of the whole war. Feltre was always safe from the worst histories of the war, but there is even now some suggestion of that time, if not in the town itself, at least in the memory of those dwelling in it. The Piave has become the sacred river of Italy, and its banks a gathering-place of pilgrims intent on living again some of that excitement and of toying deliciously with the memory of histories now almost swept away.

Our road lay farther west from Feltre towards Fonzaso and then north to Primiero and San Martino di Castrozza, so that in a short time we left Cadore behind us and entered again the fairyland of the Dolomites. There is a rich harvest of beauty, however, to be reaped in Cadore in territory deeper within the heart of the mountains and the valley of the Piave. There is the wholly delightful lake of Alleghe, one of the most beautiful of the smaller Italian lakes, with its richly clad mountain slopes and the symmetrical shadow of the Col di Lana, perhaps the only regularly designed mountain in Cadore, above. It has an eminently *bourgeois* appearance, with no fantastic *crevasses* or sharply uplifted towers of rock, but in the early morning, when there is a pale greenish colour in the sky, and the smooth waters of the lake are taking their first hesitating gleams of sun, it has its own suggestive splendour. Agordo in the shadow of the Pale di San Lucano, is one of the jewel towns of the

Alps, even as inviting as Cortina d'Ampezzo. There is one magnificent valley, glorified by some of the fiercest fighting of the war, the Valle di Visdende surrounded by lofty mountains, sun-crested with bare summits full in the glare of the sun. It is here that the Piave takes its source, with its waters hidden often beneath a sea of mist which fills up the valley on an autumn morning from mountain wall to mountain wall. Few places in Europe have the romantic suggestion and the quiet magnificence of this lonely valley which gives birth to the sacred river of northern Italy.

CHAPTER XIV

A MOUNTAIN PARADISE—SAN MARTINO DI CASTROZZA

IN the early morning we set out from Feltre on our return journey to the Alps, after having viewed the ceremony of the mail arriving in the station. The method adopted in Feltre of sorting the postbag is simple in the extreme ; a number of canvas bags is impaled on the iron railings and the mail spread out on the road first of all. Then the letters are cast into the various bags, according to their destination, while interested spectators have a look occasionally at the addresses on them and discuss aloud the nature of the contents of some of the parcels. Quite a communal system of disposing of the world's news as it comes to Feltre!

The road from Feltre to San Martino has no great attraction at first, merely a singularly bumpy stretch passing through ancient villages, where picturesque corners appear occasionally with quaintly wooded balconies and deeply overhanging eaves, past brown hillsides, where the vines seem to thrive on dust, and occasionally beside an expanse of tumbling water. Fonzaso is the first village of importance and bears with it some bitter records of the war, when Belluno, Feltre and the surrounding district were occupied by the Austrians in their push southwards. The church is probably interesting, judging from the tower which is architecturally well proportioned, but we lacked energy sufficient to examine it more closely. Beyond Fonzaso the road swerves to the right, and we climbed up by slow gradients the valley of the Cismon, one of the most magnificent stretches of mountain scenery in the whole Alps, fully as good as the entrance to the Dolomites from Bolzano. The road runs sheer beneath the mountain wall for practically the whole distance with the river foaming to the right for the first stages of the journey and afterwards to the left. The mountains are more regular in shape than the Dolomites themselves, but the Monte Avena at Sovramonte breaks into a sheer cliff, a brilliant grey-pink in the sunshine above the road, and the sensation of looking up at this bare wall, unbroken in colour by a single trace of vegetation, is that of a dangerous magnificence. The valley broadens out into narrow stretches of pasture with an occasional mill or farm, without apparently any justification for its existence, and the procession of heavy wagons loaded with timber and drawn by mules of a particularly stupid type seems to be endless. The timber wagoners of this district prefer to load at right angles to the direction of travel, so that a very small load may occupy a considerable area, especially when it comes to the question of sharing a few feet of road surface. We had one or two breathless escapes from those obstructions along the narrow roads. We were always unfortunate in coming unexpectedly on such a procession after rounding a particularly dangerous curve. These little crises added to the interest of the journey and gave a fascination to the contemplation of the landscape. We could appreciate the beauty of swelling folds of hill, filled with rich colour in the early morning sunshine, the sudden glimpses into blue distances, the flash and glitter of the water below as it emerged from shadow for a moment before dipping down into deeper shadow, when we had a vague feeling lurking at the back of our minds that the next turn in the roadway might precipitate us into the river below.

At Ponte San Silvestro, beyond the frowning mass of the Monte Pavione which thrusts up a stern shoulder of rock against the sky in an effort to imitate the fantastic savagery of Latemar, the Cismon has been dammed up so that the whole valley forms a lake—of an incredible blue shot through with the purest emerald green spread evenly, without a single ripple, over the sandy river bed from grey wall to grey wall, a perfect fusion of silvery reflection and jewel-tinted water. That single stretch of valley has a unique beauty through this alone ; there is no wind to ruffle the surface and the river has died down to a slow progression, merely a vague ripple here and there, and the transparent water seems to hold in its depth every particle of blue and emerald the sky above can give—a glory of pure colour.

Beyond the bridge we moved out from the narrow confines of the valley, the walls of rock smoothed down into rolling slopes, and the traces of cultivation, orchards, vineyards, maize-fields and even cabbage patches became more frequent. The rugged mountain splendour is blended here with something more pastoral and more idyllic, and at Primiero we enter into one of those comfortable Alpine villages, with a quaint Gothic spire, where the mountain landscape acts apparently as a decorative background. There is nothing remarkably interesting in Primiero beyond a few picturesquely timbered houses carried out in the true artistic tradition, and its main claim to attention lies in its position at

R

the opening of the Primiero Valley, one of the wonderful valleys of the Alps.

San Martino di Castozza was entirely destroyed during the war ; it shared with Cortina d'Ampezzo the honour of being among the first Austrian positions to be occupied by the Italians in their first drive forward into the Alps, and of all that village of hotels, once frequented by the vapid aristocracy of Vienna and Milan, only a mass of ruins, with a single church tower, remained when the last echoes of warfare had died away in the recesses of the hills.

After climbing continuously along the side of the valley, the sun came full upon us and an unbroken succession of mountainous landscapes presented itself to us, a warm magnificence of colour from the frail green of the pastures beside the river to the warm brown of the bushes higher up, and finally to the clear purple of the mountain edges, where the blue of the sky folded over.

There is a satisfactory solidity about the Alps along the valley of the Cismon ; they rise in solid masses, impressive through sheer bulk after the first low hills beyond Primiero are passed ; Sass Maor juts up in bare majesty above a garland of pine forests, many-scarred, with sudden clefts of brilliant colour and blinding high lights where the sun rests on the last traces of the glacier.

All along the route it rose up in a framework of pines, black foliaged against an airy purple, almost filmy through contrast. For miles, we passed through deep pine forests without a single movement in them except when a slight wind passed over in a thin wave of sound. Occasionally we came on groups of peasants from the upper slopes with their mules loaded with panniers of fruit and vegetables, and came finally into sight of that magnificent block of mountains ranging from the Pala di San Martino to the Rosetta and the Cimone della Pala.

They may be less fantastic than the Dolomites proper, but they have deeper romantic suggestion. The three peaks of the Sass Maor seen through the century-old pines bordering the road give an extraordinary impression of a mediæval knight riding on horseback into battle. The sensation of uncanny life in that figure above the snows bathed in the brilliant sun becomes more and more intense as the light deepens until the rose-coloured peaks, throned above the dark masses of rock and forest, appear a single worthy monument to all endeavour—the consummation of human history.

That, I think, is the one glory of the mountains of San Martino ; they come closer to the embodiment of an eternal majesty than any other range of Alps ; they fall naturally into groups of statuary, wonderfully formed and wonderfully aglow with colour ; there is a harmony in them deeper than the atmosphere could give, it is the harmony of life raised to something nobler and more enduring. The passage through the pine woods, with their deep shadows contrasting vividly with the snow-fields above, will always remain in the memory through this sensation of immense forces quiescent only for a moment before launching into fierce activity.

San Martino has been rebuilt with a more splendid collection of hotels than even in the palmy days before the war, and it is painfully raw at present ; everything smells of new paint and new varnish, but the hotels are undoubtedly among the most attractive in northern Italy, not only through the perfect spotlessness of the rooms, but also through the high standard of the welcome they give. They have not yet reached the complacent tyranny of a popular mountain spa. We found a quiet little inn on the outskirts of the town, the Albergo Colfosco, where many of the traditions of the old Italian inn have been preserved intact—exquisite courtesy, a true sense of human comforts and a sound cuisine. A week's treatment in that inn would have been sufficient to re-establish even a professional invalid. The host believed in the maxim of satiety being a first principle in good form. There was an interesting assortment of visitors, two world-weary birds of passage from Venice, with the Venetian characteristics suitably emphasized. One of them, with a sallow complexion and faded brown eyes, decided that the clear mountain air afforded sufficient pabulum for his delicate nature ; after much anxious deliberation with the host, he finally settled at lunch-time on an unripe peach and two flaccid grapes. We, of course, had no scruples in eating up everything at sight. The other gentleman, clad in full mountain garb, narrated with gusto his experiences in climbing to the Lago di Colbricon, a lonely sheet of water lying bare to the sky on the wild hillside. We were inclined to scoff at his remarkable adventures in climbing up the 4,000 feet between San Martino and the lake, but when we faced the ascent ourselves, an almost perpendicular track marked only by red streaks of paint on a bush or tree every 50 yards or so, through an impenetrable pine forest, we rapidly revised ideas. Our hero preened himself like a well-fed turkey-cock in the admiration of his lantern-jawed companion. The other members of the *equipage* were more interesting, four families of brilliantly clad children, vivid greens and startling reds inextricably mixed, with an inexhaustible fund of language. They formed a rich haggis of talk, and changed their formation *ad infinitum* ; one table might hold three of one family and three of the other in the morning, then change over to six different diners at night from the other two families. They were dominated by three substantial matrons, very solidly attached to *terra firma* with a sound notion of command and the dignity due to age. We spent delightful evenings watching those families entangling and disentangling themselves in the dance room, while an old lady with a multitude of rings on her fingers extracted a thin rivulet of sound from a piano in the corner. In the shadow of the mountains such an interlude of simple gaiety was delightful indeed.

San Martino lies in a cup-shaped hollow of the mountains with green meadows lying smoothly like a rich carpet over the curves and folds between the pine woods. A continual sound of water falling veiled by the pine foliage and borne to us over an immeasurable distance ! There is an air of finish about the landscape ; the colour contrasts are perfectly executed, the dark green of the forests, the emerald of the meadows, the faint blue haze over the lower slopes of the mountains and the startling rose-grey of the bare mountain walls themselves, fluted and pillared to give to every single colour tone a deeper suggestive value ! On the valley opening towards Primiero there is no edge to the opulence of the sky, and everything moving has almost a symbolical beauty, a single character on a stage of surpassing and lonely magnificence. The sunset creeps slowly up the valley, and rests on the Rosetta in a splendour of vivid rose-gold, deepening to startling violet shadows in the clefts and along the ridges turned away from the sunlight. The mountain wall has few breaks in its surface, with the result that the colour rests on it as on a screen, incredibly vivid between the dark blue of the sky and the sombre green of the forests and meadows below.

We went along the meadows parallel to the Rosetta, almost like figures in a pantomime, and at the edge where the sky seemed to close up the whole landscape we could look down on the conflagration below, the high battlements of the Vette di Feltre, the only part of that blue magnificence with a sharp edge and a fine sweep of contour. That is the glory of San Martino at sunset— a glory of colours so pure as almost to appear crude, the gold of the mountain, the sombre green of the meadows and the intense blue of the valley beyond Primiero.

In the morning we set out on a further stage of our journey through the Passo di Rolle to Predazzo and the Etschland. It was clear autumn weather, with an invigorating freshness in the air ; the lower mountain slopes had a brown tint, and the hollows were no longer a greenish colour, but a faint milky blue as if the sun-light could not pass into them. The road to the Passo di Rolle wound alternately through pine woods and into open spaces where the valley of the Cismon was unfolded in every single detail and in full sweep of colour till the last recesses of the Feltrian range were revealed. There was a Turneresque quality in the whole of that landscape dominated by the Cimone della Pala, a single sharp peak rising haughtily above the medley of other peaks, which seemed to fall into a natural symmetry the higher up we climbed towards the top of the pass. There was an exquisite gradation of mountain forms with only faint differences in colour, film by film, until the foreground met the last range of hills and completed the picture. The bluntness and the ruggedness of the

Monte Marmolata gave way here to a cultured smooth-
ness, the rich shadow of the nearer slopes contrasting
suavely with the white gleam on the distant slopes
where the sunlight rested on a glacier. No sudden
display of strongly contrasting colour—only a harmony
in silvery greys with a warmer flush on the highest
pinnacles of the Cimone.

Beyond the pass, dominated by a friendly Austrian
inn, where we took breakfast, we entered into a totally
new country, with all the characteristics of a Highland
landscape, heather slopes, lonely hamlets and rocky
columns all carefully staged to give the requisite effect.
It was bitterly cold on the top of the pass, but the
heat grew as we descended along the steeply winding
track ; the highly finished scenery of San Martino gave
way here to a more starved landscape with a greater
profusion of flowers in the valleys. We had a feeling
of loneliness more acute here than in any other part
of the Dolomites ; the hills were less impressive in actual
form, but they had a greater strength of suggestion,
simply through the feeling they gave of being secluded
in a vast world of their own.

Predazzo, the first stage of our journey from San
Martino to the Adige, is only an ordinary Austrian
hill town lying under the shadow of the Malgola ; it once
formed a centre of pilgrimage for the scientifically
minded Austrian student intent on diluting his holidays
with a little geological exploration. It stands at the
junction of two valleys, the Fleimser Valley, which
strikes up through the heart of the Dolomites and
becomes exceedingly beautiful beyond Moena, where
it changes its title to the Fassa Valley, and the Travig-
nolo Valley, along which we came from the Passo di
Rolle. The Fleimser Valley strikes down through

Cavalese, through a new and more sedate landscape punctuated by stretches of warm meadow land, quiet hamlets with Italian churches placed with unerring taste right in the heart of the picture, and, branching off to the left, goes down to the valley of the Adige. Predazzo has fallen on evil days owing to the disappearance of the picturesque Austrian rambler with his usual accompaniments; the only good hotel in the town has consigned the portraits of Franz Joseph and his consort to the rubbish heap, and established with full ceremony the portraits of the King and Queen of Italy in the dining-room. In the time of fascism he would probably find it expedient to make room for Mussolini, and then the trio would be complete. In the meantime his custom languishes, and no multiplication of symbols will attract diners to his table when they have ceased to come to his district. Predazzo is full, however, of picturesque corners in common with practically every hill town—groups of washerwomen busy in dusky courtyards round an ancient well with quaint decoration, and an occasional marvellously timbered house. We spent an interesting afternoon climbing up the hillside towards the mountain with the Bad Throat, Malgola, through a beautiful world of pines, and lying on the top we could gaze straight down to the roofs beneath as if the town were emerging from the heart of the mountain. There was a fine haze in the Fleimser Valley, so that every colour in the distance became suffused with a milky purple, flashing into gold at odd moments.

The station at Predazzo is a remarkable structure, not so much for architectural detail, since it is only a miserable little hut, but for the extraordinary capacity it has of producing officials without end. When we boarded our train there was only the station-master in sight, but every time we looked out a few more officials would appear apparently from the ground until we had a remarkably fine collection of twelve, captained by the station-master, in full war-paint. With six passengers and twelve officials the train set out for Cavalese and Ora ; we probably required some steadying influence on the train itself, for it bumped in an alarming fashion over its narrow gauge rails, and the officials were certainly a very solid lot. At every station the band filed out on to the platform, shook hands effusively with the station-master, the station-master's wife and all the local notabilities who happened to be in the neighbourhood. From the beginning to the end of the journey it was one long hand-shaking ceremony, and the band certainly enjoyed it. They also enjoyed examining our tickets after much mysterious discussion, until we arrived in Ora with tattered pieces of paper which had lost all claim to respectability.

Cavalese is a beautiful tree-sheltered town with cool avenues and wide green spaces, and the view towards Cornazzi and the Monte Agnello on the north and the unbroken series of peaks stretching from the Passo di Rolle to the Adige in the south is very splendid ; the people of Cavalese have evidently a nice taste in churches, judging by the care with which they have crowned every picturesque mound and hillock down the Fleimser Valley with simple *campanile*, wholly satisfactory in the contrast of pure straight lines against the dim curves of the mountains behind.

Beyond Cavalese we left the Fleimser Valley and entered into one of the most attractive regions of the Alps, attractive, not so much through sheer mountain beauty, as through contortions of the railway itself when it leaves the valley at San Lugano and climbs, curve by curve, towards Fontane Fredde, which is at a height of about 4,000 feet. This railway from Fontane Fredde onwards represents one of the most remarkable engineering feats of the war; the Austrian army, in its operations against the Italians north of Asiago, required a strategic railway to bring the supplies sent down the valley of the Adige up to the front line. To realize this, they simply built a narrow gauge railway up the mountain-side from Ora, without regard to gradient, and the result is interesting. There are few railways in Europe which go through the same number of contortions within so short a distance, and the descent from Fontane Fredde is exciting through the succession of hair-pin bends in which the railway line indulges. The train goes on at a snail's pace, but we could not wish it faster, for there is a rich feast of beauty disclosed at every turn, finer than anything we could ever have imagined in the Alps, the whole pageant of history lying unfolded beneath us in the valley of the Adige in a multitude of splendid vignettes brought into relief by the curves of the track.

The Austrians had a fine sense of colour values when they built this railway up the mountain-side, for every swerve in the track brings to light strange *aperçus*, each with its own series of colours, light and shadow chasing each other through the vineyards and over the bare slopes above, until the blue peaks at the edge of the horizon gleam through a warm film of light. The valley leading down from Fontane Fredde to Ora has been called the Valley of Hell, but the Teutonic mind has evidently a different conception of Hell from the Latin or even the Anglo-Saxon. There are innumerable valleys of Hell scattered through Tyrol and the Bavarian uplands, and they only seem to prove the fact that his Satanic majesty had a good eye for landscape gardening ; they have each a distinctive beauty, impressive, majestic, but scarcely as menacing as their title would suggest. Perhaps those titles are a relic of the Gothic imagination which could convert a harmless pine grove into an abode of spirits, none of them too respectable in their habits, and all of them with a strong criminal tendency.

The valley leading down to Ora is vivid with the full joy of life ; orchard stretches beneath orchard, and tree slope beneath tree slope, breaking into sudden hollows of misty colour until, at the valley foot, the radiance spreads out like the waves of the sea, and everything becomes etherealized in that fine flooding colour—a dream of beauty.

It was late afternoon when we went down the last stages of the journey, with the cliff walls rising sheer to the left of us, and the lower mountain slopes dotted with farms and distant hamlets beneath us. It was then that the real consummation of beauty was achieved, for the light deepened and softened down into an exquisite purple, shot through with shadowy gold, especially on the higher crests of the mountains beyond the valley of the Adige ; the whole fantastic mass of the Mittelberg lay beyond the dim waters of the Adige almost like some prehistoric monster rising from the flood. In the centre of its back a mysterious mediæval castle appeared, and this castle seemed to strike the note for the whole landscape ; it gave harmony to that magnificence of form and colour, a romantic suggestion to that splendour ; the Middle Ages lived again in those shadowy heights, bordered by the Adige on the one side and the placid Caldaro Lake on the other ; they had something deeper and more eternal in them than even the defiant strength of centuries, something more human and more intimate.

The high wall of the Mendola mountains rising sheer behind this foreground of rich colour closed out the sky, and in turn gave a fantastic note to the mountain pageant, where the Gantkofel dipped down abruptly and uncompromisingly to Bolzano. As the night fell, the mediæval castles, especially the castle on the Mittelberg and the fine Castell Fader on the last slopes of the Kalditsch, crept into the mystery from which in daylight they emerged and the illusion became complete ; the dark purple landscape with a single bar of rose across the higher battlements of the Mendola and the pale green sky beyond. Then the music of the night began, an endless scream of crickets, with the occasional hum of a beetle and the vicious whirr of a mosquito, and we crept along the dusty road to Ora, a typical Austrian village with the usual quaint picturesqueness of such. We met brown-faced peasants returning from the fields, sitting in bunches on flat carts or trudging wearily behind a load of pumpkins drawn by a pair of massive oxen. At Ora, relying with too great optimism on the instructions of Baedeker, we expected to find a restaurant with a good table, but discovered instead that its staple product was a particularly venomous-looking beer accompanied by a dinner of sorts.

The railway up the Valley of Hell was built by the Austrians for purely utilitarian purposes, but it is doubtful whether any railway in Europe can present such a magnificence of landscape with its twenty miles as the Valley of Hell railway ; it is superior to the Mendola railway in this respect, it deserves a pilgrimage for itself alone. We tasted at Pausa luscious peaches presented to us by one of the country girls, and the combination of magnificent scenery and equally magnificent peaches was satisfactory in the extreme. At nightfall we boarded the usual crowded train and drifted off to Trento, leaving the Dolomites in their splendour behind us, but bearing with us in their place a rich harvest of memories.

CHAPTER XV

TRENTO

A DESCRIPTION of the Italian Tyrol and the Trentino would be incomplete without reference to Trento, which acts almost as a meeting-place for all theories regarding Italian domination.

There is a deep fascination for the lover of Italian art and sculpture in tracing out the border line between the northern and southern genius as it comes to expression in the cities of the new Italian province, Venezia Tridentina ; the difference is fundamental, undoubtedly, but there are grades even in the transition which have a finer appeal than the more assertive achievement. The architecture of Verona, with its quiet old Romanesque churches, where some breath from the north has entered into the exquisite detail of the portals and strengthened the realism of the frescoes on the walls of the cathedral, differs from the architecture of Bologna in this suggestion of a northern spirit. Yet when we compare the lions of the church of S. Anastasia with the lions of the cathedral in Trento, the sharper line and more individual treatment of detail betray at once the proximity of the Gothic mind. In Bolzano and Merano, on the other hand, the Italian influence lingers in the colonnades and churches, even when we would expect all traces of the southern genius to have been swept away. This battle of civilization, tendencies

THE CATHEDRAL OF TRENTO

in life and thought, Imperial and Papal ambitions,
constitutes at once the splendour of Italian Tyrol and
its tragedy. One tradition fights against the other.
The Imperial force struggles against the Papal, the war
of the Investitures finds a parallel in the war of
1915 fought in the name of liberty; the religious
element yields to the military and strategic, but the
feeling of strife remains. This feeling colours the landscape before the eyes, and gives a new significance to
the ruins of castles perched on the hillsides. The
northern spirit filters through even in poetry as
the statues of Oliver and Duranda on the portal of the
Duomo of Verona prove, where the French epic, the
Chanson de Roland, appears to have had an ancestor
of quite respectable antiquity south of the Alps, while
the southern spirit lives in the quaint majolica tiles laid
on the roof of the church of Bolzano, tiles such as we
see in Naples and Sicily. Now, of course, there is
apparent homogeneity at last—a union, however, only
consummated in the creation of an Italian dictator
vested with the same authority as previous Austrian
dictators in the Lower Trentino. The fundamentals
remain unchanged with the change of government, the
differences of centuries are unaffected by territorial
changes; the mountains have the same radiant beauty
and the sky the same glory. Only the forests are
disappearing from the slopes of the Val Sugana, and
the landscape grows paler in colour towards Rovereto.

*   *   *   *   *

We set out from Verona on a day of rich sunshine
with the Adige swishing gently for once beneath the
hotel windows, and the hills a faint greenish-purple
deepening into intense blue in the shadows hiding the

vineyards and obscuring the valleys so that the old town appeared a frail golden-pink mass against a shimmering silk background. It is unnecessary to describe the emotions caused in us by the old Romanesque churches or the palaces of the Scaligers, old patrons of Dante. One incident is worth narrating, however, as suggestive of the hold Italy can have on the student of its past. We had been visiting the tranquil old church, San Zeno, on a warm afternoon when the sun lay in bands of flame on the square, and even the swallows swept past with a touch of listlessness. After absorbing the simple loveliness of its interior, we strolled outside to appreciate at leisure the 9th-century bas-reliefs on the portal and the bronze door. At that moment, a young American, down at heel but immensely enthusiastic, arrived with a camera and tripod, dug out two ladders from the church, leaned one against the lintel with its wooden Indulgenzia Plenaria, and the other against the round of the last pillar forming the portal. Then he suspended the tripod between the ladders with an immense length of string and balanced the camera precariously on it. His intention was to photograph a small scene on the door representing the sacrifice of Isaac with a delicious figure of Abraham, half sorrowful, half pious and wholly comical. Thus he hung, perilously balanced between the two ladders, expecting the camera to crash every moment to the ground. First of all, one ladder slipped six inches and threw the camera out of focus, then the door closed a little and came from sunshine into shadow, and finally we had to wrap up the plates, fix them in the quaking camera, regulate the exposure and always retain the focus. It was rather fine to see that figure blackly silhouetted against the glaring sky intent on reproduction of a bronze sculpture moulded at the beginning of art when the freshness and spontaneity of inspiration gave uncanny life even to the crudest symbolism. Then we photographed a Chaucerian pilgrim, perched on an amazing ass with a singularly patient, philosophical countenance, the ancestor undoubtedly of the ass apostrophized by Sterne.

After this arduous task, we proceeded to the enthusiast's hotel in the picturesque Piazza dell' Erbe and examined some very beautiful prints—the tombs of the Scaligers, with every fine detail complete even to the aged texture of the stone and some exquisite floral Renaissance decorations. He had spent the winter and spring photographing in detail the Parthenon in Greece, and was now intent on the finer and more primitive efforts of early Italian sculpture. It is difficult to imagine a richer holiday than this when the beauty of the past could be absorbed in exquisite incidents, exquisite details, cloying to the palate in combination but wonderfully satisfying at single moments, in a single flash of vision. The fascination lies surely in the rich suggestion even of the simplest decoration, not so much at the thought of something accomplished as at the thought of the spirit behind that lovely harmony of line and shadow. The beauty we admire in Italian art is a beauty of detail rather than of mass, of the delicate touch rather than of the broad stroke.

Some perception of this fact illuminates appreciation of the Alps themselves. A series of pictures, complete in every fine detail, remains focused in memory without any feeling of inadequacy before an immense expression of natural power as we experience it in gloomier countries where the atmosphere gives to low hills a dark majesty transcending the sun-lit splendour of higher mountains.

S

From Verona to Rovereto and Bolzano an infinite number of such pictures passed before the eyes—lofty hills bathed in the noonday shimmer with grey-green slopes and rosy clefts where no vegetation could grow, high walls rising sheer above the dusky green Adige, exquisite cameos of blue mountains visible beyond dusky valleys veiled in an intensity of light that gave a jewel-like lustre to the bare rock where colour itself seemed to be tossed from warm surface to warm surface. Old castles, especially at Rovereto and Trento, were seen perched dizzily on solitary heights with a goat's track sketched on the scraggy surface of the rock—white hamlets nestling almost in the sky, and, beside the river, a glory of olives and vineyards heavy with purple grapes, yellow fields of grain and orchards golden with fruit.

Rovereto, scattered over a broad hillside already in process of disfigurement through quarries and limestone works, has lost most of the authority it possessed in the 18th century when it vied with Venice and Verona in the publication of weighty volumes by church dignitaries on local antiquities and the interpretation of historical treatises. The historical school which originated in Scipione Maffei found in Rovereto an eager band of scholars intent on opening up the past history of the region and on encouraging, incidentally, the traditions of good printing upheld by Venice. Some of the finest achievements of the 18th century in Italy came from the printing presses of the provincial capital. It is possible still, reading through some of the volumes in the library, to gain a clear idea of the fashionable centre where the *litterati* and beaux of Venice took refuge in the hot summer months and used the old Renaissance palaces as centres for excursions north to

Trento and west to Lake Garda. The present town can show few traces of that time, the only memorial left being the Castello situated high up to the south where a view can be gained of the last spurs of the Alps grading down to the shores of Garda and the broadening valley of the Adige.

The change from Rovereto to Trento is more striking than the change in natural position would lead us to believe. The mountains huddling round the back of the town and projecting almost over the Adige are symbolical of the fierce independence of the Archbishopric which defied successfully throughout the Middle Ages and Renaissance the efforts of pope and emperor to annex it. Everything combines to form a unity, mountain as well as valley, complete in itself and self-sufficient. This independence, upheld by Archbishop Clesio and his successor Madruzzo, even through the long vascillations and quarrels of the Council of Trent, and triumphantly affirmed against Frederick II and Charles V, may have preserved the memorials of the past from the disaster which overtook Brescia. The cathedral, a creation of the 12th century, remains in its full glory of delicate arcades and rose-windows, the Rohr and Geremia palaces still preserve the frescoes painted on their outer walls in the 16th century by Venetian artists, while the Castel del Buon Consiglio looks down on the squares and towers as if the centuries had passed over it untouched. There dwells round the figure of Dante silhouetted against the hills a suggestion of reverence mingled with a fierce independence equalled only by the glory of the mountains. Even as far as San Michele, where the high precipices of Mezolombardo and the glowing peaks of the Brenta Alps beyond the Val di Non form a picture of rare beauty, the spirit of independence, not Italian but Trentian alone, gives to the whole district a unity of sentiment stronger even than in Southern Tyrol.

At this moment of time all the disputes and discussions regarding the Italian nature of the Trentino have been resolved into nothing through the large-handed fashion in which Italy, redeeming its own *terra irredenta*, has created a new *terra irredenta* for the German-speaking races of Tyrol. It is impossible to distinguish absolutely between the Italian and the Teutonic elements in a race which has been recognized as extraordinarily complex, even from the earliest times. The fact that the Brenner constituted one of the great high roads linking up the cold misty north with the sun-drenched plains of Lombardy led, even in the early Roman times, to the steady infusion of new blood into the old. The original population may have been predominantly Gothic and even Slav in the east, but the civilizing hand of Rome introduced a more southern influence, and this infusion has been marked by irregular patches of Teutonic culture surrounding or surrounded by patches almost purely Latin in nature. There are traces of Latin culture in Bolzano and Merano, while further west, at Schluderns and Mals, all traces of Latinity disappear. Again, beyond Welschnöfen the Latin characteristics appear and become stronger and stronger as we move towards Cortina. From Cortina southwards the mixture is fairly complete until below San Michele the Italian element comes forward in full force and reaches a triumphant consummation at Trento.

Trento formed the last great gathering place of the Italian civilization in its movement of expansion northwards, and it is impossible to forget that Trento represented even as much as Brescia or Verona, one of the great creations of the Italian genius. There is only one other town which can be compared directly with Trento—Bergamo ; the same wealth of Renaissance palaces, the same fondness for narrow picturesque streets, where the sun is only able to trace a fantastic golden frieze beneath the heavy cornices, the same quaint squares haunted by picturesque local types of humanity, earnestly engaged on doing nothing. But Bergamo has nothing so splendid to offer as the cathedral at Trento, and its towers have not the satisfactory romance and suggestive beauty of the Castello or the Torre Vanga. From the square in front of the cathedral with its magnificent fountain, Neptune lording it over a harem of sea nymphs, the centre of Trentian life and culture becomes unfolded, almost as vividly as in the 16th century. In front, the cathedral raises its Romanesque tower and its plain expanse of wall opening at the top into beautifully proportioned arcades ; on the left the street of palaces with still their frescoes intact. Every narrow street debouching on the cathedral square has its own wealth of Renaissance palaces with magnificent doorways and vaguely frescoed walls.

Trento has a history more varied and more picturesque than this survey could possibly give, and it may be possible for us to return at some future date to a more detailed appreciation and a more thorough evaluation of Trento in the history of the human spirit. A recent publication by Andrea Galante : *Trento ed il Concilio Ecumenico Tridentino* : does attempt to carry out such a work, and it should be read for the swift accuracy of touch and the clear grasp of essentials it illustrates.

History moves and pulsates through the ages, even through us, and the reality of such a movement comes very vividly to the senses when we enter the cathedral through the simple arched doorway and stand in the Gothic interior illuminated by one magnificent rose-window in a dim luxuriance of colours grading richly into the pale light cast from the deep side windows. In the cathedral the clear splendour of the south disappears and the mysterious north comes to take its place ; the cathedral of Bamberg has a closer affinity to this temple placed at the confines of the Latin culture than even the cathedral of Verona ; civilization and ideals merge and become united in a gracious moment of time, form one single instant of glory in the perception of the wanderer ere he steps into the sunlight and passes on.

There is a golden quality in the light that plays round the cathedral ; the mellow-toned walls glow and gleam with a full warmth ; the lions by the doorway, blurred and worn by the passage of centuries, live again dimly and even exquisitely, and the fantastic pillars knotted in the centre and placed on two quiant bowed figures lose their strangeness, blending into a harmony beyond architectural proportions. The abside with one perfect window guarded by griffons rises in a unique splendour beside the mass of building placed there in later centuries, and serves to strengthen the whole impression of defiance throughout the centuries which the cathedral gives. The cathedral must rank with San Zeno in Verona, and Santa Maria Maggiore in Bergamo, as one of the finest creations of the Romanesque period in architecture.

The interior has a faint suggestion of a mediæval castle through the stairs rising from each side nave to a mysterious upper chamber or gallery hidden from the eye, a suggestion which grades into the memory of the Palazzo Pretorio built into the abside, and the dimly frescoed walls with their procession of bishops' tombs do little to modify it. The tomb of Robert Sanseverino records the famous battle of Calliano fought in August 1148 when Sanseverino, the general commanding the Venetian forces, was killed. The Trentino witnessed some of the deadliest fighting in that struggle between the Venetian republic and the combined forces of France, and the Papacy and the Bishopric shared in those wars which covered the end of the 15th and beginning of the 16th century.

The Bishopric covered originally the whole territory lying between Rovereto and Bolzano, including the northern shores of Lake Garda, the Giudicarie, the Ledro and Vestino Valleys and the Valsugana, but, after the formation of the League of Cambrai by the Pope Giulio II against Venice in the early years of the 16th century, the Counts of Arco took Torbole and Nago with the Castle of Penede, Riva went over to the Bishopric while Rovereto passed in 1509 to the Empire. When Bernardo Clesio became bishop in 1514, the Giudicarie, the valleys of Ledro and Vestino had followed the example of Rovereto and the Lagarina Valley ; Pergine and the Valsugana were subject to the Counts of Tyrol, the Bishopric and Tyrol governed in conjunction the Noce Valleys. In 1531 Clesio surrendered Bolzano and surrounding territory to the Counts of Tyrol, receiving in return Borgo and Pergine in the Valsugana.

The frontiers thus delimited remained unchanged until the Napoleonic era when the Bishopric became secularized. It is important to make this delimitation quite clear since it has a bearing on the Italian claim to the Trentino. The Trentino, if we understand by this term the territory included in the Bishopric of Trento, was, at the time of Clesio, a narrow finger of country about twenty-five miles broad, stretching between Riva and Calliano on the south and Ora and Cavalese on the north, with the Adige flowing through the centre—the country surrounding it being governed by the Counts of Tyrol. Even inside the Trento the official languages were Italian and German. Acting on this evidence the Italian claim to the Trentino was smaller even than Austria was prepared to allow and certainly only a small fraction of the total now occupied. Acting on ethnological evidence, the Italian claim would cover the area south of the line, Stelvio–Madonna di Campiglio–Ora–Cavalese–Pieve–Cortina–Auronzo, with a band of territory within this area where the population would have some Italian characteristics and some Teuton characteristics. North of this line, the area of Latin penetration ended. In other words, the traveller should remember that slightly less than one half of the new provinces are ethnologically and only a small fraction historically Italian. Trento is more closely allied to Verona than to Bolzano and Bolzano to Innsbrück and Munich than Trento.

With Clesio, who seems to have had the geniality and the philosophic acuity of Bishop Blougram, Trento reached its highest level as an artistic and cultural centre ; Clesio aspired to make of it the Florence of the Alps, and in the Castel del Buon Consiglio raised a second Pitti Palace which should be his great memorial as a northern Mæcenas. As an illustration of Clesio's attitude to art, religion and life, one passage from Browning's poem may be quoted :

> There's power in me, and will to dominate
> Which I must exercise, they hurt me else :
> In many ways I need mankind's respect,
> Obedience, and the love that's born of fear.
> While at the same time, there's a taste I have,
> A toy of soul, a titillating thing,
> Refuses to digest these dainties crude.

There is something of that deeper seated force of character in the exquisite tablet let into the wall of Santa Maria Maggiore at Trento, the church raised by him as an architectural jewel of the Renaissance—two angels, solidly built, holding up the lions and the griffon of the archbishopric and, above, the empty mitre :

BERNARDO CLESIO
PRAESULE AC PRINCIPE
TRIDENTINO AUCTORE
M.D. XX.

Utter simplicity, but in itself the perfection of art ! Clesio was the first Tridentinian bishop after a long series of bishops covering almost three centuries, and his advent formed the occasion of a display equal in magnificence to the best efforts of the Sforza or the Medici, the main theme in the decoration being the marriage of the Empire and the Church.

Clesio's activities soon made themselves felt in Trento ; the Castel del Buon Consiglio which had been burned to the ground on the very day that Ferdinand, who united in his coronation the kingdom of Hungary and Bohemia, was anointed by Clesio king of the Romans, was begun anew and, in the work of rebuilding, some of the most famous artists of the time collaborated. Giulio Romano, Palma Vecchio, Palma il Giovane, Dosso Dossi, Brusasorci, Ricciarelli da Volterra, Girolamo da Trevigi, Paolo Farinato and Vincenzo Vincenzini contributed to the embellishment of the great halls, galleries and courtyards we admire now.

Other monuments testify to the munificence of Clesio—Santa Maria Maggiore, built by Antonio Medalia in the true tradition of the Como architects, who had worked in the 13th century at Trento Cathedral. In this church, Vincenzo Vicentino adds, in his choir gallery, a jewel of sculpture to the many executed in other parts of Italy by Donatello, Pisano, Roselli and Amadeo. The gallery rises up on two supports carved with bold foliage relief and forms an exquisitely sculptured " Adoration of the Kings," flanked by symbolical figures representing " Tiburtina " and " Samia." Above this sculpture the cornice projects which acts as a frame to the design. In the shadows below, a figure dreams, leaning on a pillar of scroll-work set in a square of carving fine as lace—in all, a memorable achievement !

Many of the frescoed palaces we now admire in the Cathedral Square and in the Via Bellengani, especially the Podetti or Geremia Palace, and the Tabarelli Palace, were built in the time of Clesio, and it is only necessary to wander along the narrow streets in the vicinity of the cathedral to appreciate the splendour which must have distinguished the capital at that time. Some of the portals with their graceful balconies crowned by beautifully sculptured *putti* and supported by crouched figures in vivid postures—every shadow, every limb, every piece of floral decoration carried out with economy of line and modelling—are as fine as anything Bergamo, Verona or Vicenza can present, while the frescoed walls above, drenched in mellow sunlight, glow and tremble in vague harmonies of colour. Trento lives through this picturesque combination of rich sculpture and fresco.

Occasionally we come in a quiet corner on a vivid piece of sculpture, unexpected but delicious through this alone ; the little " Goose Girl " in the fruit market near the cathedral is an exquisite creation, a fine comparison to the " Goose Boy " in Nuremburg—an Italian version of a Teutonic theme—while the northern fantasy comes to expression in the strange figure of Clesio's jester blowing into bagpipes of a Highland type. The worn stone figure bears beneath the satirical inscription :

> Quae modo festivo sonuere palacia risu
> Lugent funestae quid referunt lachrymae
> Paulus obit periere sales periere lepores
> Cum quo prodierant deperiere ioci.[1]
>
> M.D.XXXV.

Clesio's successor, Cristoforo Madruzzo, became Bishop in 1539, and was responsible for the arrangements made for holding the Council of Trent which lasted from 1545 to 1563, eighteen difficult years when the diplomacy and tact of the Bishop were strained to breaking point, and the bishopric itself brought almost to disaster in the effort to maintain the huge army of attendants and warriors the church magnates and princes brought with them. The Council met ostensibly to work out a plan of counter reform which would neutralize the work of Luther, Zwingli, Calvin and other rebels against the dogma of the Church, and there is no doubt that its labours were fruitful in holding those movements of reform in check without overcoming them. The reformation came almost as a logical sequence to the Renaissance, and the Council could scarcely hope to set

---

[1] The palaces that once resounded with laughter, are now given over to sorrowful tears. Paul died. All jokes and merry jest died, died with him who gave them birth.

back the whole tendency of the time ; the Reformation forced organization on the Church and the Council was the result.

Trento, from being a city with a limited importance, became famous internationally as a consequence of the Council, and lived during later centuries in a reflected glory. It is interesting to give a contemporary description of the town as quoted by Galante from Massanella :

" This city of Trento is subject to its bishop both in the spiritual and the temporal sense. The King of the Romans, Count of Tyrol, has a captain representing him permanently in the city. The annual revenue of the bishopric amounts to 12,000 gold ducats (£2,000). The city is placed in a plain in the valley, among wooded mountains coming down to the Adige across which goes a seven-arched wooden bridge. It has about a thousand houses, several very fine public buildings, open spaces and many palaces, among which the bishop's palace stands forth in magnificence and beauty. It is so full of varied decoration that the visitor is forced to confess that no other city has finer or more ornate palaces. Three miles beyond the city on one side the Fersina rushes down, and its waters are led into the city in such a way that no street is without running water. The surrounding country is well cultivated with pleasant hills in the neighbourhood and lofty mountains where the snows lie almost all the year round, and on some peaks are perennial. . . . The church of Trento, venerated for centuries, has eighteen canons who elect the bishop and each has an income of at least 200 gold ducats. The city is inhabited by Italians and Germans who live in separate quarters. The Germans, both men and women, wear the national dress, while the Italians follow the habits and style of the Italians, go to their own churches and listen to preachers in their own tongue."

The solution for different nationalities had been found in the Trento of the 16th century by a process of separation, which was evidently successful since we have no record of internal strife in the town. Since the 16th century, Trento went through many of the vicissitudes of the Napoleonic era after a time of minor troubles during the 17th and 18th century when the Thirty Years War and the Wars of the Succession devastated Europe, but with the Council of Trent its claim to more than local fame was exhausted, and the traveller can now enjoy the memory of those past centuries in the contemplation of what remains.

Dante stands on his pedestal gazing into the hills, and those two great influences—the force of Italian history and of culture symbolized in the stern figure outlined above and the everlasting splendour of the hills —will play their part in moulding the character of the Tridentians even after stone and mortar have crumbled away.

INDEX

Adalbert, Bishop, 31

Adamello, Monte, 135, 136, 138

Adda, river, 141, 147–8
valley of, 139, 141, 153

Adige. See Etsch
from Rovereto to Trento, 257–8.

Agordo, 237

Alleghe, lake of, 212, 218, 237
village of, 212

Allori, 57

Amadeo, 46–51

Ampezzo, mountain group, 212, 217–18.
valley, 214, 215, 218

Andraz, 197, 212

Annunziata, Chiesa Parocchiale, 118

Antelao, Monte, 214, 227

Antony d'Alemagne, 54

Arabba, 19, 212

Architecture, Romanesque, 2–3, 7–8, 254

Arlecchino (Harlequin), 68–70

Arlequin Senateur Romain, 70

Arnaldo of Brescia, 7, 99–100

Arnold, Matthew, quoted, 172

Auronzo, 215, 219

Aviolo, Monte, 137, 138

Badile, Monte, 136

Bagolino, Church of San Rocco, 121

Baitone, Monte, 137

Barbarossa, Frederick, 31

Barzissa family, 74

Bellini, Giovanni, 77, 80
Jacopo, 78

Belluno, 229–31

Bergamo, 5–6, 7, 24–33, 59–83
Accademia Carrara, 77–8, 91, 92

Bergamo associations, literary, 74–6, musical, 70–4
Casa Pesenti, 63–6
Cemetery, 71
Church of S. Agostino, 29, 57–8
Church of S. Andrea, 59, 83–4
Church of S. Bartolomeo, 59–82
Church of S. Bernardino, 59, 82
Church of S. Maria Maggiore, 32, 52–7
Church of S. Spirito, 58–9, 78, 82
Civic Library, 24, 62
families, 12, 25, 75–6
history of, 30–3
Palazzo Colleoni, 61
Palazzo Grataroli, 55, 61
Palazzo Terzi, 66
Palazzo Vecchio or della Ragione, 61–2
Piazza Garibaldi, 53, 67
Piazza Omonima, 66
school of painting, 76–9
Via Bartolomeo Colleoni, 30, 40
Via San Giacomo, 59–60

Bergognone (Ambrogio da Fossano), 77
paintings in S. Spirito, Bergamo, 59, 78–9

Bernina, Alps of, 141, 145, 147

Berzo Inferiore, 118, 125

Bianco, Monte, 136

Bienno, 116, 118, 122
Church of S. Maria Annunziata, 128

Blanchis, Andreolo de, 54

Blougram, Bishop, quoted from Browning, 265

270

Bolzano, 14, 168, 174, 179–91, 197, 254
description of, 181–2, 183–4
Bormio, 148, 149–51
Bagni, 149, 151, 152
Braulio, Monte, 153
Rocca del, 155
Valley, 149, 153–5
Brenner, highway of the, 131, 175, 180
pass, 12, 180, 197
Breno, 118, 124
Castle of, 115–16
Church of S. Antonio, 128
Church of S. Salvatore, 116
Brenta, Alps of, 14, 136, 259
Brescia, 6
art of small statue in, 110–13
Broletto, 9, 11, 62, 108
Castello at, 110, 177
Cathedral or Duomo vecchio, 87, 105
Church of S. Alessandro, 78
Church of S. Francesco, 106
Church of S. Giovanni Evangelista, 78, 84
Church of S. Maria del Solario, 104
Church of the Miracles, 48, 106
Church of S. Salvatore on Cidnean Hill, 103
condottieri at, 101–2
in Middle Ages, 99
in Roman times, 97
Lombard League and, 97, 101
Piazza del Duomo, 107
Piazza del Mercato, 109
under French occupation, 102
under Venetian republic, 101, 102
Brighella, 68, 70
Bronzino, 57, 91
Browning, 194, 232
quoted, 265
Brunnenberg, Schloss,
Brusato, Tebaldo, 101
Buchenstein, Valley of, 212
Bulgarini, G., 114

Butinone, pupil of V. Foppa, 21, 22

Cadore, 212, 213, 219, 220–38
the land of Titian, 221–2
Calisto Piazza da Lodi, 124
Campilione, Giovanni, 53, 63
Campitello, 197, 208, 209
Canazei, 196, 197, 209
Capodiferro, 56
Capo di Ponte, 125
Church of the Redeemer, 125, 126
Caravaggio, Battle of, 43
Carducci, and the Romagna, 20
Carmagnola, 35, 43, 45, 101
Cavalese, 249
Cemmo, Church of Antica Pieve di San Siro, 126–7
Cemmo, Pietro Giovanni da, 117–21
Certosa di Pavia, 46
Chiesa, Giovanni della, 21
Cima di Falzarego, 213
Cima di Piazzi, 145, 148
Cima Redasco, 145
Cimone della Pala, 243, 246–7
Cinque Torri, 214
Cismon, river, 241–2
Civerchio, 113
Cividate, 125
Cleri, Pietro, 54–5, 59
Clesio, Bernardo, 259, 263
Archbishop of Trent, 264–6
Col di Lana, 211, 212, 237
Colle d'Aprica, 138, 139
Colleoni, Bartolomeo, 7, 34–51
as a warrior, 42, 43
character of, 41, 44–5
contrasted with Sigismund Malatesta, 40
diplomatic methods, 44
relations with other condottieri, 43
relations with the Venetian Republic, 43
tomb in Colleoni Chapel, 49–50
Verrocchio statue of, 34, 40–1
Colleoni, Chapel, 8, 34, 39–40, 45–51, 52

Colleoni, Medea, described by
G. d'Annunzio, 49
tomb in chapel, 48–9
Communes, Italian, 4, 31, 36
Concarena, Monte, 136
Condottiere, 8, 35–9
as seigneur, 37–8
as warrior, 37
relations with seigneurs and
Papacy, 35, 36
Confidenti, company of actors,
69
Cortina d'Ampezzo, 196, 197,
215–18, 242, 260
a funeral procession at,
216–17
Costalunga, Pass of, 208
Cristallo, Monte, 210, 214,
215, 217
Cristallo (Bormio), Monte,
150–1
Croda da Lago, 210, 213, 214,
217

D'Annunzio, G., quoted, 49
Dante, 15, 259, 269
Darfo, 135
Desiderio, king in Brescia, 98,
104
Dietrich von Bern, 162, 168,
170
Dirupi di Larsec, 208
Dolomites, 15, 192–219, 247
main characteristics, 193–4
seen from Ritten, 200–2
seen from Vigiljoch, 198–200
Donatello, 43, 48, 111
Donizetti, Gaetano, 24, 25,
70–4
criticized by Mazzini, 73
memorials to, 70–1
principal operas, 72–3
Dosso Pedalta, 132
Drei Zinnen (Tre Cime di
Lavaredo), 218
Duccio, Agostino di, 48
Dürrensee, 217, 218

Ebenferner, 153, 157
Edolo, 117, 123, 136–8
Eggenthal, 197, 200, 202, 204–5

Eisack, valley of, 165, 201
Erbanno, 116
Church of S. Maria del
Restello, 123
Ermengarda, wife of Charle-
magne, 98
Esine, 118, 122
Chiesa Parocchiale, 122
Church of the Assumption,
120–1
Etsch (Adige), river, 168, 251
valley of, 173, 179–80, 206,
250
Etschland, 161, 164, 201
compared with Dolomites,
185
view from railway to Ora,
250–3

Falzarego, pass of, 196, 197,
212–13
Feltre, 231, 232–7
frescoes by Morto da Feltre,
234
older town, 11, 232–4
Feltre, Vette di, 246
Ferramola, 93–4
Florence, 5, 59, 136, 194
Fontane Fredde, 250
Foppa, Vincenzo, 21–3, 93
Francis I, 102, 114
Franzenshöhe, 157, 158

Galla Placidia, 104
Galsworthy, J., quoted, 173
Gambara, Lattanzio, 90
Ganassa, Alberto, Italian actor,
69
Gantkofel, 184, 252
Gaston de Foix, 102
Gattamelata, statue by Dona-
tello, 43, 45
Gelosi, Compagnia dei, 69
Giordano, Luca, 55–6
Gnochis, Alessandro, Italian
actor, 70
Gonzaga, Francesco, 38, 43
Gorzone, 116
Gottfried von Strassburg, 169
Gritti, Andrea, 102

Grosina, river, 147, 148
  valley of, 147
Grosotto, 147
Gufidaun, Schloss, 165

Hawkwood, John, 35
Hell, Valley of, 250–2
Hofer, Andreas, 17, 176
Hölderlin, quoted, 159

Investitures, Wars of, 5, 31, 255
Isabello, Pietro, 55
Iseo, 132

Kalvarienberg at Bolzano, 16
Karer Pass, 194, 197, 206
Karersee, 15, 193, 206–7, 218
  Hotel, 207–8
Karneid, Schloss, 167, 204
Klausen, 16, 165, 166
Klobenstein, 200, 201
Königsspitze, 151
Kues, Nikolas von (Cusano), 234

Lago di Colbricon, 218, 244
Lago d'Iseo, 130–1, 134
Lamberti, Stefano, 89, 106, 113
Langkofel, 202, 210
Latemar, 193, 199, 205
Laurin, peak, 162
Lebenberg, Schloss, 164
Liberale da Verona, 10
Lodi, massacre of, 31
  Peace of, 102
Lombardi, Tullio, 14
Lombardy, Northern, 11, 13
  plain of, 14, 16, 19, 26–7
  share in Italian history, 5, 6
Longarone, 228
Longhi, Cardinal, 57, 74
Lotto, Lorenzo, 10, 77, 80–3
  André Maurel on, 81
  paintings in Alzano Maggiore, 81
  paintings in Brescia, 80–2
Lovere, 131, 134

Madatscherferner, 153

Madatscher Glacier, 156, 157
Madruzzo, Cristoforo, 259, 267
Maffei, Scipione, 12, 158
Maggi, Berardo, 101, 108
Malatesta, Pandolfo, 32, 101
  Sigismund, 8, 32, 38, 39–40, 177
Malcesine, Castle of, 163
Mantegna, A., influence on
    Butinone and Zenale, 22
Maretsch, Schloss, 162
Margaret Pocket-Mouth, 175
Marmarole, Group, 218–19, 223–4
Marmolata, Monte, 199, 210
Marone, Raffaelle, 113
Massarella quoted, 268
Mascheroni, Lorenzo, 76
Masuccia, Monte, 145
Mendola, pass of, 183, 201, 252,
Merano, 15, 162, 174, 175, 179–91, 200, 254
  a centre of Austrian fashion, 185–6
  Burg at, 164, 177
  the Kursaal, 187–8
  under the Italian regime, 186–8
Meredith quoted, 195–6
Misurina See, 217, 218
Moderno, il, 111
Montone, Braccio di, 42–3
Moretto of Brescia, 10, 77, 83–7
  compared with Lotto, 83
  main characteristics of, 83–4
  paintings in Duomo Vecchio, 85, 87, 105
Moro, Lodovico, il, 32
Moroni, G. B., 10, 77, 90–2
  portraits in Accademia Carrera, 91
  religious paintings, 92
Morto da Feltre, 234
Muffetto, Monte, 135

Nadro, 115
Nullo, Francesco, 25, 32
Nuvolau, Monte, 197, 212, 213

Oberbozen, 198, 200

T

Oglio, river, 134-8
  valley of, 95, 134
Ora, 250, 251
Orbetello, 37
Ortler, 153, 156, 158-9, 183, 200, 206

Padrio, Monte, 138
Padua, Sala della Ragione, 6
  Seminarium, 13
Pala di S. Martino, 243
Pale di S. Lucano, 237
Palladio, 1, 109
Pallaus, Schloss, 164, 165
Palma Vecchio, 77, 79-80, 265
  compared with Titian, 220
Pasquale, Monte, 149
Pedenollo, Monte, 153
Perarolo, 227
Piano, Monte, 218
Piave, river, 226, 227-32, 237, 238
  valley of, 219, 226, 227-9
Piccinino, Giacomo, 37, 38, 43, 102
Pier della Francesca, 39
Pieve di Cadore, 197, 215, 222-6
  a glimpse into Cadore, 223, 226
  Titian and, 220-2, 225
Pieve di Livinallongo, 196, 212
Pisogne, 122, 128, 131, 134
  Church of Our Lady of the Snows, 128
  Church of S. Maria, 128
Pius II quoted, 37
Piz Popena, 215, 218
Pizzo dell' Orto, 131-2
Pizzo Umbrail, 156
Planta, Schloss, 168
Pomagagnon, 214
Pordoi, pass of, 196, 209-11
Poschiavo, Valley of, 143, 147
Predazzo, 246, 247-8
Presanella, Monte, 135
Presolana, Monte, 136
Previtali, 10, 58, 77
  paintings in Bergamo, 55, 78

Primiero, 237, 241, 245
  Valley, 242, 245
Pustertal, 175, 197, 215, 218

Radisca, Monte, 153
Reichenberger See, 218
Reiffenstein, Schloss, 164
Riccardina, Battle of, 43
Riccio, il (Andrea Briosco), 41, 112
Rienzi, Cola da, 6, 99-100
Rimini, Church of San Francesco or Tempio Malatestiano, 8, 38-40, 48, 178
Ritten, 183, 198, 201
Roccatagliata, Niccolo, 112
Rolle, Passo di, 246-7
Romagna, plain of, 19-20
Romanino, 10, 77, 121-4
  compared with Moretto, 86
  paintings in Cathedral of Cremona, 88, 90
  paintings in Cathedral of Trento, 88, 90
  paintings in Padua, 88
  paintings in S. Francesco, Brescia, 89
  paintings in Val Camonica, 121-4
Romano, Chiesa Parocchiale, 92
Roncagli, Silvio, Italian actor, 69-70
Rosengarten, the, 15, 168, 174, 183, 184-5, 199, 206-7
Rosetta, Monte, 243, 245-6
Rovereto, 258, 263
Runkelstein, Schloss, 162, 164, 168-73

S. Julian l'Hospitalier, 63
  frescoes in Bergamo, 63-6
S. Leonard, 17
San Glisente, Monte, 125
San Martino di Castrozza, 237, 239, 242-6
San Michele, 14, 259
San Paolo, island of, 131
Sand in Taufers, 167

Sanseverino, Roberto, 263

Santa Croce, painter of Bergamo, 79

Sass Maor, 242–43

Savi, Bartolomeo, Italian actor, 70

Saviore Valley, 136

Savoldo, painter of Brescia, 94

Scaligers of Verona, 7, 41, 163
  castle of, at Sirmione, 163

Scheffel, Victor von, 162
  quoted, 173

Schiavoni, Andrea, 230

Schlern, the, 183, 199, 202

Sella, Monte, 198, 210, 212

Serafino da Brescia, 114

Sforza, the, 38, 102, 163

Sigismund of Tyrol, 177

Sigmundskron, 167, 168, 184

Soardi, family of, 42, 55

Sobretta, Monte, 148

Sorapis, Monte 197, 210, 214, 217

Sottocastello, village of, 224–5

Southern Tyrol, 2, 14, 18, 160–78

Spino, Pietro, biographer of Colleoni, 41, 74, 75

Stelvio, pass of 156, 157–8

Talfer, river, 169

Tasso, Bernardo, 74
  Torquato, 74
    sonnet to Pietro Spino, 75

Tenno, Castello, 163

Theodoric at Brescia, 98, 103

Tiepolo, 10, 51, 58

Tirano, 141–4
  Church of the Madonna, 114, 142–3

Titian, influence of Cadore on, 220–2

Titschen, morning on the, 182

Toblach, 197, 215

Toblacher See, 218

Toblino, Castle of, 164

Tofana, Monte, 14, 197, 212, 213

Trafoi, 158

Tre Croci, 215, 218

Trentino, Upper, 2, 3, 14, 254–5, 260–1

Trento, 8, 14, 15, 181, 259–69
  Archbishopric of, 263–4
  a sixteenth century description of, 268–69
  Castel del Buon Consiglio, 163, 259, 265
  Cathedral of, 17–18, 65, 254, 259, 26,1–3
  Church of S. Maria Maggiore, 265, 266
  Council of, 267–8
  Palazzo Geremia, 259, 266

Treviglio, 21–4
  Cathedral of, 21, 23
  Church of Madonna delle Lagrime, 23
  Church of S. Martino, 21, 22

Tristan and Isolde, legend of, 169, 172
  frescoes at Schloss Runkelstein, 169–72

Trostburg, Castle of, 165

Tyrol, Castle, 17, 164, 173–7

Tyrol, Counts of, 17, 174–8, 263

Umbrail, Group, 156
  pass of, 156

Vajolettürme, 206, 208

Val Camonica, 115–28, 129–36

Val Cavallina, 132

Val di Cismon, 240–3

Val di Dentro, 150

Val di Non, 16, 259

Valle di Sotto, 150

Valtellina, 131, 148

Varagio, Jacopo da, author of Golden Legend, 64

Vecellio, Cesare, 226, 231

Vela, Vincenzo, 71

Venice, Republic of (Serenissima), 32, 37, 101, 102

Verona, Church of S. Giorgio, 11, 92
  incident at Church of S. Zeno, 256–7
  medieval market town, 6
  palaces of Scaligeri, 11, 256

Verona, romanesque churches at, 7, 8, 9, 254, 256
Veronese, Paolo, paintings in Brescia, 92–3
Verrocchio, Andrea, 40–1, 45
Vigo di Fassa, 197, 209, 247
Virgl, 183, 202
Visconti, 7, 43
 Filipo Maria, 32, 43, 101
 Gian Galeazzo, 32, 41–3, 101
Vittorino di Feltre, 11, 232–4
Vogelweide, Walther von der, 15, 161, 176
 quoted, 166

Vogelweide statue at Bolzano, 181
Vogelweiderhof, 166

Weisser Knot Inn, 158
Welschnofen, 205, 260
Wölfflin, Heinrich, on the criticism of art, 9

Zannoni, Atanasio, Italian actor, 70
Zebru, Monte, 149
Zenale, pupil of Foppa, 21, 22
Zoppa, Paolo, 93

Printed in Great Britain by
UNWIN BROTHERS, LIMITED, LONDON AND WOKING

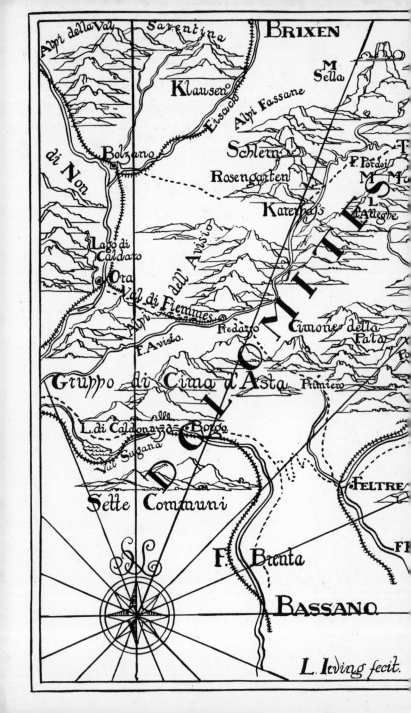